edition **+ plus**
MATHIAS VOELCHERT GMBH

About this Book:
Conflicts, grueling power struggles with difficult children, and destructive behavior daily challenge both teachers and parents. The main cause for disobedience and lack of discipline is a deeper-seated relational conflict between adults and children. Children want to learn; and they want to cooperate - provided their personal integrity and individuality are acknowledged and maintained in a respectful manner. This requires truly true dialogues with children.
Juul and Jensen emphasize the significance of relational competence as the core concept, changing the very nature of how we see education. They offer relevant alternatives to conventional education and solutions for difficult situations. They seek valid alternatives and give teachers the support that is so urgently needed.

About the Authors:
Jesper Juul, born in Denmark in 1948, family therapist, supervisor and author, was the founder of the renowned Kempler Institute of Scandinavia, now Danish family therapy institute (dfti.dk) and represented by the DDIF.de and IGfB.org in the German speaking world. Besides training family therapists, this institute provided over 3 decades hundreds of Scandinavian teachers with training on how to treat children and adolescents. Juul is one of the most influential family therapists and authors on family topics in Europe. His books have been sold in record-breaking numbers. His international project *family-lab* is committed to enabling parents and professionals to transform emotional love and commitment into loving behavior and is active on several continents (www.family-lab.com).

Helle Jensen, clinical psychologist, family therapist and supervisor was responsible for conflict counseling at the Kempler Institute in Denmark and Norway for many years. Alongside her work at her own institute, she currently teaches courses all over Europe. She is a well-known author of numerous articles and co-author of the book *Empathy: It's What Holds the World Together* written together with Jesper Juul, Peter Høeg and others. Her current main focus is the project *training empathy* (trainingempathy.com), which is an international training course for teachers and other professionals.

Jesper Juul
Helle Jensen

RELATIONAL COMPETENCE

Towards a new
Culture of Education

Translated by Svenja Grabner
Edited by Robin Menges

Title of the Danish original edition:
Pædagogisk relationskompetence – fra lydighed til ansvarlighed
© 2002, Jesper Juul, Helle Jensen
Udgivet af Forlaget Apostrof, København

Copyright © by Jesper Juul, Helle Jensen & Mathias Voelchert GmbH
Compilation: Robin Menges & Mathias Voelchert GmbH
Cover design: Mathias Voelchert GmbH
Display and processing of data: Julia Kraus, München
Production: Books on Demand, Norderstedt

ISBN 978-3-935758-71-0
Also available as E-Book: ISBN 978-3-935758-70-3
Copyright for the english edition 2017
© Mathias Voelchert GmbH Verlag, 94336 Windberg, edition + plus
1st edition 2017

Alle Rechte vorbehalten. Reproduktion, Speicherung in
Datenverarbeitungsanlagen, Wiedergabe auf elektronischen,
fotomechanischen oder ähnlichen Wegen, Funk und Vortrag,
auch auszugsweise, mit schriftlicher Genehmigung der Copyrightinhaber.
Contact: mvg@mathias-voelchert.de
www.familylab.de
www.bimw.de

Translated by Svenja Grabner
Edited by Robin Menges
Coverphoto: Photodisc V90, Summer Scrapbook 90095

Important information:
All rights reserved. No part of this publication may be reproduced, stored in a retrieval system, or transmitted in any form or by any means, electronic, mechanical, photocopying, recording or otherwise, without the prior written permisson of the publisher, Mathias Voelchert GmbH.

www.jesperjuul.com
www.psychologhellejensen.dk
www.familylab.de · www.familylab.at · www.familylab.ch
www.twitter.com/family_lab
www.dfti.dk
www.ddif.de
www.igfb.org
www.familylab.de
www.familylabassociation.com

The only alternative to
paternalism is dialogue.

VILLY SØRENSEN

Contents

INTRODUCTION TO THE ENGLISH EDITION 2017 — 10

part one:
GENERAL ASPECTS — 19

Chapter 1: Educational Landscape — 20
- A Colorful Picture — 20
- Adults on the Defensive — 25

Chapter 2: Family — 32
- Parents are Partners — 32
- From a Social Necessity to an Existential Decision — 34
- From Education to Inclusion — 36

part two:
PERSONAL ASPECTS — 40

Chapter 3: Integrity — 42
- Definition — 43
- The Role of Disobedience — 49
- Integrity and Cooperation — 54
- The Universe of Cooperation — 55
- The Existential Conflict — 59
- Integrity, Equality and Democracy — 65
- Integrity, Self-esteem and Self-Confidence — 68
- Self-Consciousness — 82

Chapter 4: Personal Responsibility — 84
- Definition — 84
- Children's Personal Responsibility — 86

Adult Guidance	97
Children with Special Needs	101
Adults Personal Responsibility	104
Authenticity and Authority	108
Integrity and Educational Ethics	113

part three:
RELATIONAL ASPECTS   118

Chapter 5: Interpersonal Relationships   120
Levels of Interaction: Content and Process	122
Adult-Child Relationships	126
Peer Relationships	130
Teacher-Parent Relationships	135
Conversation and Communication	137

Chapter 6: Relational Competence   141
Modern Infant and Attachment Research	142
Adult-Child Relationships between Now and Then	145
Defining Relational Competence	148
Relevant Moral Concepts	149

Chapter 7: Professional Development   153
Professional-Personal Development	154
Collegial Reflection	165
Supervision	174
The Role of Superiors	176
The Children's Role	185
The Parents' Role	195

part four:
BUILDING RELATIONSHIPS 200

Chapter 8: Teaming up with Parents 202
Approaches to Conversations 203
Cooperating on a Regular Basis 210
Daily Cooperation 216
Cooperating on Problematic Issues 219
Responsibility and Power 221
Preparing Necessary Conversations 223
Authentic Contact as Prerequisite 232
Who is Responsible for What? 236

Chapter 9: Understanding Conversation 238
Personal Language 242
Personal and Private 245
Verbal Aspects 247
Nonverbal Aspects 248
Insight and Development 249
Differentiation and Respect 258
Equal Dignity 259
Acknowledgement 262
Acknowledging Communiation 264
Evaluative Communication 271
The Quality of Contact 275
Individual Student-Teacher Dialogues 278
Existential Conversations 283
Conversation and Conflict Resolution 288

Chapter 10: Challenging children 294
A New Approach 297
Examples and Analyses 301
Psychology and Education 317

Notes 320

INTRODUCTION TO THE ENGLISH EDITION 2017

Since this book was first published in 2002 understanding of what makes for good schools has developed considerably. Many elements have been researched on and new insight in many areas has been taken serious. The the concept of multiple intelligences (Howard Gardner), for example, has proven valuable for everybody involved in public education. But what has not been established is an overall concept of what we call *"relational competence"*. A competence of the individual, which not only improves the academic learning and the well-being of children and adolescents, but simultaneously supports the well-being of teachers.

Some languages do not have a term for this competence. One reason might be that it has been a basic assumption of pedagogy that teachers just know how to establish fruitful relationships to their pupils. In a similar way, earlier generations believed that emotional love was sufficient to ensure healthy relationships within families. And the basic presumption was: this is a personal trait and cannot be learned.

The subtitle of the original book – *from obedience to responsibility* – describes a new paradigm for understanding child rearing and pedagogy. And it seeks a new culture for the way adults relate to children. The common paradigm believes that children must first learn to be obedient and cooperative, before a constructive and dynamic relationship between adults and children can be established. Over the past decades we have witnessed serious attempts to break away from this in several countries around the globe. One common way was by forming *democratic schools*. Some of these were successful and some not. One reason might be that they were built on an ideology more than on what we now know about children's real capacities. That is, their way of learning and interpersonal needs.

To develop a new paradigm, we have also established a new terminology. In the following, we give a brief overview of the terms we use and which are described at length throughout the book.

Relational competence

The term *relational competence* refers to the teachers' ability to see each child on their own terms and to adapt one's own personal behavior accordingly without giving up the leadership. It also describes the ability to remain in contact with the child (or parent) authentically as well as the ability and willingness to take on full responsibility for the quality of the interaction.

Relational competence is both a matter of pedagogical trade/craft as well as a matter of ethics. Therefore, in our understanding professional competence is determined by the sum of a teacher's *teaching competence* and *relational competence*.

Equal dignity

Equal dignity is not an existing term in many languages, which why we constructed it by combining *equal* (often used in a political or hierarchical way) with *dignity*. In our understanding, equal dignity is not a political term. We do not claim that children are or should be equal with adults in terms of power. The term *equal dignity* calls attention to the fact that the cognitive, verbal, non-verbal and emotional reactions of children are meaningful messages and need to be taken equally serious. The term also points out the fact that the human needs of both adults and children are equal and need to be encountered in a dignified way. Children's messages show relevant aspects of the current relationship and thus are helpful in order to adjust the quality of interactions.

Professional-personal development

A common assumption is that difficult relationships to children, can only be adjusted if the child can be motivated to change its behavior. In the last decades, we have seen thousands of clinical examples of how powerful even small adjustments of teachers' behavior can be and how quickly this can enable children to learn on all levels (personally, academically and emotionally). The term professional-personal development relates to the fact that the person (in the role of a teacher) is the most influential factor when it comes to relational challenges.

Self-esteem and self-confidence

For a long time, pedagogy and psychology have been trying to strengthen children's *self-confidence* in order to support their learning. This makes sense because self-confidence is all about what a human being can do and how this can be improved. We have however seen, that enhancing a child's *self-esteem* is much more productive for many children. Self-esteem describes what a child knows about themself (emotions, thoughts and behavior) and how it feels about that (most children simply mirror the attitudes of their parents and teachers). A child needs to feel *seen*, recognized as the person it really is, so the gates to enhanced learning as well as increased self-confidence can open.

Personal authority

All formal roles and authorities are experiencing, what they call a *lack of respect* for their roles. But this is also true in many partnerships and between parents and children. In all cases, one or both parties find it increasingly difficult to ensure that their boundaries are respected with help of traditional means.

The way to *mutually* respectful relationships – both personal as well as professional – goes via personal authority. Personal authority that builds on understanding our personal boundaries and our ability to express them firmly and kindly and – very importantly: on inviting the other person to do the same. This always leads to both stronger mutual respect as well as self-respect. This does not alter the professional relationship into a private one, it simply adds a personal dimension.

In 2017 expecting obedience seems to be fading and slipping into the background for both teachers and parents. But in a way, it looks like functioning has replaced obedience, without changing much of the underlying dynamics or ways of thinking about each other. Children, as well as their families are expected to in a thoroughly structured world. Consequently, we see both increasingly dysfunctional relationships and children that are being marginalized. Many parents and teachers experience that time for dialogue and contemplation is not readily available to them. This is mainly due to a complex host of political and cultural phenomena and the situation varies from country to country. The key concepts described in this book do not go into depth on these phenomena, but rather offer relevant support for the personal time we have with children and the time we choose to spend with them. Every day when teachers, children and parents meet, they share the same desire: to feel of value for each other and be successful in their roles and jobs.

For the English edition, we especially want to express our thanks to our esteemed colleague, psychologist and family counselor Robin Menges who very committedly helped translate the book from German and edited the text with meticulous accuracy as well as Jessica Joelle Alexander – the author of *The Danish Way of Parenting* for her support in editing and finding the best English sayings and Trent Murray for his support and questioning the translation.

Jesper Juul and Helle Jensen
Denmark 2017

Introduction

This book seeks to identify and describe the processes that form relationships between teachers and students. This approach may appear unusual, because we differentiate interpersonal processes and pedagogical processes. Our personal experience is that most schools pursue a professional educational approach. Many institutions, however, are uncertain concerning underlying principles and values and their practical implementation, even though they know these are the foundation for successful education and cooperation.

The perspective that relational processes are the foundation for every pedagogical approach is up to debate continuously. Frequently we encounter the opinion that achievement and success have the highest priority and everything else comes after that. This attitude also shows the enormous responsibility teachers have, and the necessity to abide to regulations and standards provided by law. But it also reflects the remnants of schools conceived of as institutions.

All institutions working with children share the same kind of responsibility. The responsibility of caring for the personal, intellectual, and social development of children. In practice, however, this responsibility is often split between daycare facilities and schools. While daycare facilities tend to focus on the personal and creative development of children, schools are expected to provide intellectual and social stimulation. Although circumstances, goals, and contents change as children move from daycare to school, the relationship between children and adults as well as the underlying processes stay the same. To understand relational competence in professional relationships, we do not see a need to divide different types of educational institutions.

Our experience shows that academic goals can best be achieved if teachers are committed to good student relationships. This foundation for cooperation and involvement influences all further activity in the classroom. In many educational settings, *relational competence* – the key concept of this book – is the *missing link*, to enabling all parties to receive care, attention, and respect.

The term *social competence* is often used in this context as well. Despite strongly varying definitions, the word social primarily describes the children's ability to cooperate, be considerate, or build friendships – in other words, to be a constructive member of the community. Since this term was introduced, the focus on children's social competences has risen and gained importance. But as independent experts in conflict resolution, we have observed that in the end, it comes down to the adults' relational competence that provides the necessary basis that children can internalize these social competences. In everyday life, it is difficult to draw a clear-cut distinction between relational competence and social competence. *Adults develop relational competence by interacting with children, while children simultaneously acquire relational and social competence.*

This mutual and equal learning process plays a central role in our understanding of relational competence. Neither young, nor experienced teachers have fully developed relational competence. It is a life-long learning process. And all children lack social competences and are in a learning process.

Of course, one may say that universities do not teach relational competence and parents should prepare their children for social life in school, but everyone involved has to cope with the competence level they have attained at the given moment. Both teachers and children have to make the best of their common reality, both in the classroom and in working with peers.

Another concern of this book is to show a way out of the culture of obedience. This culture of obedience has shaped society and education over a long period and is still often thought of as the most effective means to combat antisocial and individualistic attitudes. But obedience in itself does not give sufficient inner strength and stability to face the cultural changes, unpredictable challenges, and historically unique polarization of values in postmodern society. People need strong self-esteem and personal integrity.

Besides this concern, our prime motivation to promote a paradigm shift in the field of education, and to suggest substituting obedience with responsibility is grounded in psychological, existential and pedagogical knowledge. In fact, we are convinced that this shift is not only the next logical and necessary step for teachers but for every individual and society at large. We believe relational competence is fundamental for personal development and the social progress of humanity. In addition, it establishes an ethical foundation for qualitative improvement of social communities. These ethics are an important basis for building successful professional relationships between the four parties involved – teachers, children, parents, and society.

The majority of this book builds on our experience; our desire to share the experience we gathered each on our own and together in over 30 years of practice in education, psychology, and psychotherapy, studying interpersonal relationships in families, schools, therapy and many other settings was the motor for this book.

The literature cited draws on relevant issues, we encountered while trying to keep up to date professionally. They are not the result of systematic study. We conceive of ourselves as practitioners and aim to substantiate and pass on our practical knowledge.

This book builds on values, and concepts we consider essential for pedagogical work. Values and concepts relevant for students, freshly graduated teachers, directors, and experienced pedagogues wanting to reevaluate the quality of their work. Readability and practical application have influenced the writing and use of specific language in this book. We have consciously spared scientifically concise terms due to their rare use in daily interactions and discussions.

We are aware that we are sometimes seen as taking sides with children, but we do not see ourselves this way. Actually, we do not act in the interest of any parties involved. Our focus instead is on the relationship itself. In other words, we advocate for the relationship, for only intact relationships benefit both children and teachers.

Pedagogical literature usually classifies children in different age groups – ranging from infants, toddlers, preschoolers, school children, middle-schoolers, etc. In this book, however, we let this classification go. This decision is due to the fact that the constructive qualities of professional relationships are largely consistent over all ages, from birth until death. We use the term *'early childcare'* and *'day care'* to describe institutions caring for children up to school age*. The term *'school'* includes all types of schools including private schools and special schools. *'Educational institutions'* is used as a collective term.

For the same reason, we do not differentiate different types of educational institutions, nor do we expand on schools based on specific pedagogical or philosophical ideologies. The fundamental values and concepts promoted in this book build on underlying human interactions, true for all and also apply to universities, hospitals, or even nursing homes. The necessary qualities in professional relational processes are the same regardless of the goals, content, framework, or structures of an institution. The same holds true for the ethnical, religious, and cultural background of children and their teachers. Our international work has shown us that the values and interpersonal principles described in this book are, to a large extent, valid across differing cultures. They are equally acknowledged and appreciated everywhere in the world, despite differing norms and cultural patterns which often impede their implementation.

---

* In most countries, this is between 5 and 7 years of age

Please be aware of the limitations of written words when reading a book of this kind - a book which talks about relational processes *between the lines*. This book builds on real examples and personal interactions and the described interactions cannot be applied in general. The choice of words is always unique to specific situations and the actors involved.

Some examples have been selected because they are exemplary, others for the opposite reason. If we describe inappropriate professional behavior, we do not claim that the persons involved acted deliberately. These examples show radically different value systems and illustrate that, values and actions often do not correspond.

The book is divided into four main parts. The first part is devoted to conditions influencing educational work. The main focus is on the changing adult-child relationship and the significance of family. The second section deals with personal aspects which are common to both children and adults and play an important role in developing professional relational competence. The third section describes how interpersonal relationships influence professional development. In addition, it offers a definition and description of our key concept: relational competence. The fourth and last part of the book provides a detailed view on specific relational situations. The final chapter touches issues dealing with difficult children and emphasizes the need for a new educational approach.

While working on this book, we exchanged experiences, examples, and thoughts. Jesper Juul was the driving force of the project. We would like to thank our friends and colleagues at the *Kempler Institute of Scandinavia* for their substantial contribution of a wealth of experience, which the institute collected from 1979 on and thereby provided a strong foundation for our ongoing work. We would equally like to express our thanks to the educational institutions whose openness and trust we appreciated in particular. In addition, we would like to thank our editors Elsebeth Jensen PhD, vice dean, director of Studies Teacher Education, VIA University College and Ole Varming, PhD for their interest in this project and for giving us invaluable input and feedback.

Part One
GENERAL ASPECTS

Chapter 1:
The Educational Landscape

A Colorful Picture

Looking back at schools we have worked with over the years, we see an educational landscape which is anything but consistent. Of course, national, political and cultural differences have influenced the framework in different countries. But the differences within individual countries are often more salient than the differences between countries. Looking at the educational climate within institutions, we have encountered everything from deserts, minimalist kitchen gardens, to fertile greenhouses. We have worked with dynamic private schools and excellent public institutions, but also with complacent and static institutions – both private and public. We have worked with schools with an ongoing drive for development regardless of political and economic circumstances while neighboring institutions remain static, basing their lack of drive on the exact same circumstances. There are preschools and schools that feel honored and are committed to being cultural providers for their country, while others oppose the prevalent values of their society. Similarly, there are principals and teachers, whose careers and identity are characterized by seeking professionalism. Others see themselves as mere public officials and then there is everything in between.

On the relational level, we have encountered institutions where the adults formed a closed but lively circle, showing activity and commitment within their sphere of influence. Yet, we have also met institutions where cold passivity or stubbornness led to self-righteous power plays between teachers and students. The prevalent thinking in these cases often is, that everything will be fine in the end, but if things do not work out someone is to blame. The awareness how this behavior influences the relationship between children and adults varies. Early childcare institutions are often more aware of this interplay, due to the more direct way younger children react to adult interventions.

Another relevant factor are the significant changes that have occurred in society as a whole within just one generation and strongly influence the quality of interpersonal relationships. The most important changes, which have prompted institutions to seek new educational perspectives are:

1. The questioning of authorities in the 1960s.
2. The women's fight for political and social equality, changed gender roles, and equal treatment.
3. The general emphasis on human rights and specifically, the 1989 United Nations Convention on the Rights of the Child as a political response to the growing awareness for human integrity.
4. Modern infant and relational research, as well as clinical work on interpersonal relationships in families, institutions, and professional occupations.

1. Questioning authorities

The politically motivated questioning of almost every form of official authority marked the beginning of the end of the *role play* which influenced the adult-child relationship strongly. I.e. the interaction between the teacher's *role* and the student's *role* rested primarily on the student's fear/respect for – or fearful respect for – the teacher's *role-based* authority. In educational institutions, this was not discussed openly and consciously. Almost overnight children claimed a *full-fledged* self and refused being reduced to the predefined role, which they had been taught to fulfill previously. Approximately at the same time, corporal punishment was forbidden as an educational measure. Subsequently, children as well as teenagers began to draw attention to the social and existential discomfort and pain which characterized their relationship with adults. They also started to show their creativity, their spontaneity, and their directness. Character traits which have always been part of being a child. Teachers who had been denied the privilege of showing their true selves as a child, continued to cling to their professional roles. Today, it is becoming very clear that this role-based authority is outdated and must be replaced by *personal* authority, if teachers want to create meaningful teaching conditions for both parties involved.

2. Women's fight for equal rights

In this context, women's fight for recognition is particularly relevant. It triggered public discussions about the so-called *soft* values in families, institutions, and society as a whole. Parallel to the political fight for equality and more power, women clearly also struggled for personal recognition. This fight on the interpersonal level was soon also adopted by men and children. Besides a general recognition, personal acknowledgement also includes closeness, contact, care and empathy - values which rarely dominate the male world, but are not specifically female. These values are better described as human values and needs. The increased significance of these values has enhanced knowledge on relationships in general and expanded psychological and pedagogical concepts of the individual.

In addition, the new focus on a *psychology of oppression and violence* was an enrichment to society. The oppressed and the violated finally had the opportunity to express themselves freely. Surprising and shocking statements confronted those who stood for an opposite ideology.

3. Human rights

End of the 1950s, Scandinavian countries witnessed an almost unnoticed but revolutionary shift in the general view on children. A group of researchers, including Åse Gruda Skard, Aase Hauch, Jens Sigsgaard, Thomas Sigsgaard and Nic Waal specialized in infant psychology. They initiated a major change, which helped schools shift their attention from seeking *conformity* to enabling *development*. The objective no longer was to raise obedient, well-assimilated humans impelled to *other-directedness* (David Riesman[1]) but to stimulate each child's motoric, linguistic, intellectual, and creative development consistent with the individual's potential. The reason for this shift was, without a doubt, of a practical nature. The focus on individual development should simply create a broader foundation, for educational work and the child's *role* as students. But in the light of the political, social and psychological movements of the subsequent decades and because of the growing economic wealth, children not only demanded individuality which made them profitable members of society, but they also demanded the right to simply be themselves.

The fight for political and social children's rights peaked in the UN Convention on the Rights of the Child[2]. This instigated a progression in the Western world, where the wellbeing of children was not just the concern of parents any longer but also of the society at large. The political significance of children's living conditions directly correlated to psychologists' growing interest in children's inner experiences. In course of the last century, adult employees experienced a similar development. In addition to working conditions such as work hours, safety, the right to have a voice, or fair payment, the *psychological work environment* was given more and more attention.

Comparing these changes in work environment with changes in children's learning environment reveals a rather bleak picture. For example, at the turn of the millennium, Denmark was faced with the decision to either pursue improvements of the learning environment for children (investing in new furniture, regulating the number of children allowed per square meter, and providing proper ventilation) or to combat a provoking social phenomenon through a nationwide campaign against bullying. The decision was made for the campaign against bullying and, thus, became another example of how adults abuse their power over children while maintaining their image as responsible, caring, and child-focused human beings. Later in the book, we will revisit this example in order to demonstrate that such choices are commonplace in education.

4. Modern research

Modern infant and relational research[3], represents a paradigm shift and is turning the majority of former discoveries and previously held opinions about development on their head. Research focusing on infants, bonding and interpersonal relationships has developed over the past decades and focuses mostly on the relationship between mothers and children up to the age of two. But despite this short time span and the early age of children studied, the findings coincide with our 30 years of clinical and therapeutic experience working with experiential family therapy. Up to the present day, none of the scientific observations in the field has contradicted our personal experience of adult-child relationships.

Furthermore, brain research supports our thinking[4]. Evidence has been found to show that children's awareness is not a blank slate, as developmental psychology believed for a long time. From these insights and others, we conclude that the currently prevalent concepts of learning and educational practices need revision.

The willingness and ability to integrate new knowledge is greatest in early childhood. Even if early child care can be reduced to mere supervision in some cases, it usually pursues social, developmental and psychological goals for good reasons. Schools, however, generally tend to focus on more specific and accomplishable tasks. Its deep-rooted tradition demands separating the children's intellectual abilities from their existential and psychological being.

Educational research on the other hand is continuously refining its areas of academic expertise. Former activities and subjects are being replaced; new branches have been introduced; language teaching has changed its form and methods just like teaching creative classes has. Kindergartens are faced with the decision to abandon interactional aspects and concentrate on preparing children for school. In all educational settings, quality is taken very serious, despite lacking a satisfying definition of what *quality* means in this context.

These processes as well as the perpetual desires and demands of educational experts represent a natural step in the development of society as a whole. Groups and individuals who invest their energy and enthusiasm in order to change and improve circumstances have always been at the heart of educational institutions. Even if this commitment, that sometimes borderlines fanaticism, isn't always given credit and immediate success, it is imperative in raising important questions and finding answers. The same applies to educational research and its wealth of topics and fundamental principles that are hard to keep track of for teachers out in everyday life.
In the process of these developments, unfortunately many children are defined or diagnosed as outside the norm and, consequently, marginalized.

We say *unfortunately* because these diagnoses very often lack a sufficient basis. Similarly, children in earlier times were denied help or support for no apparent reasons.

And adding to the full picture, a strikingly high percentage of teachers would change their job if they could in Europe. Many teachers who quit soon after starting, do this in their own words *because of the children's inappropriate behavior or their poor bringing up.* These issues are not issues politicians like to focus on.

Adults on the Defensive

The most noticeable difference between today's children and those of 50 years ago, is that today's children walk the earth in the belief that they have a right to be here. They express their opinions and feelings naturally, ask questions, provide arguments, and expect to be taken seriously. They have gained a certain amount of confidence. Even more relevant, more and more children wake up every morning not fearing adults like children of previous generations did; and some of these have grown up to be parents and teachers themselves.

A quarter of a century is a long time. Today we can hardly imagine how provocative it was to be inexorably confronted with this development. On the one hand, this struggle involved adults who had been taught to live in humility and restraint and sometimes even in self-denial. And on the other hand, children who, unaware of their role in this development, took the newly gained privileges for granted. Adults who had fought for the rights and the improvement of children's living conditions, and delighted in enabling children's freedom, were all of a sudden faced with ungrateful children who took this freedom and their rights as granted.

To counteract the general sense of helplessness adults felt, new categorizing methods were established. The emergence of a *new child's character* was one of the earliest attempts to explain this new difficult relationship. Ever since then, *pedagogical debates have focused more on the question why adults have difficulty working or getting along with children instead of focusing on how to create a basis for healthy cooperation between children and parents.*

This does not mean that the adults' difficulties with children have not been real. And vice versa it also is true for children. The largely reactive behavior and the inability of those in charge to handle the situation have caused a lot of insecurity and confusion. Since conflicts between children and adults were previously more or less hidden power struggles, adults often misinterpreted the situation and considered the children as the *winners*. Actually, we are dealing with a mutual relationship in which both sides are at a disadvantage if the relationship lacks specific qualities.

Interestingly, the widespread helplessness and defensive attitude of adults soon was an international phenomenon, despite differing approaches to education, value systems, democratic traditions, and economic developments in individual countries. Even politicians picked up this defensive attitude and only suggest restrictions, punishments or anti-campaigns. The head of a Danish boarding school gave an interview that illustrates the problematic nature in this situation. Rather upset, he told how his school had introduced a smoking ban in compliance with new the regulations passed by the ministry of education. A couple of students ignored the ban and smoked at school anyway. The principal described with righteous indignation that he went so far as to call the ministry and ask for permission to interfere, but he was denied this option.

This little anecdote exemplifies a central issue: in Scandinavia, today's children are said to lack *social competence*; in Germany, there is talk of a substantial *crisis of discipline*; and so, every country has its own version of the same problematic situation. What all of the countries have in common, is their incessant search for possibilities to change the behavior of *children* without recognizing that this is the wrong track.

We do not deny that there are children with destructive behavior towards themselves and others that is socially unacceptable, or that there are teachers who are forced to cope daily with violations to an extent which no one should have to put up with. One's ability to tolerate or be broad-minded varies greatly from person to person and yet we do not doubt that there are numerous damaging adult-child relationships and that they require limits. The way out of this social plight, however, does not lie in restriction, campaigning, control, regulation, prohibition, or punishment. These all too familiar methods go back to an old saying *'Those who don't listen must feel'*, meaning that if I can't reach you by reason, I have the right to implement consequences or punishments regardless of the infliction of personal borders This approach not only ignores the actual adult responsibility and the significance of relationships but also subjects children to adult manipulation and their exercise of power.

Furthermore, it is a defensive strategy – a reactive response to the child's behavior. Defensive strategies do not produce satisfying outcomes for the parties involved in interpersonal conflicts. Whenever adults are in defense, the following three scenarios can be observed:

- adults lose the initiative and perspective of the situation; their collaboration with the child is reduced to a tiring struggle of being right.
- children become insecure and lose their trust in the adult's leadership;
- both adults and children lose faith in themselves.

These observations are not only a snapshot of the situation schools are in. They also apply to families and show the widespread social helplessness we feel in the face of free individuals. Similar conflicts occur when a family with small children sits down for lunch, kindergarten groups go on excursions, school children do not want to do the assigned group work, high school students ignore the teacher and text each other, university students miss a class and then demand that relevant information be repeated when they are present, or local authorities plan to disavow a small group of second-generation immigrants within a community.

In the educational world, teachers are left to figure out how to react best to this defensive helplessness of any given situation. Individuals such as Birthe in our next example are expected to fend for themselves while figuring out how to integrate new teaching methods and cop with the institutions changing structure and demands for teamwork. These are sometimes overwhelming social expectations.

Making a collective problem the issue of an individual teacher is never adequate and leads to teachers being labelled as *incompetent, problematic, psychologically unstable* and the like. Often the social and political expectations as well as the institutional structures need to be revised and questioned. On the other hand, however, personal professional development for individuals like Birthe has gained importance in the educational field.

EXAMPLE

Birthe recently assumed a new position as a first-grade teacher, even though she had not worked with first-graders in a long time. She was a competent Danish teacher with high career ambitions. And had high expectations for the new school year, but first-grade students require patience and cannot be expected to learn as quickly as older students do.

After the winter break, she realized that her pupils would not reach her goals set for the current year. Despite her commitment to differentiated teaching, she wasn't seeming to have success. Since she defined her worth as a teacher by her student's progress, she was gradually developing doubts about her ability. Her reaction was similar to how many of us react to the feeling of being unworthy: we either withdraw frustrated, become more and more self-critical, depressed and inactive or show our despair in the form of anger and aggression.

Birthe did both. She wondered if she was too old to teach first-graders or if she was suffering from burnout. She also considered the 'new children's character' and 'stressed-out parents too busy to properly raise their children' as possible causes for her professional failure. Either way, she didn't reach a satisfactory explanation.

Birthe lost the sense of being a valuable teacher along with her awareness of her personal boundaries and needs. She started to neglect her responsibilities, and let the children get by with things which affec-

ted her professional integrity. The children sensed Birthe's insecurity about who she is, what she wants, and what she does not want. Consequently, they also became insecure. And they were hurt by Birthe's critical and reproachful remarks and her complaints.

Birthe is a competent and experienced teacher with a positive and affectionate attitude towards the children she works with. For this reason, her story is a good example that psychological instability or personal issues are not the reason, when we fail to establish healthy relationships with today's children. For many years, her qualifications and role-based authority served her well but now she is challenged in an entirely new way.

A similar crisis could have emerged just as easily in her marriage, in raising her own children, in living with her mother-in-law, or in any other relationship where her commitment alone would not have gotten her any further either. In this sense, her conflict is a personal one. In order to regain her confidence and develop personal authority, she needs personal help from outside. She can only find confidence in herself, not in widespread attitudes and opinions. Criticizing her teaching methods and ability to teach first-graders will not help her any more than the well-meant support by colleagues who deplore the behavior of today's children and their parents.

In her case, Birthe did not receive much support at work. She had to rely on a psychologist's assistance. As is often the case, her difficulty with the first-grade pupils mirrored difficulties in other essential relationships, both private and professional. This shows that her temporary crisis was more connected to her personal developmental than to an *educational problem* or a sign of personal weakness. She soon learned that her relationship to the children improved in correlation with her ability to recognize when and how to take herself more seriously.

Birthe was raised and educated in a school culture shaped by implementing corrective measures on a child's behavior to solve problems. It was common practice to invite to parent-teacher meetings to draw the parents' attention to their child's inappropriate behavior, to summon additional teachers focused on the individual to motivate children to cooperate, or to ask a school psychologist to examine and analyze groups of pupils to find solutions. Having grown up with and been taught these kind of strategies, Birthe is now challenged to question her own role in relation to her students. She is urged to find a way to improve her relational competence allowing her to change the in-class working climate *together* with her pupils. In a culture with a long tradition of accusation, taking on responsibility and feeling guilty often get mixed up or used synonymously.

EXAMPLE

Karen has worked as a teacher in a daycare center for 20 years. Her story shows how a professional relationship can produce a similar existential reaction.

Karen had integrated several routines in her daily work: she used these routines with the children at any given opportunity. She seized special occasions such as public holidays, the change of season or the like. She did not question her practice and relied on her personal experience, thinking that the established routine was effective and made children feel good around her. After several years of working with the same partner, she was confronted with a new colleague – a young graduate who wanted to discuss everything they did and question how they did it.

As a consequence, Karen started to develop doubts. She was not used to putting her pedagogical approach into words. Thinking that her work and experience was being questioned, she felt offended and tried to defend her position. Her new colleague, mistook this attitude for a lack of openness to discuss professional issues. The cooperation between the teachers soon became problematic.

Karen developed sleep disturbances and lost interest in her work. She talked to her immediate family a lot about how she was unable to find common ground with her new colleague. The children also were affected by this situation and no longer felt secure, and so Karen's decreasing self-confidence slowly developed into a self-fulfilling prophecy.

These two examples illustrate the scope of individual psychological and existential phenomena which have to be considered in modern educational settings, regardless of whether they are related to the child's or the adults' behavior. For generations, personal issues were kept private and only expressed in case of severe illness. From a health standpoint, it is a healthy development that this kind of individualization and keeping personal reactions taboo are in decline.

Moreover, the examples demonstrate the need to offer teachers counseling and opportunities for professional development, as well as the need for heads of institutions to improve personnel management, and for staff to maintain teamwork on a high qualitative level.

As we see personal, professional, and social aspects merge into one. And even though the wellbeing of teachers and children is at stake educational institutions lack a tradition of integrating this fact. Even though other work environments are confronted with similar issues, the difficulties are especially visible in relationship shaped by learning, supervision, socialization, and care

CHAPTER 2:
Family

Parents are Partners

Over the course of the past decades, parents have become partners with whom many teachers have difficulty finding common ground. There are confident and self-assertive parents placing demands on teachers; parents hiding beneath an anxious mask of an arrogant know-it-all attitude, coming well prepared, but still missing each other's point in interaction with teachers. And we also find parents whose willingness and ability to enter a dialogue with flexibility facilitates fruitful cooperation.

A widely discussed issue is the reproach that parents are no longer raising their children properly and instead are leaving the responsibility to institutions. A task they don't see themselves responsible for. One could say that institutions have always had an educational purpose, but since the children today are no longer socialized so homogenously, schools have to take the responsibility more serious and be actively committed. The children's needs have also become more complex. They insist on being treated with respect and on being acknowledged as individuals before showing a willingness to cooperate. The extent to which parents raise their children today, however, has not considerably changed. What has changed is the decreased importance parents place on preparing their children for school. Today's children are expected to learn, live, and function in many different realities, including cyberspace, which makes it almost impossible for parents to socialize their children for just one area. *School and parents must therefore work together to teach their children personal integrity and inner responsibility, so they can move and act within a reality which allows freedom to choose all directions. Drugs and hardcore pornography compete with sports, literature, and the arts.*

We find it equally saddening and alarming that the pedagogical world has unquestioningly adopted the assumption that the children's decreasing (and changing) social competence can be traced to their parents' lack of time (and reluctance!) to raise them. We do, however, also see that today's lifestyle creates challenging circumstances for all private relationships which are the psychological basis of a family. But we do want to emphasize the strong influence day-care centers have on the lives of preschoolers. And, want to draw attention to the fact that only two generations ago children largely acquired social competence by playing with other children. Nowadays, childhood is strongly affected by almost uninterrupted adult surveillance and instruction. These are often adults who avoid personal conflicts and are hesitant to allow children to learn through normally arising everyday conflicts (both socially and personally).

Two factors *characterize* the majority of modern-day parents and have a significant influence on their way of interacting with teachers and schools. They have abandoned patriarchal family models and authoritarian parenting styles and have reached an experimental stage in which they literally have to reinvent relationships and redefine parenthood for themselves. Many countries are stuck in the discussion about traditional and consequential methods versus so-called *loose* parenting styles, Scandinavian parents have sought a third approach to parenting. They have become international pioneers of child-rearing and had to manage without examples or role models. In addition, they have partially relinquished the idea of perfectionism and false feelings of guilt, which pushed many generations of parents to withdraw from public in shame and humility whenever their children did not *function properly* or required more assistance than normally expected. Just like all parents, they have a natural tendency to protect their child beyond all reason. They feel insecure and helpless when it comes to parenting in a more competent way and therefore trust teachers to have useful knowledge and expect they are also willing to share it.

Parents do however demand an equal dialogue, and with good reason expect experts to lead the cooperation. This attitude isn't new, but has become more manifest.

For a long time, it has been commonplace for children in Scandinavian countries to spend most of their childhood in educational institutions. Among other things, this brought about a shift of on who defines values. Educational values developed in the school setting now serve parents as a source of inspiration and teachers provide good examples for them. One of the benefits of this is that parenting has become more objective and is no longer exclusively based on morals and habits of the individual. One of the drawbacks is that experts are not aware of the crucial differences in the adult-child relationships. In educational settings, the relationship is built on theory and pedagogical methods, and in the family, it is built on love.

In light of this new development and their increasing function as role-models, teachers in Scandinavia have assumed a heavy responsibility. Because of the large amount of time most children spend in institutions, teachers are also responsible for the wellbeing and development of young people. The socially enacted division of children's lives into school and family does not correspond to a child's needs but rather to the requirements of the labor market and the gross national product. Consequently, it unavoidably demands a closer analysis of the decisive roles parents and experts play in the lives of children.[1]

From a Social Necessity to an Existential Decision

The predominant power structures in families were well defined and established before 1970. In the 1970s, however, the concept of family has experienced a major shift. The change was so dramatic and rapid that people were predicting the very institution of family might die. Gender roles were being questioned; the way of interacting with children became subject to democratic thinking. Women were educated, took on jobs, had bank accounts of their own and could get a divorce if they did not feel comfortable in their marriage. Around this time the term partnership surfaced, describing a love relationship between people who were not officially married. Men had to give up their relatively isolated position as the chief provider of their families and actively engage in a care-taking family infrastructure. Within just one busy decade, marriage and family life changed from a social necessity to an emotional and existential decision.

The institution family never died.[2] It continues to thrive and in many ways still has the existential significance it always had. The general framework and content have drastically changed – not to the extent many would have desired but still with greater vigor than in any other historical period of just 25 years. Society was split. On the one hand, it depended on the women's contribution to the national economy; on the other hand, it regretted the loss of reliable and ever-caring housewives who run the house. The touch of panic may have subsided, but the situation has remained unchanged up to this day: the financial minister pursues the goal of maximizing the number of people in employment and the period for which they are employed, while the social minister works to create conditions so parents can spend more time with their children.

Parallel to this, families are genuinely grappling to develop a structure supporting loving adult relationships in which men and women are equal and children receive sufficient attention. Through experimenting, families are trying to establish a reasonable balance between work life, private life, and family life; but a perfect solution has not yet been found. Some sacrifice family life for the sake of work life - very often at a high price. Conversely, others sacrifice themselves for the sake of family life without ever receiving the expected reward. Most, however, successfully make the best out of their situation. People criticizing the modern family rarely have something to add to the conversation. They either spread cynicism and mistrust or corrupt the idea of family in lieu of romantic memories of what it was like in the *good old days*. These nostalgic ideals bear little in common with today's reality.

In this shift a large degree of newly developed tasks and responsibilities have fallen to the children. Already at the age of one year, most children are expected to take on daily *jobs*, just like their parents. Their work environment, however, is often more physically and psychologically straining than most adults would ever accept. At the age of three, children become aware of the possibility of their parent's divorce, if not a reality. Many three-year olds are forced to cooperate to cope with the disappointment and separation through a divorce. They live in patchwork families, are stepchildren, stepsisters, stepbrothers, half-brothers and sisters and struggle to meet the expectations of different groups of grandparents.

In return, children have been freed from physical abuse, have been given a voice and money, and their childhood has become the subject of a growing body of research.

From Education to Inclusion

From the middle of the last century, the values, objectives, and means of child education have changed considerably. Back then there was only one valid method of educating children, while today there are innumerable methods. Over generations, school and family values were largely in harmony. For the most part, both sides agreed on when children behaved well and when they did not - that is to what degree they met the adults' expectation of obedience. In former times, children were treated like some kind of *raw material* which required refinement. It was the responsibility of parents and teachers to bring children in line with the prevailing moral, social and cultural standards of society. On the one hand, there were the labor market requirements concerning future employees' knowledge and ability and on the other hand there were personal skills. Childhood was seen as a preliminary stage, which served to prepare for adult life. Authoritarian and hierarchical power relationships dominated family, school, and the labor market alike.
The key concepts of child rearing were obedience and conformity. Still, there were differences in how parents and teachers handled situations. In some cases, the demand for conformity was approached flexibly; in other cases, children were expected to fully identify or even submit to this notion. Knowledge about children, their development and internal disposition was rather limited, compared to today's understanding. Education was pre-

dominantly based on moral concepts. Parents, teachers, and psychologists were not interested in *who* a child was but rather in *what* he or she would become and how to guide them towards this adult life goal. For this same reason, the professional focus was placed on pedagogical instead of developmental psychology. Doctors and health authorities first and foremost looked into children's physical development. Only later on did they take into account the interdependence between physical development and social circumstances within the family.

The development from 1980 onwards was much more complex due to influences from two fields representing differing values: the political and psychological-existential[2] sphere. Although the two value systems overlap to a certain degree, for the most part they contradict each other.

By the mid-90s, educational researchers and clinicians had defined three distinct styles of parenting. It is summarized below by the Norwegian researcher Kari Killén:[3]

Both researchers and clinicians have developed a keen interest in parenting styles. The prime focus of research has been on the differences between authoritative, authoritarian and indulgent parenting as well as their influence on children (Darling & Steinberg, 1993). Authoritative parenting relies on love, commitment, strict but reasonable rules and open dialogue. Studies have shown that children raised authoritatively tend to be emotionally stable, confident and socially competent (Baumrind, 1989). Authoritarian parenting is characterized by emotional distance, rigid rules and a certain kind of ignorance towards children's individual needs. Authoritarian parenting is very often related to anxiety, antisocial behavior and a high aggressive potential (Baumrind, 1978; Patterson, 1982). Indulgent parenting places minimal demands on children concerning the compliance to adult rules and norms. Children receive little guidance how to structure their lives and observe limits. Indulgent parenting often causes immaturity with low impulse control, social responsibility, independence, and cognitive abilities (Baumrind, 1978). Both indulgent and authoritarian parents have been shown to have difficulty communicating with their children.

Ever since these findings were published, generations of parents have struggled on their own to redefine authoritative education and create a new balance between necessary parental authority and children's needs as well as vulnerability. Like educational researchers, parents have also done their *research*.

The shift from top-down parenting approaches emphasizing obedience to a family structure based on equal-dignity has necessitated bold attempts to renew parenting. Many parents have had difficulty maintaining the balance, for their idea of *new parenting* was unclear compared to their own experiences and their rejection of traditional patterns.

Interestingly enough, most parents are determined to provide their children a better life than they have had themselves. Consequently, they invest a lot of energy to avoid the practices applied by their own parents. In doing so, however, they do not deliberately reflect on what kind of childhood they want their children to experience. In countries where the population struggled with extreme poverty over generations and parents had to deny their children almost all material wishes, we now observe that adults are willing to do anything to fulfill their children's material wishes. But very often, the parents' efforts only result in disappointment and severe conflicts. Lacking the personal historical experience of their parents, children do not experience happiness or a sense of satisfaction. On the contrary; they become demanding and discontented persons.

In Nordic countries, a similar phenomenon has arisen, though material poverty belongs to the past. Parents who were taught to be obedient, who were denied any kind of influence and not taken seriously when they were children now allow their children's random longings to determine what the family's day looks like. This kind of relationship produces constantly frustrated, demanding, and socially incompetent children as well as helpless parents.

In our estimation, the above described approach to parenting is in decline. More and more parents are ready to genuinely commit to values which best shape family life and their children's childhood. The school system is challenged by the fact that parents are quicker concerning this development and has to take on a new role. In the end both the parents and schools need each other in form of a loyal and inspiring cooperation.

Part Two
PERSONAL ASPECTS

CHAPTER 3:
Integrity

Introduction

We see maturing the individual's personal integrity as the natural goal of 21st century child rearing and pedagogy. The personal integrity of a newborn encompasses their basic needs and boundaries. In the process of growing up, a child's integrity develops into an increasingly complex entity, constantly advancing and shifting. Therefore, the development of the individual's integrity is not only an educational goal to be achieved in the child's future; nurturing the child's integrity rather has to be the central function of all educational practice.

Fostering an individual's integrity is always, closely connected to moral and ethical demands at all levels of society. The degree to which responsible adults meet these needs determine the child's mental health and social development. Yet, there is no guarantee – not even in the most progressive societies.

Therefore, we want to take a look at the possibilities available to ensure the integrity of both children and adults within the educational framework. Infringements of personal integrity are very often, evaluated differently depending on the viewpoint. For example, verbal and physical attacks on teachers are seen as infringements with more severe moral significance than violations of children's integrity. The explanation for this phenomenon does not lie in diverging moral attitudes but rather in the historical fact that violations of adults' integrity by children has always been prohibited, while the reverse has been acceptable over a long time. Generally, violations of children's integrity are subtler albeit more frequent and regular – a fact which influences adult-child relationships in a destructive way.

Definition

Psychological and pedagogical dictionaries define integrity as *intactness, unimpaired condition; completeness, wholeness; as the autonomy and invulnerability of a human being.* A German dictionary describes the term as the ability to autonomous, honest action in line with personal moral principles, which leads to personal autonomy. The word itself traces back to the Latin *integritas* which means intactness and integer which signifies unspoilt, undamaged.

In summary, we understand a person's individual integrity as their feeling of wholeness and a balance between inner and outer responsibility.

Inner responsibility is an individual's responsibility for him- or herself and, thus, for their personal boundaries, needs, emotions, and goals. In philosophical terms, we speak of an existential responsibility: a responsibility for one's own life because of one's own uniqueness despite all the similarities with other humans. There is no other person on earth just like me and, consequently, no one can know me better than myself. But this also leads to the necessity to take over responsibility for my own life, without assistance from others. From a psychological perspective, inner responsibility is a developmental process based on emotional perceptions and experiences. The quality of this development depends primarily on the quality of the child's emotional interaction with their parents, as well as brothers and sisters.

Outer responsibility is the responsibility each person develops towards social and cultural values as well as value systems, he or she lives in. These are based on cognition and are determined from outside the individual person.

INNER RESPONSIBILITY:

- Builds on emotional experiences with others

- Independent of social belonging, of competences and talents

OUTER RESONSBILITY:

- A system of values outside of the individual person, builds on theories, thoughts and is learnt

- Dependent on social and cultural belonging and intellectual development

Internalization/ Integration

In earlier times, individuals had to submit to external values and customs. If these did not make sense or stood in contrast to one's inner responsibility, one had to hide or suppress the arising conflict. Common terms used to describe the individual's ability or willingness to comply with and accept external values as a moral superstructure were *strong character* and *weak character*. In cases where inner experiences contradicted outer requirements and doubts emerged about what is *right* and what is *wrong*, this moral superstructure provided guidance. A person with a strong character showed the will (or acknowledged the necessity) to subordinate personal experience to collective beliefs concerning right and wrong.

With the collapse of the culture of obedience and postmodern value pluralism, obedience has been replaced mainly by processes of internalizing and integrating. That means a cognitive and emotional process by which the individual attempts to complement and balance personal perceptions and experiences and to integrate aspects of external values and traditions into their own context.

This process entails the continuous analysis and evaluation of experiences; it is the core of what we call personal development. But since the process relies on interpersonal experiences of inspiration and validation, it may be more appropriate to define it as the individual's psycho-social development. Internalization and complementation add a dialectic dimension to the process of socialization. More than ever before, we are now forced to build our own opinions and put our lives in context while continuously trying to answer the question of who we are.

By taking over the prevalent value system and building one's own opinion on external factors, others are able to define who you are. In this sense conforming is a personal choice, just the same as the possibility to pursue individuality. Obedience has become a personal decision: it is no longer authoritarian requirement and / or a social necessity.

The internalization and integration process is prerequisite to the feeling of wholeness. The experience of personal integrity is built on the individual's perception of balance between inner and outer responsibility. It is not a fixed and predefined entity but a relational feeling which constantly shifts and, ideally, constantly grows.

The significance of the concept of *social responsibility*, defined as the responsibility each of us has for other human beings, varies greatly from culture to culture. For example, Scandinavian countries have a long tradition of emphasizing the individual's and society's responsibility for the weak, for children, and for those who fall victim to events beyond their control. Interestingly enough, the rise of criticism of the individual's low social responsibility coincides with growing social democratic welfare societies. Originally, welfare societies were meant to assume social responsibility - while individuals could take on social responsibility indirectly by paying taxes for example. We have come to realize that welfare institutions can take over social responsibility for the individual only to a limited extent. In addition, professional experience *shows that care, assistance, and support must be based on a dialogue between the inner responsibility of the provider and the inner responsibility of the recipient.* In other words, both the provider and the recipient of social services have to agree on what care, help, and support mean to them.

Difficulties understanding integrity also arise from the fact that integrity is based on individual perception and, consequently, unique to each person. And on top of this, the subjective experience of integrity is vague. It can be hard to pin down with words and explain to others. Still, it is vital that each of us has an understanding of another person's integrity in order to live and work together in respect and equality. As long as parenting and education are primarily focused on obedience, the individual's search for integrity remains private and lonesome. At best, it turns into an emotionally determined trial and error process, involving the people close, verbalized, if at all, only in private terms. In fact, the process of searching one's own integrity is often so lonely that it does not reach verbal expression at all. It may well be this lack of personal expression that drives people to seek therapeutic help in order to obtain a clear vision of personal integrity and its verbal expression. But therapy is limited in comparison to the social space.

The public has already given some attention to the aspect of personal integrity representing *human boundaries:* when society acknowledged humanistic values, it also created a common verbal foundation in form of written as well as unwritten laws. These can only protect the individual to a certain degree, but they provide justification for feeling violated.

One of the first laws acknowledging intellectual integrity was granting religious freedom. Much later physical, psychological, and sexual integrity were acknowledged.[1] In Denmark, it was not until 1967 that the teachers' right to use physical violence as a pedagogical method was denied. And since 1997 physical violence as a means of parenting is also prohibited by law. Opponents of these bans argued that violence – euphemistically referred to as *physical discipline* – was necessary to secure an obedient culture – and they were right about that.

Becoming aware of our individual, personal integrity and the ability to express this sense of wholeness – be it verbally, nonverbally, or bodily – is an ongoing rational process. This process is interrupted by meditative pauses in which the feeling of having found personal integrity and the feeling of having lost it alternate in irregular intervals. The process of becoming aware of our integrity is shaped by the need to constantly expand, refine, and redefine this sense of completeness. A painter's way of working may serve as a simplistic illustration of the underlying internal processes and the limited role of external witnesses. The artist is likely to work on the canvas for several weeks, months or even years before he or she feels confident enough to deem a picture complete. But anyone except the artist him- or herself may consider the picture *good* or *bad*, at any time in the process.

We all run through a similar process. Our canvas, however, is the interpersonal space. We are challenged to refine our ways of expressing ourselves. We must express ourselves first to be able to evaluate the quality of our expression and the degree to which our inner perception matches our verbal-emotional articulation. Other people may be sources of inspiration, provide support or pose challenges; but they cannot act as judges. This is why no one else can take responsibility for our own integrity and the activity or passivity it derives from. This is also why it makes sense to use the term *inner responsibility* to describe the way we treat ourselves in contrast to obedience. Obedience in line with *outer responsibility* is the opposite of staying true to oneself. Obedience means to act according to the expectations and wishes of others and it enables handing over the responsibility for one's own actions.

In a child's world, this is relevant on two levels:
For one, the conflict is central to a child's psychosocial development. Children often claim *It wasn't me, I didn't do this.*
This can have any of the following meanings

- that they actually did not do it
- that they are frightened by their own action to the extent that they cannot handle the responsibility for it
- or that they actually did do it but not in compliance with their *true* self, and at the moment "I am unable to distinguish or unify the two sides".

Secondly, this conflict also influences a child's moral development. Adults carry a decisive role model function in this situation. For generations, parents and teachers have confronted individuals and groups of children with double standards shown in the attitude *If my relationship to (the group or class of) children is a success, it is my personal success or the success of my education. If the relationship fails, it is the children's fault.* Children have always known better, but they did not have the means to counteract the injustices arising from adults' arbitrary avoidance of responsibility.

Interpersonal relationships follow a well-documented pattern. In equal adult relationships, the failure of one person to take on their responsibility pushes the other person involved to take over dual responsibility. In adult-child relationships, the child experiences guilt and shame alongside dual responsibility. Guilt, shame, and a passive dual responsibility imposed indirectly are the three major reasons, that impede developing a balanced awareness for oneself and one's inner responsibility. In this way, the adults' lack of moral integrity, combined with the unwillingness to accept responsibility for the relationship, directly affect the personal integrity of children. This explains to an extent how violations are inherited and violated children grow up to become violating adults themselves.

Children fall victim to the double standards of adults in their immediate social environment very often, while at the same time fathers and mothers of society handle responsibility in the media in a similar way: most stories show adults trying to hand off their responsibility. On a daily basis, children are confronted with adults acting like persons without integrity. with children on the issue in a reflexive and philosophical way. Classical literature, such as Carlo Collodi's Pinocchio[2], can serve as a valuable example. Let us compare the Italian story about a wooden marionette written in 1883 with its film version released by the Walt Disney Company in 1940.

The original text tells of the development of the young boy Pinocchio from being *externally* directed to becoming an *internally* directed human being, in other words from an obedient to a responsible child. The character Jiminy Cricket embodies Pinocchio's (bad) conscience, who tries to remind him to be obedient whenever the boy acts independently, yet he occupies a rather minor role.

Disney's version assigns him a dominant role as a moralist and representative of outer responsibility. The film version's moral of the story is that children are wise to keep to adults' expectations. Collodi's compelling story of a child's inner development has been reduced to plain pedagogy.

At the age of two, children begin to grapple with the ongoing conflict between integrity and cooperation. Over the course of growing up, the topic comes back time and time again in varying degrees of intensity in relationship to their parents, in kindergarten, or school. Pinocchio's story could provide ideal input for discussions, exercises, and insights.

Public and private child education have had this inner conflict for generations, just like in Collodi's times. They have upheld obedience as a basic value, method and goal, expecting it to grow into inner responsibility. The adults' expectation was that by obeying parents' and teachers' rules for the first 14 years, a child will learn how to take responsibility for him- or herself. In line with this belief, educational institutions welcomed children with lectures about norms and rules before showing any interest in who they are as individuals.

The most extreme examples are found in socio-pedagogical institutions, where children are declared well-educated when they showed the ability to *adhere* to the institutions' norms and rules at a particular point in time. The pedagogical goal of obedience explains why punishment, consequences and new rules of conduct became legitimate methods of training obedience. Most children raised successfully this way, have difficulty coping with the world outside of institutions. This is a problem we will discuss in more detail in Chapter 10.

The Role of Disobedience

Very often, disobedience as understood in everyday language, marks a child's first step towards their personal integrity and inner responsibility. Therefore, we need to stop trying to assimilate the disobedient according to our expectations and start taking them by the hand on their way to an identity whose nature and goal is not yet known. *We have to give them experienced company on their way to themselves.*

Children's disobedience is neither an expression of social irresponsibility nor an intentional attempt to overturn the power of adults. It is much rather a reactive attempt to stay intact and regain the authenticity and integrity required to return to society. And society also needs to change its character. It is rarely an intellectual process adults go through when they withdraw for a shorter or longer period of time to find themselves; it is an emotional process by which humans learn how to listen to their inner voice telling them if and possibly how they can re-enter society. The time (and energy) necessary to retreat and integrate the experiences vary between children and adults. The time periods may stretch from only a few seconds to several months or even years. But due to higher emotional flexibility and behavioral adaptability, children usually need less time than adults.

The fact that the culture of obedience is in decline has logically raised the question whether society can exist, if all members are disobedient. The question, however, is a rhetorical one, because it doesn't take the individual into account.

In this thinking disobedience is not seen as an important link to personal and social development but merely the exact opposite of obedience.

Similarly, we are confronted with the question whether kindergartens, schools or teamwork can function well without obedience. The answer is that allowing space for disobedience actually enables constructive development of each person involved in these social constructs and thus for the institutions themselves as well.

The relationship between an individual and the group is always dialectic, even if the individual's ability and right to express their integrity are inhibited or even prohibited. Both children and adults express their integrity more indirectly and in a distorted way, the more limited their opportunities are. This commonly results in aggression, poor communication, and a collective sense of meaninglessness. The introduction of countermeasures based on rules and discipline have been shown to have little effect.

The quality of guidance and reciprocal interaction adults offer a child however has an immense pedagogical significance. Poor quality does not bear risks for society per se; it rather bears the risk of children seeking refuge in other authoritarian communities instead of strengthening their inner responsibility. These seem attractive because their norms differ to the well-known cultural and family norms. Very often these are systems adults have good reason to stay away from. So, in order to strengthen a child's integrity, adult guidance and interaction should not be based on what is (culturally, religiously, morally, or legally) acceptable or inacceptable at a given point in time. On the contrary, it is essential to be committed to children as individuals: to their personal experiences, boundaries and potential. In doing so, adults endow children with a sense for social values and what they mean to them. But if adults refuse or fail to fulfill their central role in this relationship, it gives rise to antisocial individualism and social isolation.

Asked about where the interaction with adults went wrong, isolated children always give the same answer: they did not experience what it was like to be seen, to be heard or to be taken seriously. These three relational qualities strengthen more than admonition, prohibition and restriction, in both children and adults.

EXAMPLE

A 19-year-old young man who grew up in a children's home talked about what usually happens when education is dominated by obedience and shallow morality. As a protection against the educators' power, the children created their personal 'community of disobedience', which allowed them to stick together (and keep their mouths shut). In this situation, neither the educators nor the 'community' were concerned with inner responsibility and personal integrity. The young man explained, "We learnt how keep silent. Should I ever be interrogated by the police, I would not say a word. I know how to withstand pressure from the outside."

> *The man had a reputation for being aggressive and running riot. He always ran riot whenever he did not want to admit an offense. As a pedagogical measure, the institution would gather all children involved and pressure him collectively. If this did not show any effect, he was confronted with six or seven pedagogues urging him to admit his misconduct. He described his experience, "When I got tired of this game, I found out how to behave in order to get out of it. It was easy: I only had to conform to the rules and, when I did not, admit to my failure. This was how I escaped. But in our own world, in our secret community, we did whatever we wanted. The pedagogues never found out about this because none of us would give it away."*
>
> *The pedagogical philosophy and methods of the children's home thus provided the young man with nothing more than a new version of the 'street smartness' he already possessed before.*

This story is not an example of how a young man with a well-established personal integrity was denied his need to become a part of society. It is rather an example of how society denied him the possibility to become part of it. It is not a coincidence that adults who show a high degree of personal integrity are often referred to as *lone wolves*, in the positive sense of the word, and thus distinguished from *conformists* or *opportunists*. Until now education has never emphasized developing inner responsibility. People who develop inner responsibility nonetheless or who have grown up in families with a different attitude are rare exceptions.

It would be a quantum leap forward in educational practice if children's healthy and natural urge to discover themselves, and themselves in relationships, were no longer tainted with shame and guilt. Shame and guilt are two existential factors, which most often trigger self-destructive behavior. Shame and guilt are also the prime cause of destructive social behavior. In situations where people do not know what to do or feel provoked, they have a tendency to resort to demanding obedience and respective patterns of action. In Scandinavian countries, this often happens with great regret, while people in other countries see it as part of their value system. An educational psychologist described the issue this way:

"The central question is whether our teachers have a genuine interest in improving their relational competence, or are merely attempting to regain their previous power."

It is a deep-seated conviction that teachers are successful when the children they work with do what they are told to do. For generations, obedience has been the ideal. The Grimm Brothers' tale of *The Stubborn Child*[6] represents a counterpart to Pinocchio's story:

> "Once upon a time there was a stubborn child who never did what his mother told him to. The dear Lord, therefore, did not look kindly upon him and let him become sick. No doctor could cure him, and in a short time he lay on his deathbed. After he was lowered into his grave and was covered with earth, one of his little arms suddenly emerged and reached up into the air. They pushed it back down and covered the earth with fresh earth, but that did not help. The little arm kept popping out. So, the child's mother had to go to the grave herself and smack the little arm with a switch. After she had done that, the arm withdrew, and then, for the first time, the child had peace below the earth."

Pinocchio's story represents an exemplary approach to education, asking the readers themselves to find a solution. Whereas the Grimm tale and the Disney version of Pinocchio provide their own moral.

The main difference between the past and today in terms of education can be found in the general knowledge people have about child-development and psychology. The multiplication of new insights has dismantled the paradigm of obedience from within. We constantly pass on knowledge and values to our children. Both our current society and the newly gained knowledge, however, necessitate that we do so in equal dignity, in which each and every person is capable of creating a sustainable synthesis of the past and the future.

Integrity and Cooperation

The urge to discover yourself in relation to others is not just a healthy and natural urge of childhood. It is also the existential human condition common to all, which has been known, sung about, praised and described ever since people began to express themselves. But the conflict between the need to care for and develop one's own personal integrity and the wish to be acknowledged as a valuable member of groups is part of an important process in the psycho-social development of children and in the personal and professional maturation process of adults.

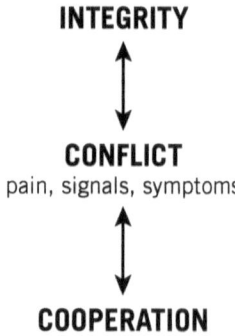

Over the course of time, this fundamental conflict has been described from various points of view. Politics have referred to it as a conflict between the *individual* and *society*; psychology has seen it as a conflict between *individuality/autonomy* and *conformity*. Because of our relational perspective, we use the terms *integrity* and *cooperation*. We do this partly because of our positive experience with the terms' vigorous effect in educational settings and partly because of the to the point description of what the conflict feels like *from within* the individual.

Integrity: Infants are able to fully show their personal boundaries by sounds and gestures. Their physical and psychological development depends on their parents' and other caregivers' ability to understand these signals and act appropriately. Infants are not able to avoid experiencing adults' failures in responding to their basic needs or to prevent violations of their boundaries. Serious failures and severe or repeated less severe violations distort or inhibit healthy development. But with increasing motor skills and verbal expressiveness the ability to protect themselves also grows. In many cases, however, they learn to cooperate with the behavior of their primary caregivers. Children's cooperation in such cases reflects that their need to maintain the relationship with their caregivers is greater than their ability to protect themselves from intrusive influences.

Cooperation: A child's ability to cooperate is built on their tendency to *imitate* their parents' external and internal behavior, and encompasses verbal, physical, social and conscious as well as unconscious patterns. In our experience, children usually mainly imitate the behavior of one parent. Cooperation in this context also includes the urge and the ability to establish contact in personal interaction. This is a capability humans possess from birth on, as infant and relational research has been able to show.

A child's ability and willingness to cooperate provide the essential foundation for personal development and developing a survival strategy. That is an unconscious strategy which enables a child to keep their personal integrity intact without damaging the relationship to relevant caregivers.

The term *cooperation* replaces *conformity,* even though the ability to conform is an essential component of children's ability to cooperate. In our understanding, the term *cooperation* describes the active part in building relationships better, especially when cooperation takes place *in reverse*.

When observing children whose mothers are not able to be present actively and empathically, we see that about half of them cooperate in accordance with (i.e. imitate) their mothers' behavior: That is, they become more and more passive and begin to repress their needs as well as their frustration. At first sight, they are often mistaken as *easy to handle*. But taking a closer look at their behavior, we see that they show resignation. The underlying message is: *I see/experience that you are unable to care for me, which is why I try to demand as little as possible.* Ignoring the sad aspect of this situation and the long-term consequences for the children's development, we may mistake the cooperation for compliance with our expectations or demands. The children are expected to come to grips with what they do or do not receive and to adapt to these conditions.

Other children in the situation described above respond with striking activity. They express their deprivation and frustration verbally as well as physically. In contrast to the other children, these children cling to their mothers, when they want to be fed by breast or bottle. It almost seems like they are trying to climb back into their mothers' wombs to establish a relationship. The message behind their cooperative behavior is: *I realize that you are unable to interact with me, therefore I will do the work necessary.*

Both types of cooperation show comprehensive social competence; the behavioral strategies of both groups of children are a *gift* to their mothers. The first group sacrifices themselves in order to give their mothers what they need most in this situation. The second group fights for their integrity and, thus, gives their mothers what they both need in the long run. But it is a thought-provoking example of how immediate cultural prejudice makes us define children as *easy-to-handle* or *difficult*, ignoring the significance of the children's integrity. (Please be careful not to generalize the above findings: not all children that are daily categorized easy or difficult are necessarily struggling with an existential conflict and many have competent parents, who are capable of relating in a good way.)

As mentioned above, both behavior patterns are expression of high social competence, yet with very different social, emotional and existential consequences - for both mothers and children - as well as their relationship. Which kind of behavior causes which consequences depends on external factors such as possible help and support by the social network the parents receive, or if and to what degree the children alter or correct their unconscious survival strategies. As a general rule, introverted and extraordinarily unassuming children show little tendency to change their strategy as preschoolers. Often, their conflict does not show until puberty, when their self-destructive behavior becomes more obvious. Active children occasionally show a tendency to give up. Usually, however, they draw attention to their conflict with more aggression. They have a considerably higher risk of being objectified (as problem, client or scapegoat) due to their longing for a responsible subject-subject relationship.

The above described phenomena, and other similar ones, should make teachers/professionals very sensitive when evaluating children's social competence and enable rethinking the definitions they rely on. Unfortunately, *professional systems have a strong tendency to almost exclusively react to the children's survival strategy (shown in their behavior) instead of their underlying existential dilemmas.* We must be aware that the children's inherent ability and willingness to cooperate, facilitate the integration of the needs of both the group and the individual more than we would have ever thought possible.

The Universe of Cooperation

Without doubt, the pedagogical ideas and strategies of parents and professionals would be more readily applicable if we could jointly pin down the phenomena, which have an adverse or even destructive effect on the children's (proper or reverse) cooperation. That is, the effects the parent-child relationship or the parental relationship has on their individual ability and willingness to cooperate. The same applies to teacher-child relationships, which can both increase and relieve the children's pain and, in some cases, are the dominating cause for their pain.

But this is not easy because children not only cooperate with adult's conscious behavior. Children also cooperate with internal and external behavior patterns that adults are not aware of. For most of us, such patterns make up more than half of our behavior. They include all unconscious thoughts, emotions and interactions as well as what Daniel Stern calls *representations*.[4] In short representations are the aspects of adult behavior which belong to the non-self and show the outcomes of both successful and failed cooperation with their own parents.

Children cooperate equally with both sides of adult behavior, that is with the expressed aspects of the *self* and the aspects that represent the *non-self*. If the relationship is, however, dominated by the adults' *non-self*, children become significantly more insecure.

For this reason, we warn of offering good advice to parents, that might be theoretically well founded and make general sense, if it is not in line with the actual conditions of this specific adult-child relationship. Even well-informed and generally acknowledged advice that doesn't take the concrete reality of this parent-child relationship into account bears a great risk of reinforcing the parents' *non-self* and, thus, the children's insecurity. Children have a strong awareness of reality and perceive adult representations as unauthentic.

Some parents practice and maintain a conventional and loving, but impersonal *role*. A role corresponding with the role of parents of the past, partly influenced by the parents' personal experience with their own parents, and partly by cultural representations. In such cases, the children's security is built on the consistent lack of authenticity as well as the consistent presence of authority.

In addition to confusion arising through the mix of representations and authentic reactions, we have to also cope with the processes any relationship goes through. Often, we become aware of the nature and significance of these processes months or years later. But irrespective of the degree to which adults are aware of these processes, children sense them and are forced to cooperate.

As an example, a family might have two parents who, have learnt (from their family of origin) to hide their emotions from the outer world under all circumstances, and thus have developed a certain numbness on the inside. Their children have two possibilities to handle the situation. Firstly, they can cooperate *properly* and develop an emotional behavior without ups and downs. They will even stick to this if their parents actually ask them to express their feelings. Secondly, they can cooperate *in reverse* and develop very emotional behavior in everyday life, even if their parents demand the opposite. If there are two children, frequently one of them, (often the older one) cooperates as the family code expects, while the second cooperates in reverse. The parents are generally puzzled by their children's opposite behavior, because they have been raised in the same environment. But family processes, just the same as other ongoing relationships, are never stable. Regardless if the general conditions, attitudes and rituals remain the same.

Consequently, we are not able to perceive and follow the phenomena children have to cooperate with over the course of growing up in their entirety. We may be able to pick out a few relevant educational principles, attitudes and actions. But children are still confronted with a whole range of interpersonal phenomena they have to react to spontaneously. By means of video recordings, researchers are able to capture some aspects of this interpersonal universe and study them picture for picture. But the rest of us must be humble in the face of all that we will never know. All we can do is try our best to maximize the quality of what we are able to influence and increase what we call relational competence (refers to professional relationships).

The Existential Conflict

Both children and adults are confronted with the same conflict between integrity and cooperation, even if it shows in different ways. For this reason, we have decided to step out of line and veer away from conventional categorization. In doing so, we hope to be able to illustrate the inappropriate polarization which often occurs concerning this conflict within the framework of professional discourse. Usually one party takes the children's side, while the other steps in for the adults.

We know today that both children and adults have to cope with a range of more or less challenging conflicts every single day. The existential importance of these conflicts depends on the individual's own cognitive evaluation of the content's relevance, no matter if adult or child. This fact helps understand what the Norwegian pedagogue and researcher Berit Baa[5] calls the "adult power to define". The historically evolved adult power to define includes the adults' power to decide, for both sides, whether a conflict with a child is significant or insignificant, necessary or unnecessary, right or wrong. Only a few generations ago, marriages were also often determined by the masculine power to define. The power to define may well be the one component of adult-child relationships which denies a child the sense of being acknowledged and seen to the largest extent.

EXAMPLE

Anna (5), was interviewed about conflicts in kindergarten for an educational film.[6] The journalist asked her, "Anna, what do you think is the worst thing about grown-ups making all the decisions in kindergarten?"

Anna thought it over carefully and answered, "If they don't allow us to be angry."

"But is that really true, Anna? Are children not allowed to be angry in kindergarten?"

Again, Anna took her time to think carefully before she said, "Well, yes, ... you are allowed to be angry, ... but only if you have a good reason to be, ... and the grown-ups decide if our reason to be angry or not is good – for me, that is the worst."

The above is a typical example of adult power to define. Anna's kindergarten probably doesn't represent a carefully balanced and holistic approach to education. The teachers involved possibly have the widespread but illusionary idea that children will develop social wisdom if taught the difference between *right* and *wrong* rather than experiencing it through adult guidance.

Yet, it is not the *actual* power that denies children the feeling of being seen and acknowledged. The actual power that decides e.g. whether or not a child is allowed a scoop of ice cream; it's the *procedural* power that interprets the child's craving as irresponsible, disloyal, inappropriate or a sign of indulgence. Although children sometimes express themselves as though they want to be right or have their own will, they – just like adults – primarily strive to be taken seriously in a situation where they know they are dependent on the others' decision.

This is a central aspect. One of the most essential indicators for hearing and understanding existential undertones in conflicts, is the child's immediate reaction in the respective situation. The child's immediate reactions to adult decisions are phenomenon which adults have traditionally condemned the most and handled with the least success.

An ordinary, healthy child can process the fact that their longing for ice cream will not be satisfied within a few minutes. If the conflict is not resolved after this short period of time, either the adult involved has not been clear enough on their decision or he or she has abused the procedural adult power – in many cases both is true. Then the conflict is no longer just about ice cream but about the quality of the relationship. The conflict could have just as well arisen from a disagreement about clothing, breakfast, the child's participation in a group assignment, or the return of another child's toy.

From our clinical experience and our knowledge of infant and relational research, we have learnt that children often opt for cooperation instead for their own integrity when confronted with an existential conflict with adults they are very close to, such as parents or surrogates in particular. The clinical work with couples and other adult relationships has revealed that the same applies to adults. Everything points towards a general tendency to cooperate rather than protect our own integrity. The entirety of experiences we have gathered around the conflict between cooperation and integrity during our childhood and youth determines the quality of our contribution to later private and social relationships. These established patterns, however, do not necessarily remain unchanged; through personal reflection and relational feedback, patterns can be renewed in new relationships.

The dominant tendency to choose cooperation above integrity is also one of our most important strengths. It is, for instance, the reason for children's enormous social and cultural flexibility and adaptability. Children born in Denmark behave like Danish children within only a few months, and children born in France quickly behave like French children. Similarly, children of French parents who have moved to Denmark or of Danish parents who have moved to France fit characteristics of both cultural profiles. Their inherent flexibility allows children to socialize in most diverse settings without losing touch with reality. An ordinary, healthy child also manages to change from life in a core family to life in two smaller families consisting of the child him- or herself and new brothers and sisters without serious adaptive difficulties. And it can easily handle one or several groups of grandparents at once as well as the transition from one form of care to the other or from kindergarten to school. The success of the adaptive process does not depend on diversity as much as it depends on the ability of the adults involved to acknowledge and protect the child's personal integrity. In situations where the child's integrity is ignored or violated or their cooperative capacity exhausted *adaptive difficulties* will arise. The cause of such difficulties is hardly ever a lack of the ability or willingness to adapt; it is usually much rather the result of overconforming.

This can be observed, for example, in migrant families: the child sometimes gives up their personal integrity for the sake of their parents' cultural identity and integrity. This is part of the desperate attempt to adapt to a new cultural identity. The children concerned are often plunged into painful existential crisis, which usually become manifest as social crisis. Similar incidents occur within religious groups which demand children and parents to give up their personal integrity for the sake of an ideological identity. Such demands very often cause life-long existential struggles for children (and others) who do not have the opportunity to make an independent decision guided by their inner responsibility. Often, their conflicts do not surface until much later. Authoritarian communities and obedient systems still attract many people by promising security. Members of communities which are entirely shut off from the surrounding society often find particular relief in not having to make any personal decisions; they content themselves with being acknowledged for their ability to cooperate and being promised a better life after death.

From time to time, similar communities develop within the educational world. Alternative institutions are founded by young and passionate educational ambassadors whose lack of personal and professional integrity prevent them from developing a sense for their students' integrity. Institutions and projects like this are always seen as a success from the inside. Even viewed from the outside, they are often given an exemplary status. But once one of the pupils or employees develops sufficient integrity to reveal the truth, discrepancies become obvious. Luckily, however, most alternative projects are established on adults' well-founded sense of children's integrity and a professional vision protecting and facilitating the development of children's integrity.

As mentioned previously, adults also have a similar tendency to cooperate beyond their own needs. Teachers are often adults whose positive attitude towards children encourages them to give up their own integrity and wellbeing in order to serve others. Along their way, they put up with repeated hurtful behavior by superiors and colleagues as well as severe violations by the children. In addition to the negative personal and professional effects on themselves, they are also poor role models for both children and younger colleagues. As long as we do not see this as a *relational* phenomenon, we lose ourselves in moral indignation and endless discussions about who is to blame. But even if we manage to agree on who is to take the blame and remove this person, peace is short-lived. For the deep-rooted disposition to over-cooperate and deny oneself bears the constant risk of new violations.

Luckily, severe violations are not very common. But the transition from role-based authority substituting personal integrity to personal authority is a new challenge. Consequently, many teachers find themselves trapped in a psychological vacuum – an empty space, marking the situation where the old no longer applies and the new has not yet come to be. In all respects, this phase is exhausting, and in many cases unsettling. If transitional phases occur at the beginning or as a consequence of a personal crisis, we find it hard enough to persevere. But if such a transition occurs, as in the case of education, as a cultural mass phenomena, we may have even more difficulty passing through it. This is also influenced by the fact that the next steps and decisions depend on a large number of other people and not just ourselves.

If our need to pursue our own interest and the need to cooperate is out of balance, it becomes painful. All of us are able and willing to acknowledge this pain to varying degrees. At the beginning, most of us experience it as
- a type of fatigue that can increase to the point of burnout,
- a lapse of concentration which may develop into an impaired short-term memory,
- a low frustration tolerance which can become manifest in impulsive aggression,
- or an increasing depressive mood which might evolve into serious clinical depression.

Should the readers find themselves showing similar stress symptoms, they are probably right. Especially negative stress affects the organism's homeostasis, which is the unconscious process by which we maintain our balance. In the case of biological or psychosomatic imbalance, the organism may opt for supplements, like insulin to provide the body with the substances it is temporarily unable to produce. In the case of psychosocial imbalance, however, it is more healing to establish a connection to one's own inner responsibility and accept support and advice from outside. Support from others can be helpful in developing an attitude of taking oneself seriously, (which is often wrongfully decried as selfishness). It is also wise to activate the personal social network, which is usually part of the problem and can, therefore, also be part of the solution.

Both children and adults, who have had to cooperate with phenomena contradicting their inner responsibility, express their conflict in anti-social behavior. Children lack the necessary experience and cognitive insight to find a civilized way of distancing themselves from the group. Therefore, they need the knowledge and guidance of adults. But adults sometimes have similar deficiencies and, consequently, also need support and caring guidance through their colleagues. Most of us do not give up cooperating unless our integrity has been violated so long that it urges us to invest our last energy for its protection. To give up cooperating may be perceived as antisocial or selfish, but in truth it reflects both our fundamental social disposition and the necessity to protect our own identity.

None of us are able to prevent fluctuations in cooperating with others over time. But the healthier our self-confidence and, hence, the relationship to our inner responsibility, the less dramatic are imbalances. We cannot expect good results to be achieved within the first 18 years. At the same time, there is no rule according to which certain developmental processes cannot kick in before the age of 40 or 50. It is often more a question of personal values and social expectations

Integrity, Equality and Democracy

Democratizing the adult-child relationship in families and educational institutions has probably been the most successful attempt of the last generations in trying to modernize education. Many believed that such democratization would suffice to protect children's integrity, but this is not the case. Democratic values are about distributing power and influence and, thus, about ensuring the *rights* of the individual.

Although we are convinced that democratic values provide an ideal foundation for supporting the individual's personal and social *development* and *existence*, we also see that they do not per se ensure the best possible conditions to facilitate and protect the individual's needs.

The belief that the children's right to participate in the process of decision-making would constitute the final humanist step was proved false in both families and schools. Parents were confused, when they experienced that children still did not thrive and develop properly despite being allowed to decide for themselves. And schools were disappointed, that introducing democratic values did not suffice to restore the calm and harmony of the classroom, not even in activities and topics children were allowed to determine themselves.

What we still lack is adult guidance combined with values like creating opportunities for an equal dialogue with adults in which children

can discover themselves, or to simply giving children enough space and time to discover themselves on their own, with little instruction. This means adults who have an ear and sense to discern when children shout out what they truly want or do not want and when they are merely echoing their friends' or teacher's words. Adults who begin to know and listen when children actually voice their innermost wishes, needs, and goals. And, children need adults who are able to distance themselves by personal authority and, when they are not able to, are willing to learn from the children's reactions.

Bringing democratic values into family life and schools was an important and necessary step. But we need to take it a step further. We need to establish a holistic approach that takes into account the individual as well as the fact that the professional and social quality of our present community is not, by definition, determined by the majority – no matter if these are adults or children.

Today's children are often described as lacking discipline. If this means they act undisciplined in given conditions as well towards rules and guidance, it is certainly right. Yet, it is not right to say that they lack the ability and willingness to discipline. Just think of chess clubs, karate clubs and all the other sports associations, which are living proof of children's ability in this. The difference between children of the past and today is not in their general ability to comply, but rather in demanding the right to choose to say yes to the discipline expected.

Most children easily come to terms with the fact that they have no influence on whether they have to go to kindergarten or to school. Their openness grants institutions as well as individual teachers the opportunity to build a relationship with the children in which they are invited to say *yes*. But for over 30 years, a reluctance to accept unquestioned discipline related to authoritarian rules and obligations has influenced adult behavior. The feeling of being treated with respect and accepted as equal is what we need to enable a full-hearted *yes* to expected discipline. The situation has thus been reversed: discipline today depends on the respect a person of authority brings up towards the individual. While in earlier times, discipline was dependent on the individual's respect towards authority.

In cases where children lack *self-discipline*; that is the ability to formulate personal and objective goals and to pursue these with joy and frustration, the situation is more complex. But whether the number of children lacking self-discipline is lower or higher today than 25 years ago, remains an open question. Taking a closer look, we see that most of these children lack a sense of *self-esteem*. Two different factors we see that influence this are one: deliberate disturbances or neglect of the child's development of personal integrity and two: tendencies to follow children's wishes as a family rule. Growing up in families with such tendencies, children feel no need to think about what defines them beyond immediate cravings or temporary needs and the frustration they sense when they do not get what they want. Although usually temporary, such feelings of frustration can easily grow into a more profound frustration and doubts about whether they are *someone* at all. Doubts of this kind impede personal goals and drive children into seeking relief in short-lived, shallow, and material goals. This is not because they are shallow themselves but because they have not yet been able to get in touch with their deeper needs.

A few generations ago, self-discipline and the ability to pursue personal goals were rarely accompanied by a healthy feeling of self-esteem. Developing these qualities was motivated by the contemporary overall goal of becoming *something* or fulfilling a certain role. This could have been an officer, a carpenter, a housewife, a family's breadwinner, or a businessman. In combination with the schools' one-sided focus on teaching knowledge and facts, such social ambitions and familial requirements produced a mass of people who, in fact, managed to become *something* – but something they did not feel comfortable with.

Today's contemporary values are more about creating a balance between social and personal goals. It is about creating a balance between the goals of becoming *something* and becoming *someone*. The emphasis of institutions is to provide children with knowledge for life. Parents' ambitions are more often existential than social. From the perspective of individual health, this is a huge step forward, even if it isn't completed. It seems like we are still looking for safe ground on which to stand with both feet.

Integrity, Self-Esteem and Self-Confidence

Integrity and self-esteem are closely related in a dialectic way. Growing up among adults who consciously foster a child's personal integrity and respect their attempts to discover and define themselves provides ideal conditions to develop a healthy self-esteem. This in turn, is essential for the introspective process underlying the ability to connect directly to one's inner responsibility. Provided that a child's integrity is intact, their sense of self healthy, and their relationship to adults fruitful, the introspective process happens intuitively and only takes a second. But if one or more of these three conditions is missing, the process can take up to several minutes, months, or even years.

The close and dialectical relationship between integrity and sense of self becomes more obvious when trying to answer the question *what can you do to develop and strengthen your feeling of self-esteem?"* The answer is to *act congruently with your own integrity.* With good reason, this answer is often perceived as ironic, for we depend on ourselves, even if we are unable to find ourselves. We can establish relationships that provide support, inspiration, and challenges, but the process of developing self-esteem will always remain personal and lonely.

Relationships become more transparent when we think of self-esteem as a two-dimensional phenomenon with both a quantitative and a qualitative aspect:

The *quantitative* dimension is about how much and how good we know ourselves. Put simply, the quantitative dimension focuses on the introspective process first. In everyday language, we call this gaining self-awareness. The *qualitative* dimension, on the other hand, is about how we behave towards what we know about ourselves.

EXAMPLE

Imagine the interaction between an infant and his mother, who just prepared lunch and is ready to feed her child. The child, however, is not

hungry and refuses to eat by lowering his head, turning his face away from the spoon, and pressing his lips together. The true reason behind the child's refusal to eat may vary: the child might actually be hungry but not have been given enough time to wake up and feel his appetite; he might actually be hungry but not like the smell of the food; he might just not feel like socializing or had a bad experience with the last meal. Anyway, the infant senses a reluctance to accept the situation. He sets clear signals about his current position in relationship to his mother and the food she has offered. His behavior demonstrates all qualities required to maintain a healthy relationship. The behavior is
- *personal: it expresses the child's current feelings,*
- *social: it actively relates to the current incident in the relationship,*
- *and authentic: it is clear, honest, and in compliance with the child's emotions.*

In response to her child's behavior, the mother starts to worry. At first, she remains calm and says: "Okay sweetie, let's have something to eat. You haven't eaten all day ... Mommy knows you gotta be hungry." The child, however, still refuses to eat. Consequently, the mother becomes more and more concerned and increases the pressure on the baby. Since the mother fails to take her child seriously, her contribution to the relationship in this situation lacks all the qualities the child's behavior shows.

It may well be that her worries, visible in her facial expression, are personal and authentic; but they may also come from her idea of what a good, responsible mother's reaction in such a situation should be like. In either case, we are unable to know, because she does not express herself personally in her words. She does not describe her personal being but her fantasy about the child's needs and feelings. Her entire expression is authoritarian and unsocial. This happens because she does not enter in a dialogue which takes the needs and boundaries of both herself and the baby into account. She creates a reality of her own in herself and acts accordingly. And thus, her loving and caring intentions are transformed into authoritarian and impersonal behavior.

If this conflict is not an exception but one of many of that kind, the child will soon find him- or herself in a deep existential crisis, torn between trying to protect their own integrity and adapting to the mother's needs and wishes. Soon, the child will either start to cooperate properly, transgress their boundaries and give in to the mother's wish despite not wanting to eat, or cooperate in reverse, and fight tenaciously for integrity.

In either of the cases, the child's self-esteem is affected. A child *cooperating properly* has to abandon their feelings of not being hungry and replace them with the mother's fantasy that they must be hungry. The mother's facial expression and the persuasive, worried, demanding, painful, or maybe even threatening tone of voice push the child to take the mother's emotions more serious than their own. And this is reinforced because the mother seems pleased when the child gives up their integrity.

Reversed cooperation quickly puts the child in a situation, which is no longer focused on the question whether he or she is hungry or not. Meals themselves are then associated with confusion, anxiety and the feeling of being stuck. Sooner or later, the child will stop fighting for integrity and instead combat the mother's authoritarian behavior. Ironically, the mother's first assumption that the child is hungry becomes true, which upsets the child even more and fosters the mother's fantasy. Just like when cooperating properly, the child loses touch with their actual appetite and becomes more attuned to the mother's feelings than the own. Children cooperating properly say: *I eat because my mother is worried.* Children cooperating in reverse say: *I do not eat because my mother is worried.* The quantitative dimension of self-esteem is inevitably damaged in either of the cases as soon as the mother's emotions are more relevant than the child's. The qualitative dimension is also impaired in either of the cases, albeit for different reasons. In cooperating properly, children learn to care more about their mothers' feelings than their own and, eventually, stop taking themselves seriously. In reversed cooperation, children mistake their own integrity for the cause of the conflict with their mothers and, consequently, develop feelings of guilt.

The quantitative and qualitative loss of self-esteem arises from specific situations like this disagreement about the child's appetite. This loss is the result of what infant research refers to as present moments[7]. Reinforcement occurs because children have ultimate faith in their parents. Therefore, they lose faith in their own feelings and perceptions before they give up faith in their caregivers. In cases of severe violation, however, children lose faith in their parents alongside the faith in themselves.

In addition, the parents' love and care can in itself pose a challenge to in the development of quantitative self-esteem, because it is the accompanying process of a child expanding their knowledge of and faith in personal experience. One aspect of this process requires particular attention, because it can be easily mistaken for a normal learning process.

EXAMPLE
A father, who was taking a walk with his daughter loved the woods and knew a lot about nature. It was important to him to pass this passion on to his daughter. In the course of their walk, he therefore offered one piece of knowledge after the other.

"Maria, look: this is a pellet, something owls spit out after they have eaten."

"Look up there! Can you see that bunch of twigs in the tree? That's a buzzard's nest, where it lives taking care of its babies."

"Or look over here! Do you see that snail? It's a Burgundy snail, and it is edible. But you can't eat it straight from the ground; you have to clean it first, then cook it –and then it tastes delicious."

"Maria, look: this is a fir, it looks just like a Christmas tree. Can you remember our Christmas tree? And that is a pine tree. The pine tree has longer needles than the fir. Do you see that?"

This fathers eagerness to teach his daughter about nature strongly influences her process of building up self-esteem. If he were able to take himself back a little more, Maria could pick up things herself, ask her father questions, or develop her own fantasies about what she sees. She might look up herself and wonder about the cluster of dead branches in the middle of the tree's green and, maybe ask for an explanation. She might have fun drawing her father's attention to the *long-haired* fir tree or to touch the big snail and find out what it is.

But in this situation, Maria's attentiveness and her chance to use it are at stake. She is not given a single opportunity to determine her own rhythm of paying attention to nature, to her inner experience, or to her father. Her father's behavior and her love for him urges her to give him all attention. This turns him into a filter through which she perceives the world. Maria is learning a lot about nature but not about herself, her own observations, fantasies and her own needs for additional information. Her ability to reflect and to question is neglected. Maria might inherit her father's passion for nature or only his knowledge; but her attentiveness might become too confused and manipulated to be able to maintain either the passion or knowledge of nature.

The abilities to question and to reflect are key processes both for the development of quantitative self-esteem and for the capacity to learn about the world outside of the self.

The importance of self-esteem as a strong foundation for learning is an essential reason to change the focus of teaching away from giving information and learning to the pupils' perception.

The above example does not necessarily represent a serious or regular situation in Maria's life and the father-daughter relationship. But it does illustrate a typical adult-child relationship and a common situation also arising from the tendency to not allow children to be alone or to play with other children without being supervised, instructed, or entertained by adults. *Children live slowly and need time and quietness to reflect and question their lives.* This also includes qualitative time with adults who offer their full attention instead of challenging the child's attention. Nowadays, the culture around children in family, school and leisure time is focused extremely on activity and productivity. A child's ability to focus, to question, and to be attentive are usually inborn. If these abilities get lost over the course of growing up, it makes sense to take a look at the quality of past and present relationships. Not to draw attention to possible failures but to find the key to building helpful relationships in the future. The knowledge of relational components which were missing in earlier relationships can help detect destructive elements and, thus, provide an essential foundation for creating healthy future relationships.

Quantitative self-esteem develops over our whole life-span regardless of how we live our lives. The longer we live the more we learn about ourselves. Whether the current state is perceived as sufficient or not differs from individual to individual. Some adults seem to be content with their lives without thinking too much about who they are. Others, however, struggle with the consequences of low self-esteem in professional and private relationships all their lives.

It is the adults' responsibility to aid children in developing self-esteem. We are convinced that professional ethics require teachers as well as all other professionals to continuously evaluate their own self-esteem and inner responsibility. And wherever necessary take care of possible adverse effects on the relationships in their jobs. This usually entails personal interaction and reflection both on the qualitative, as well as the quantitative dimension. But the focus usually changes from one area to the other several times in the course of our adult life.

As mentioned before, the qualitative dimension of self-esteem describes how we treat what we know about of ourselves. How we think about ourselves, shows in many different ways:
- In large groups, I am reluctant to interact and consequently, feel uncomfortable.
- I blurt everything out that comes to my mind and, in doing so, often embarrass myself.
- I have short legs and small breasts; I hate my body.
- Whenever confronted with a new group of children I get nervous; I think that is embarrassing and unprofessional.
- I easily dominate other people and reproach myself for doing so.
- I feel stupid, because I am bad at spelling.
- I have a strong need to talk but feel ashamed to take another person's space.

These expressions of self-awareness *(what I know about myself)* are followed by a negative evaluation of these aspects *(how I judge how I am)* All of them represent low self-esteem. Healthy self-esteem is not the opposite; expressed in praise and positive remarks about ourselves. Praise is the opposite of criticism and represents a judging inner dialogue just the same. To develop healthy and dynamic feelings of self-esteem we need to replace judgement with *acknowledgement.*

Our own tendency to judge or acknowledge is largely determined by our early relationships with our caregivers. *Negative assessments of the self are never authentic; they are inner representations of personal criticism vocalized by others.* Usually these were people we cooperated with and imitated, because we believed that they knew better or because we feared the consequences of staying true to our own perceptions and feelings. Children even *invent* negative descriptions of themselves to explain their parents' failure. This happens e.g. in situations where children have been put up for adoption, neglected, sexually assaulted, or abused physically as well as psychologically. In some cases, the negative evaluations of the self are so painful they can't be integrated and the self is cut off from the own feelings. Consequently, the children concerned get stuck in existential crises. Their self-esteem is low and dominated by negative feelings. And the situation prevents them from being able to work with their self-esteem and achieve any kind of improvement. Although introspection is invaluable to a person's development and building prosperous relationships, it can be rather daunting. Due to negative experiences in previous relationships, people therefore simply stop to try and give up their authenticity. They can, however, regain authenticity if they are able to gain trust in a person who helps them develop the courage to revise their previous distrust in themselves and others. This other person can be a teacher who enables trust. Trust builds on the same foundation as relational competence: experiencing acknowledgement without being devalued or betrayed.

Low self-esteem and thus resulting difficulty to connect with and consult one's personal integrity and inner responsibility inhibit setting constructive and personal goals as well as the ability to perceive life and cooperation with others valuable and satisfying. So obviously, low self-esteem has important implications on our health, social life, as well as our existential and intellectual competence.

These implications are determined for one by the phenomenon itself: the individual's attitude towards him- or herself. And for another by ways people interact with the way low self-esteem shows.

People with a well-developed feeling of self-esteem can easily be recognized by their natural authority, authentic profile, and sober as well as accepting perspective of themselves. Low self-esteem, shows differently from person to person. But the two categories introverted and extroverted can help understand reactions. Here are a few characteristics as possible examples.

Introverted people tend to suffer from social timidity, social anxiety and different forms and states of depression. So-called *quiet* girls and boys often develop eating disorders and thoughts of suicide. In some cases, they do attempt to commit suicide. Usually, society responds to introversion with sympathy, care, support, praise, or the like.

Extroverted people are often perceived as consistently craving for validation, being monotonously preoccupied with the *biggest*, most *expensive*, or *best*, aggressively criticizing others, rejecting any kind of fault and responsibility or are in continuous rivalry. In contrast to introverted behavior, extroverted patterns are often confronted with criticism and rejection.

Another important difference between the two types is that it seems easier to involve introverted people in rational educational contact than extroverted people. But experience has shown that it is equally difficult to help them with issues related to their low self-esteem. While introverted people see their issues, and are convinced that improvement is impossible, the extroverted deny having a problem at all. *What all manifestations of low self-esteem have in common is the inner experience of not being able to achieve one's true being because of having spent one's life in borrowed costumes.*

The better adults succeed in protecting a child's integrity and help them learn on their own, the better the chances of developing a healthy self-esteem.

While the terms discussed above are existential concepts, the term *self-confidence* is an issue in educational settings. Not because it is solely relevant to professional relationships, but because it is about abilities and skills. Our degree of self-confidence is determined by the quality of our mental, physical, and creative performance. The better we are at something, the higher our self-confidence – in the respective field. The more areas we are good at, the higher the level of our overall self-confidence.

The term was introduced to child rearing towards the end of the 1940s and quickly became a key concept of pedagogical work as well as an important goal of parents. Children without self-confidence were considered a *mess*. Children with low self-confidence were thought to be in desperate need of increased self-confidence. The pedagogical solution for this problem was praise. Praise children as often as possible, inappropriately praise them for bad performances as well as appropriately praise them for good performances, incidentally praise them for mediocre performances as well as objectively praise them for performances which truly deserve praise. However, also arbitrarily praise them just to emphasize one's own position.

Up until the 1920s, experts on child education spoke up against praising children for their behavior or specific performances. People assumed that praise would convey the impression that *correct* behavior was not as natural as it was supposed to be. Therefore, adults were advised to criticize children whenever their behavior did not meet the (adult) standards.

Undoubtedly, the emerging interest in children's self-confidence was sparked by modern American psychology, which was dominated by a strong commitment to the development of self-esteem in both children and adults.

As explained before, self-esteem has different underlying psychological patterns than self-confidence. Self-esteem is our ability to know ourselves and the way we react to what we know (high versus low self-esteem). Self-confidence in contrast develops from our experience of competency and is limited to these areas.

The terms self-esteem and self-confidence were originally defined in American Psychology with a similar meaning as we are giving it in this book and taken over by European Psychology. Over more than half a century they lived their own life on the two continents. In Europe self-esteem disappeared or was absorbed by self-confidence, which then became the goal for parents and teachers – i.e. focus on skills and performance. In America self-esteem was confused with self-confidence to a degree, where todays parents, teachers and psychotherapists want to give children (as well as insecure adults) a lot of self-esteem. They attempt to do so by supporting their self-confidence. In both cultures, the result is the same: a lot of people with a lot of self-confidence (winners) but without or with very weak self-esteem. The most obvious outcome is a many good performers and competitors with low emotional and social intelligence.

In practice, both terms are often understood synonymously. Therefore, the preferred method to achieve self-esteem is mistakenly also seen in praise:

Goal:
self-esteem = self-confidence

Method:
praise

This has especially influenced educational psychology and families, but also played a certain role in developmental psychology and psychotherapeutic practice. One of the most far-reaching consequences is that children were raised with an inflated ego but little self-esteem and hardly any inner responsibility. Today, the inflated ego is very often seen as a main cause for children's' inability to get over small disappointments and failures and the violent aggressions resulting from such small frustrations. Researchers as well as the public were surprised by the fact that children, who hurt or even murder their classmates and teachers, are often perceived as *'ordinary, well-adapted children from stable families'* who might have had a *'tendency to introversion but never caused any problems'*.

To show the difference we described the vital difference between self-esteem and self-*confidence* in an article published in 1990[8]:

Goal:
self-esteem
self-confidence

Method:
acknowledgement
praise and critique

The situation is complex especially in educational settings. One of the fundamental principles of *psychology of performance* is that success leads to success, or at least is more likely to lead to success than failure. Educational psychology and practical pedagogy internalized this principle and advocated *'small everyday successes'* as the pedagogical key to restoring the self-confidence of neglected children. The implementation was crowned with little success, because the children concerned suffered primarily from a lack of self-esteem. Self-esteem cannot be fostered by strengthening self-confidence as a loosely defined prime goal of education. This does not mean that it is not also important to support self-confidence in respective areas and find joy in it. But in areas, where self-esteem and self-confidence do not directly correlate with each other, the emphasis on self-confidence can cause a neglect of the emotional side. This is also an issue in remedial education: where the focus lies strongly on children's intelligence and performance as well as their conduct.

In a picture, the difference between self-esteem and self-confidence can be illustrated as follows:

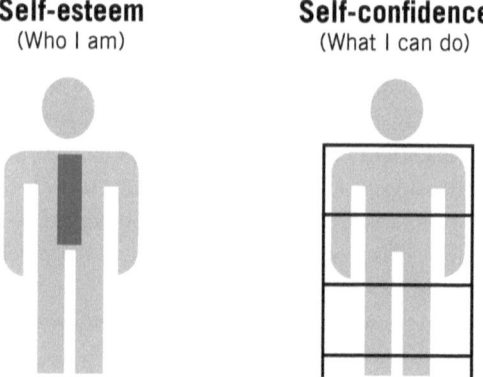

Self-esteem
(Who I am)

Self-confidence
(What I can do)

Self-esteem represents inner standards, enabling us to react to external expectations, requirements, temptations, etc. It assists us in making decisions we support and take seriously. Self-confidence is an external framework, which we can draw on for support. Self-confidence is not shallower or less substantial than self-esteem. Self-confidence and self-esteem each belong to a distinct dimension – on one hand personal competencies, that can be learned and on the other the existential dimension – and, for this reason, do not allow any kind of comparison. They are both important in their own way. The connection between the two seems rather weak. Although people with high self-esteem tend to be more objective and accepting of their level of self-confidence in different areas. In contrast, people with low self-esteem tend to overemphasize their deficient or extraordinary self-confidence in respective areas.

Children hardly express their existential dilemma or suffering openly, which is why their problems are often ignored or trivialized. Most commonly, they are expressed through psychosocial signals and symptoms or learning difficulties. (But not all learning difficulty should be traced to existential issues!) In order to categorize these signals and symptoms, educational and clinical child psychology has spent years exploiting all resources available, but they have not been able to produce more than a few methodological approaches. The outcome of research does not justify the efforts that were put into it.

From our perspective, the missing link is understanding ways of supporting a child's relationships to him-/herself as a basis for social and cognitive performance.

This is not due, however, to a general lack of interest in the wellbeing of the children. But schools' emphasis on performance and efficiency has never been interrupted: teachers alike have stuck to traditional performance parameters instead of developing new parameters suitable to foster children's sense of self-esteem. As far as we know, not a single culture on earth has yet been able to develop such parameters.

Objective praise and criticism are the pedagogical tools necessary to strengthen children's (as well as adults') self-confidence. Already by the age of five or six, children have developed a sober attitude towards their parents' praise. Most of them have figured out that their parents' unjustified or exaggerated praise is simply a sign of their love. They do however, expect objective and justified praise and criticism from teachers.

Music teachers, dance teachers, math teachers, and gym teachers as well as all others play an equal role in developing a child's self-confidence. Their task is to honestly tell the child when their performance is good and when it requires improvement. If, in addition to that, they also accompany the pupil's process of working on the performance. In this way, they not only fulfill their responsibility as teachers, but they also contribute substantially to the child's self-confidence.

This process also entails that children must realign their career aspirations as well as their personal goals time and again. At times, this also makes them unhappy. This fact cannot be changed. It can be helpful if experts and parents become involved in the personal learning process and provide support as well as advice, but children should not be underestimated. When they realize, for example, that their dream of becoming an elite student or pop star is unattainable, they do not need to be comforted by giving them praise for their mathematical talents.

EXAMPLE

Rune was in fifth grade. He was an average student but had learning difficulties, especially in reading. Even the simplest first grade texts were a huge challenge for him. This handicap made it difficult for him to get by in school. In addition, Rune had developed a strong tendency to behave aggressively. Consequently, he very often acted up in the heat of the moment. He destroyed things, beat up classmates, and approached adults with stubbornness whenever he didn't feel like meeting their expectations. His teachers tried hard to help him, especially by strengthening his self-confidence. Whenever he became nervous reading and had little success, the adults offered comfort by saying something along the lines of "Rune, just think about all of the other things you are good at: you can build caves, you are very skilled with your hands, and you can invent games which are fun to play. You see: everybody is good at something."

Every time he expresses his struggles through action or words, and is given similar answers Rune is left alone with an overwhelming amount of feelings and experiences. He does not receive relevant feedback to immediate expressions of his inner conflict and, thus, hardly any opportunity to develop his self-esteem. He does not receive reactions that help him find a way to get in touch with his struggles. In this sense, it isn't a surprise, that his feelings of frustration only express themselves in the psychological superstructure he constructed himself. In this case, this superstructure could be described as an e*motional excess as a result of a lack of acknowledgement*.

To help Rune recognize this difficult side of himself, to come to terms with it and integrate it in his identity, he needs adults that react differently. Once important adults start to respond to Rune's open frustration, he can learn to as well. By leading a dialogue with Rune, or with people in similar situations, we experience that the persons' actual needs surface.

The following dialogue is an example of how to initiate a process: *"Rune, I can imagine that it is difficult and tiring for you to sit in class, not being able to read, while others are."* Rune answered immediately: *"No, it's not, because I know I am good at other things."* The immediacy of his answer created a doubt about whether it is his own answer – it almost seemed like he answered automatically. Therefore, we continued: *"Oh, I see. I was just asking because I recently met a boy at another school. He went to fifth grade, just like you, and had difficulties reading. He told me how mad he was at himself as well as his classmates because everything came so easy to them ..."* As we continued with the other boy's story, we saw that Rune was gradually recognizing himself. He became interested and listened carefully. Maybe this was the first time that he ever received an opportunity to talk about what makes life so difficult for him. During our first conversation, he chose just to listen, but already on our second meeting, he became more engaged: *"Have you talked to the other boy in the meantime?"* In this case this was the beginning of a series of conversations in which Rune was able to find words for his experiences reading.

Rune started seeing the educational psychologist *after* he had developed several symptoms. It would have made more sense, if these conversations had complemented daily classes from the onset of Rune's difficulties.
Once teachers learn how to communicate with children in situations like Runes in a way which enables them to get an understanding of what their

problems feel like, they will discover how painful it must be to grapple with the same challenging task day in and day out. They realize that there is no point in sending children like Rune to a psychologist, for the psychological superstructure is not Rune's personal problem; it is a problem in relationship to the teachers. Therefore, it makes more sense to provide teachers with psychological expert knowledge and supervision. They can be enabled to talk with the children about their issues in a productive and effective way on an everyday basis, supporting the children's development of self-confidence as well as self-esteem.

Despite the weak connection between self-confidence and self-esteem, most of us master the challenges in education and professional life largely or solely on the basis of self-confidence. But, pedagogues must question if this is desirable for children of today and tomorrow and to content themselves with this situation.

Self-Consciousness

Children's increased self-consciousness has delighted and fascinated but also annoyed and provoked. Within a period of just 30 years, children's non-existent, sporadic or well-hidden self- consciousness has evolved into an open, collective and almost natural phenomenon.

While self-esteem as mentioned above is an existential issue and self-confidence an issue of competence, self-consciousness is a social phenomenon.

It is a term wide-open for interpretation. The way we use it in this book describes the phenomena that since the turn of the century children are no longer creeping along the walls trying to be invisible. They are behaving as if *they have a god-given right to take as much space as they need* (Juul, 2000)[9] It shows as a societal phenomenon, by the advertising industry vigorously focusing on them as an important target-group in their own right. But self-consciousness is also a collective phenomenon, and it is not related to the individual child's self-esteem or self-confidence. Actually, the discrepancy between the child's private, personal universe and the way they show themselves to the world is usually substantial.

Another factor supporting this development is the fact that a distinct child and youth culture has developed. The significance attached to childhood is new: childhood is now appreciated for the sake of childhood itself. In addition, children's living conditions have become of interest. In the past, there was nothing like child-oriented charter flights, hotels, or meals; there were no playgrounds at gas stations, no child car seats; McDonald's had not yet started to give out plastic toys with their meals to attract children as new customers. Also, no one had any reservations about buying Oriental carpets possibly produced by low-paid children under bad working conditions.

We could elaborate on many facets related to these developments, but we want to focus on one specific aspect, which is often overlooked and has a great impact on the way we relate.

There was broad agreement that children should not ask if they were not asked first. This restriction affected all wishes and needs in children's lives, be they small as a burger or toy, or more significant as the wish to be heard and acknowledged. Both families and schools adhered to this unwritten rule and expected the children to act accordingly. Today, children take it for granted to be able to express their wishes and needs. This is an expectation that has its limitations. While expressing one's opinion like asking for pocket money, having a say in the family, wanting a scooter, new clothes or a trip to Disney World, are seen as self-evident ways of participating in family life, more fundamental existential needs are still withheld. This is due to the lack of means to express these needs. There are hesitations because of a child's loyalty towards their parents and, maybe, even more relevant, to a basic doubt about whether they are allowed to - or have the right to - express themselves personally. Family therapy sessions are full of examples of children carefully wording their true needs, while their parents are surprised that they have not done so earlier.

Children's *social* self-consciousness has experienced a rather sudden boost. But this development, has not facilitated the development of healthy feelings of self-esteem at an existential level.

CHAPTER 4:
Personal Responsibility

Definition

In this context, personal responsibility denotes the individual's ability and willingness to assume responsibility for their personal integrity and actions as well as the minor and major life decisions resulting from them. In countries around the world, political and cultural circumstances limit the individual's external freedom to take decisions and threaten the development of personal integrity to different degrees. Also, different religions acknowledge, support or suppress the individual's ability to make independent decisions.

Regardless of the outer circumstances, our individual perception of quality of life and the quality of our relationships is essentially determined by the degree to which we actively take over personal responsibility. Or on the contrary how much we submit to the expectations of others or social and cultural conventions. By definition, other people's needs and expectations, as well as cultural and subcultural conventions, threaten one's own personal responsibility. Each of us is challenged to make decisions for or against ourselves. We are guided by the extent to which we are aware of the processes and/or the degree to which we feel an emotional, intellectual or mental discrepancy.

Personal responsibility is the most important factor concerning relational competence because it is both a way of intervening and the goal of child rearing and pedagogy. Strengthening personal responsibility is the most fruitful alternative to oppression and humiliation. It essentially adds to relational quality and ensures the development of responsible communities.

We have encountered many opposing views from experts who shun giving children more responsibility; in addition to what many of them have to deal with already. We share the opinion that children who grow up in families where they have to assume exceptional amounts of *social* responsibility (e.g. for their parents) should not be given additional responsibility. However, it is not the *personal* responsibility which strains children of addicted, mentally ill, or merely incompetent parents. It is the overload of social responsibility, which has far-reaching consequences for the children concerned. And one of the most serious consequences is that too much social responsibility *prevents* children from learning how to acquire personal responsibility and protect their personal integrity. Social responsibility may teach children how to get by without parental support; but this is an entirely different ability.

Children in troubled families should not have to take over increased social responsibility over an extended period of time. If this is the case, they will unconsciously integrate this responsibility as an essential part of their existence and behavior. Even after being relieved from the burden of responsibility for their parents and brothers and sisters, they are left alone with a self-destructive sense of responsibility overload, which drains vital energy and affects future relationships. According to our experience, the only effective means to create a healthier existential and social balance is the increased focus on a child's personal responsibility.

As practice has shown, an individual's perception of their personal responsibility and the access to it is predominantly determined by the degree to which the social environment recognizes and encourages the development of personal responsibility in childhood – especially during the first eight to ten years. This is, of course, closely related to the way adult caregivers perceive and care for the personal integrity of the children they are responsible for.

Since clinical research has, as mentioned above, focused on children's personal responsibility only recently, we will first of all take a closer look at the aspects on which we have well-founded evidence.

Children's Personal Responsibility

To begin with, we want to list areas in which children from zero to six years are able to take over responsibility for themselves. These include hunger, taste, closeness, distance to adults, choice of friends, clothing style, hair style, taste in music, etc. Later, children also develop a sense of responsibility concerning pocket money, homework, bedtime, getting up, religious and political affiliation, education, love relationships, eroticism, etc. Note that the above list is brief and incomplete, yet it suffices to illustrate the point that the spectrum of children's ability for responsibility is manifold.

There is a correlation between the child's age and their willingness to assume responsibility for specific tasks, as well as differences from child to child. Another important influence is the parents' social responsibility and the way it supports or inhibits the child's personal responsibility.

EXAMPLE
> A family friend visits to see the newborn baby. She places the baby, who is eyeing the stranger carefully, on her lap. Just like most adults would, she starts a spontaneous dialogue with the child. At a distance of about a foot, she holds the baby in front of her so that they can look each other in the eye. She opens her eyes wide, plays with exaggerated facial expressions, and talks at a higher pitch than usual, 'Hello, little guy' – pause – 'So, who are you?' – pause – 'You are such a cutie!' – pause – 'Hello, I'm Anna' – pause – 'Hi there' – and so on.
>
> Whenever the adult pauses, the child responds by seeking eye contact and maybe moving their arms and legs. It tries to imitate the adults' facial expressions and lip movements. It may even try to smile. At some point, the baby turns its face to the side and thus signals that it wants to end the conversation or at least make a break.
>
> Infants take responsibility for their need for social contact and their sense of how long contact feels good to them by seeking or ending contact independently.

This example illustrates how even very small children are capable of taking on personal responsibility, but need a corresponding environment. If adults are not sensitive enough to recognize the child's needs and boundaries and lack respect for the child's integrity, an inner conflict between integrity and cooperation arises. Small children, such as the baby in the example above, give up their integrity in most cases to comply with the expectations of adults and become more and more passive in contact. But some of them start to fight for their integrity. In either case, however, it is hard to establish a close and harmonious relationship.

The older children get, the clearer they can mark their boundaries and protect their integrity – provided that they grow up under healthy circumstances and are not neglected. They develop the ability to express their boundaries in words and to develop arguments for their right to take over their personal responsibility. Before illustrating this in more detail, we want to take a look at the natural dialectical interaction between the child's personal responsibility on the one side and the parents' social responsibility (parental responsibility) on the other. We would also like to look at the dialectic interplay between a child's responsibility for him-/herself and the parents' necessary and/or chosen exercise of power.

In most cultures, parents express their love and care for children by assuming full responsibility for their needs. Without doubt, this guarantees the survival of children. Yet, it is also necessary to enable space for expressing personal responsibility. This does not mean that parents should forget their sense of responsibility and exclusively focus on a superordinate responsibility. Allowing this extra space adds on to and extends their social responsibility with a new facet, that enables their children to learn how to take over responsibility for parts of their own lives. In other words, parents have to learn how to be sensitive to their child's way of showing where they are taking over responsibility for themselves. It is important to recognize and respect this self-responsibility to the extent they are able to and to the degree to which they can let go of their adult power.

Two important competences are beyond a child's capacity. The ability to take over responsibility for the relational quality with adults and the ability to care for themselves.

If a kindergarten or school child gets up one morning with the wish to stay at home, it confronts parents with a decision on several levels of responsibility including

- their responsibility towards the institution
- the responsibility towards their own employer
- the responsibility for the child's needs and wellbeing
- the responsibility to take the child seriously
- the responsibility for their own personal limitations and needs and the responsibility/power to make decisions

When it comes to child rearing, many adults have a tendency to think in terms of opposites rather than alternatives. In this example, this could be putting the idea *'school should not be neglected'* up against *'allowing the child to decide if it wants to go to school'*. The underlying principle of this common reasoning is simple but not very appropriate. It does not take into account the other areas of responsibility named above. Alternative ideas are offered later in the chapter under the title "Parental guidance". The main point of the above example, however, is that the child obviously has something on their mind, which requires their parents' attention and acknowledgement. In addition, it demands taking over parental responsibility *in accordance with the child's needs* instead of decisions on the child's behalf. By considering the child's needs and possible alternatives, parents gradually accompany their children how to learn to make decisions not only based on their current feelings and desires but to also take other factors into account. In addition, adults learn more about who their child really is and more aware of other, well-founded alternatives, instead of rules. The weak point of rules is that they exclusively teach children how to be obedient or disobedient. Rules do not facilitate the children's development of personal responsibility or ability to make qualified decisions, nor do they teach adults how to exercise power with as much care as possible.

A child's ability to take personal decisions over the course of growing up is closely related to the intactness of their personal integrity and stability of their self-esteem. These also strongly influence the way the child gets to know their needs and limitations and allows him-/herself to express them. The quantitative dimension of self-esteem, that is the child's connection to him-/herself, widely determines the ability to recognize what they want and what they don't want in the first place. The qualitative dimension, however, determines their willingness to openly express themselves towards adults with equal dignity.

Consequently, the child's existence is clearly shaped by a dialectical relationship between three central phenomena:

In the pedagogical context, there are two possible starting points, partly influenced by the child, and partly by the attitude of the pedagogues. When talking to pedagogues, we find two types: one group has the opinion that the development of a child's personal responsibility should not be supported specifically as long as they manage to adapt to the demands and expectations. The other group is actively committed to supporting the development of personal integrity. Pedagogues of the first kind are very successful with most children. But there are always children who inevitably give up the cooperation sooner or later. In our experience, the second attitude benefits all three essential parts best: the adult, the child, and the relationship between them. And to tell the truth we see no other reasonable choice than committing oneself to the child's development of personal responsibility.

The chapter about challenging children will provide further arguments in favor of this choice.

The main focus of process-oriented educational approaches is the dialogue between expectations, demands, and institutional goals on one side and the children's personal responsibility on the other. Again, the quality of this process depends on the teachers' relational competence.

EXAMPLE

In a kindergarten where the lack of space forced the team to go to the wood with at least twelve children every day, the teachers had several options to handle the situation:

1. The teachers could choose to simply divide the children into groups of twelve, and exercise their power by determining which group has to go to the wood each day, and announcing their independent decision via a list of names on the black board. In doing so, they establish a form of benevolent autocracy, taking into account the kindergarten's spatial shortcomings as well as the children's need for exercise and play. The institution's leadership has to act accordingly and not allow children to take any influence on institutional or pedagogical decisions. The children will learn to conform and that their individual desires and needs do not play a role in adult decision-making.

2. The teachers can also choose to merely make the overall decision that each day twelve children have to spend the day outside but include the children in deciding who the individual children will be. This entails a number of dialogues such as the following:

Teacher: What about you, Louise? Do you want to come with us to the wood today?
Louise: No, I don't want to go to the wood. It's nicer in kinder garten.

Teacher: Have you been looking forward to something in particular?
Louise: Yes ... to playing with Trine ... and it's raining outside.
Teacher: But it's most important for you to be with Trine, right?
Louise: Yes, Trine is my best playmate in kindergarten.
Teacher: Okay, Louise. I understand that this is important to you. So, we have two options: we can ask Trine if she wants to come with us to the wood or find a child who could trade with you. Kids, listen! Louise would love to play with Trine here in the kindergarten. Would any of you like to go to the wood with us instead of Louise?
Alexander: I would.
Teacher: Okay, Alexander ... but I'm curious: do you want to come with us because you want to go to the wood or because you feel sorry for Louise?
Alexander: I just want to play in the woods.
Teacher: Great, then we just need two more kids to come with us.

If no one volunteers, the dialogue could look as follows:

Teacher: I'm sorry, Louise, but it looks like you've got to come with us. Do you want to have a couple minutes with Trine to make a new date?
Louise: Yes, but I'd rather play with Trine now.
Teacher: Yes, I know, it's stupid. But I hope the rest of the day will be better for you. Don't you want to run in to tell Trine before we head out?

In the above dialogue, the teacher shows respect for Louise's wishes and feelings and carefully confronts her with reality, in which we do not always get what we want most, without giving a lecture. Beyond this the teacher can contribute to Louise's day by asking her during break time *"So, Louise, how do you feel? Do you still miss Trine?"* Louise did not get what she wanted most, but in this case, she received what she needs most in the long run: The feeling that she is seen the way she is and that her individuality is neither antisocial nor irresponsible.

Louise's ability to express her feelings and desires and to take over responsibility for them become even more obvious when we compare her to Pernille in the example below. Pernille always acts contained and conforms without protest. Adults easily mistake her behavior as social competence, which is why her teachers need to take more time to find out the reasons for her introversion:

Teacher: Listen, Pernille. I noticed that you hardly ever say what you want. My idea is that you don't say anything because you sometimes don't know yourself or you don't want to annoy anybody.

Pernille: I don't know …

Teacher: That's okay, but would you like to think about this a little? Because I would really like to know what you think or if there is something you don't like.

Of course, Pernille is not able to answer the question. Her exact answer, therefore, is not relevant. What is important, is that the teacher invited her to think about it. Over the course of time, Pernille's reaction will show if she needs more support in perceiving and expressing herself.

EXAMPLE

Per was in eighth grade. His teacher wanted to talk to him one on one. After having addressed several issues, the teacher said, "Listen, Per, I would also like to talk to you about your homework. I just think that you don't do enough and the results aren't good enough, considering what you actually know. I'd like to know what you think about this yourself."

Per: *(apparently embarrassed) Yes, I'm aware of that … and I promise to try harder.*

Teacher: *I don't like the way you look at me, as if you let me down or lied to me.*

Per: *(not taking up eye contact) Well, I don't know ... I just find it difficult to sit down and do my homework when I get home after work at the store.*

Teacher: *(sticks to the common thread) Okay, let us talk about your homework later, Per. But then I'd like to know why it is so difficult for you to tell me about this.*

Per: *Well, you just have to do your homework, right? You say that we have to do the homework.*

Teacher: *Yes, that's true, because it would be good to learn as much as possible as long as you go to school. But, at your age, it is not enough to just do your homework because your teacher wants you to. Although, I'd like to see you doing your homework, I'd rather see you taking your own decision and defending it.*
I don't think it's good that you sit here in front of me as if you're a little boy who stole money from his mom's purse.

Per: *What do you mean?*

Teacher: *Well, I want you to tell me, for example, that you work at the store every afternoon and afterwards usually decide not to do your homework – because isn't it you who decides what to do every day?*

Per: *Yes, but if I say so, you will be angry with me.*

Teacher: *You can take the risk to make me angry when you don't do your homework. People at the store would be angry too if you didn't do your work, right? But I think it's more important that we can look each other in the eye and that you don't risk your dignity. In my case, it is just about work, but in your case, it's about life.*

Per: *(confused, because he is used to being criticized and has developed a habit of avoiding confrontation): I don't know what you're trying to say ...*

Teacher: *Yes, I know, and I think it will be difficult to explain, but I'll make a suggestion: what if you get home from the store and*

> start a conversation with yourself about homework, or, wait, you could even do that before you get home. Then you make a decision without making stupid excuses. You could tell yourself: "Today, I decide not to do my homework", or: "Today, I want to do my homework". If you have decided that you don't want to do the homework, I want you to tell me the next day. Just tell me: "Yesterday, I decided not to do my homework." What do you think about that?

Per: But what if you get angry anyway?

Teacher: Sometimes I'll get angry, and sometimes I won't. That doesn't matter, as long as you start taking your own decisions – without feeling bad about them!

Per: That's not that easy ...

Teacher: Yes, I can know. That's also why I wish we had had this conversation much earlier. So, are you in?

Per: Yes, I'll try.

Teacher: If you decide 'to try', you don't actually decide to do it. Do you want to do it or not?

Per: Well, yes, I want to.

Teacher: Okay. In case you change your mind when you get home, let me know.

Per: Are we done now?

Teacher: I'm done. And you?

Per: Me too.

This dialogue is a good example of a teacher who focuses on two essential aspects in Per's life: his school work and his inability to take personal decisions with dignity. Per will not benefit from his knowledge, as long as his relationship to authorities is shaped by promising more than he is able to give. This way of interacting will also affect private relationships with friends, partners, and future children.

The exercise the teacher suggests, however, shows a fundamental human mechanism:

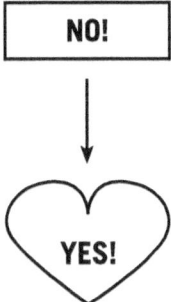

In relationships with people who are very important to us but do not seem to fully acknowledge our *No!* we find it hard to give a wholehearted *Yes!* If not given the opportunity and acknowledgement necessary, children like Per continue to signal No! through their *behavior*, which will become increasingly aggressive the more pressured they feel. In further consequence, the lack of personal dignity and the increase in bad conscience will foster the feeling of not being worthy and, in turn, stir aggression. In addition to the school situation, there are many other factors which essentially determine whether he will *only* express his aggression verbally or also physically and/or quit school. Therefore, it is of great significance that the teacher in the example above decides to put existential issues above the child's performance. His goal is to improve Per's commitment to school alongside restoring the sense of equal dignity in their relationship.

Of course, responsible schoolteachers with an intact professional integrity cannot promise children like Per to ignore their homework. But they can see that children who commonly answer with *Yes, of course, I'll try* and *Yes, but ...* and never keep their promises must first learn to say *No!* without feeling bad (about themselves). Then they can wholeheartedly and responsibly say *Yes* to requests and expectations of their environment. The same holds true for adults: if our refusal of social expectations is not based on true *yes* to our own needs, the social refusal will eventually become an aggressive and self-destructive *No* directed both towards society and ourselves.[1]

A more common way would be to *motivate* Per by telling him more about the significance of homework for his school career and future, informing him about consequences or even threatening with short-term penalties, and maybe asking the parents to support the school's attitude and take over (shared) responsibility for their child's homework.

But adults who pursue such strategies do not only underestimate the intelligence and knowledge of a 14-year-old but also give him the feeling of being even more out of place and humiliated than he already feels anyway. *In addition, strategies of this kind are usually without effect, though they make teachers feel like they are acting responsible.* Even if the method seems successful, the reason why it works is the wrong reason. Moreover, this approach will not work for parents who have not been able to aid their son develop personal dignity and responsibility in the first place. Without professional advice about their fundamental relationship to Per, his parents will be limited to solving the problem through authority and control or by embarrassing their son because they want to live up to the expectations of a frustrated teacher. In either case, Per would become the target of measures that have never produced satisfying outcomes and are humiliating for the child.

In reality, the school requirements do not contradict Per's needs. Schools are designed to contribute to developing students' active responsibility for their own education. Yet, Per urgently needs the guidance of an adult who can show him the way to his self and his personal responsibility. The difference between Per's and the school's needs is that their shortcoming has far more serious consequences on his future than it does for the school.

The suggested approach to achieve pedagogical goals doesn't take more time or resources than conventional strategies. On the contrary, it hardly ever takes longer to treat humans right than to treat them wrong and ignore their needs. Experience shows, we can achieve professional and social goals faster and better if we base our decisions on personal responsibility instead of waiting for an *awakening* of external or social responsibility.

Adult Guidance

A child's (and teenager's) development of personal responsibility depends on their parents' and teachers' ability to lead, and on the degree to which adults show personal and social responsibility in interacting with them. We know that children develop best if surrounded by adults who are willing and able to act as leaders. Children raised by parents who are not able or do not believe they are able to take on the leadership usually lose their faith in their parental guidance and get trapped in an existential and social vacuum. The same applies to children who become victims of misused adult authority. As we will see in Chapter 10, these children and teenagers also need guidance, which facilitates their personal responsibility.

While small children need their parents to come forward as leaders, older children need their parents to step back from their dominant role and take a more passive role accompanying and advising.

Adult guidance which equally fulfills the needs of the child, the adult-child relationship, and pedagogical goals consist of the following components:

AUTHENTICITY
INTEREST
ACKNOWLEDGEMENT
PARTICIPATION
DECISION
CONFLICT

Authenticity
Authenticity, describes the ability and willingness of adults to openly express their personal thoughts, perceptions, values, goals and limitations.

Interest

Interest, in this context, is the interest in who the child is. It directly corresponds to what we described as the ability to *see* children according to their own premises. By definition, parents are interested in their children, and teachers are interested in the children they work with. But, paradoxically, only few adults know how to express their interest by creating meaningful conversations; conversations, which are not perceived as meaningless like the question *what school was like*. This type of conversations is similar to a one-way interview in which adults only ask questions without providing information about themselves as though it's some sort of hearing which shows the adults' distrust in the child. Or it is like a lecture, which often concludes an interrogation.

Few adults from our generation remember situations in which our parents talked to us out of interest in who we were. Consequently, many of us grew up lacking role models as well as a tradition of conversation.

Just like in many other areas, parents and teachers seem to have yet to develop a language that fits their commitment and interest for children. For example, we encounter teachers who are suspicious of parents who, pick up their children from kindergarten and immediately ask them whether they ate their lunch. The lunch question is simply a modern version of the question *did you behave?* Both formulations contain hidden expressions. What these questions actually say is *did you live up to my expectations today?* or *See how responsible I am!* Once we confront parents with this reality, they quickly recognize the irrelevance of these questions for the children's lives and want to know what else they could say or ask in respective situations. Once they are looking for alternatives, they are on the right track. Because, *only the one asking can find the answer, what he/she is interested in.*

In pedagogical context, adults' interest in children is very often limited to their current behavior or actual performance, except for when a child is obviously sad. All other feelings seem to exclusively activate the use of evaluative and defining language.

Later in this book, we will consider the role of teachers as committed and interested dialogue partners in more detail.

Acknowledgement
Acknowledgement is verbalizing and emotionally confirming, what the adult sees in the child. It is giving words to things the adult has figured out about the child in this given moment. If possible this facet or insight needs to be confirmed with help of the child's own words or, where they lack words, through the use of emphatic language.

Participation
Once adults have seen and understood the child's emotional state, needs, likes and dislikes, dreams, goals, etc., their responsibility is to include this knowledge as far as reasonable and feasible into the future relationship. This ensures that children develop a sense of being taken seriously. In cases where adults fail to find a way of including the child into future decisions, they have to either ask the child about possibilities or acknowledge that there is no possibility. Even in these situations, children can feel that they are taken seriously.

Decision
Of course, most decisions lie in the adults' responsibility. (An exception would be decisions that are part of a democratic process, and are clearly understood to be taken by an individual child or a group of children.) In an educational context, this means that adults need to take decisions based on their experience, insight and responsibility as teachers, and acknowledge that this will often fail including all children concerned. Due to this fact a variety of conflicts can arise.

Conflict
These conflicts are absolutely necessary for the relational quality - in respect to both content and process. Conflicts will change with the children's increasing age and linguistic development, but the components always remain the same:

needs/desires – *no* – fight/negotiation – loss/frustration – rest

Children do not *set up* conflicts with adults to sabotage their decisions or undermine their authority. And it doesn't make sense to end conflicts (and restore obedience) by simply saying things like *No is no – now, I don't want to hear any more about this.* Conflicts are necessary for a child's inner balance and a prerequisite to wish to continue cooperating.

Conflicts arise in situations in which the child expresses their desire or need for something. Once the adult says *No*, the child begins to actively fight for what it wants, which is a sign of healthy development as well as a necessity in all present and future relationships, be they private or job-related. If the child fights for their needs or negotiates, but still does not get what it wants, it is confronted with a loss. It may appear somewhat exaggerated to talk of *loss* when we are talking about everyday conflicts, and yet psychologically this term is appropriate. It is the loss of satisfaction, the loss of a fantasy, a dream, an idea, social wellbeing or simply the loss of something the child has had a small but strong craving for. Each child reacts to conflicts differently, depending on the individual disposition and their family's conflict style. Yet all children have to find a way of processing the loss emotionally. Some will cry, others will complain or get in a huff, while again others will get angry and frustrated or even show indignation. Their reactions are not directed at a specific person; they are part of the organism's homeostasis, which is the process by which we restore inner balance and our ability to participate in society. If adults inhibit the process, turn it into ridicule, or even forbid it to take place, the child's frustration accumulates. Later, the child will inevitably express their frustration, usually in an irrational way, which takes the adults' energy and attention away from the child in addition.

For these reasons, it is important to allow children to take the time they need to come to terms with their frustration. Some children will require more time, others less.

If we allow children to take time to process conflicts, and thus resulting losses, we also enable them to maintain their personal dignity and develop the ability to accept adult decisions. If we do not, we do not leave a choice for the children but force them to give us a *Yes*. At first sight, the children's agreement may look like it honors adult authority, but in the long run it undermines it. A child's reaction is not much different than the way adults react in similar situations.[2]

Children with Special Needs

Children with special needs be they of pedagogical, psychological, physical, motoric or medical nature, confront us time and again with the existential fact that they are dependent on continuous personal support to develop and maintain personal integrity and responsibility. This existential kind of support cannot replace other types of specifically adapted support. It must rather complement all offers of help a child with special needs receives so help can be effective.

In many cases, there are more important issues than homework or other school activities: in fact, in some circumstances, personal responsibility, which we also refer to as existential responsibility, even concerns the survival of a child.

EXAMPLE
Elisabeth was 13 years old and attended a special school for learning-disabled children. Elisabeth suffered from a rare hereditary disorder, from which she could die. But correct medical treatment and an adapted life style guaranteed that she would be able to live with her disease for many years. Elisabeth had learning difficulties. In many respects, she was a difficult student. But the principal had a good relationship with her.

One day, Elisabeth's condition became worse and she was taken to the hospital. After several days at the hospital, she told her parents and doctors that she wanted to die. Everyone tried to convince the girl that she must and should go on, and that the world would look so much different once her condition improved. In response, Elisabeth refused to eat. Her family and friends tried everything, without success to make her eat. Her nurses even asked the chef of the in-house kitchen to go to Elisabeth and ask her about her favorite meals.

Elisabeth gladly talked about her favorite meals, but she refused to eat them. She quickly lost weight. Everybody started to panic. One day, Elisabeth's psychologist asked her if she could think of a person she would really like to talk to. The girl mentioned the principal whom the parents immediately called for assistance. Elisabeth's family and friends trusted the teacher's pedagogical skills would help dissuade her from her wish to die.

The principal felt pressured by the enormous responsibility placed on her. And, she felt strongly tempted to pursue the parents' and nurses' strategy to convince Elisabeth that her decision to die was wrong. She hoped to be able to motivate Elisabeth to live on, but on her way to the hospital, she reminded herself not to let her own feelings take over and to focus on Elisabeth's existential personal responsibility instead.

Her visit was rather short, but right after she came in, a very decisive dialogue took place:

Teacher: Elisabeth, people told me you want to die. Is that true?
Elisabeth: Yes, I don't want to live anymore.
Teacher: Elisabeth, I want to tell you that I would be incredibly sad if you died. I wish there was something I could say or do to make you want to live. But I can hear what you're saying and I know you're serious on this. So, I'm here to support you if you want me to.
Elisabeth: I just want to die.
Teacher: I respect that, even if it's hard.
(The teacher now took some time to tell Elisabeth about what had been going on in class since she had been taken to the hospital.)
Teacher: Elisabeth, I'm going to go now, but I want to ask a huge favor of you before I leave ... Will you ask your parents to call me before you die?
Elisabeth: Yes, I'll do that.

About 24 hours later, Elisabeth started eating again and her health improved quickly. Soon, Elisabeth was discharged. After 13 years of being the object of worried parents, doctors, teachers, psychologists and special pedagogues who thought they knew what was best for her and took over responsibility for her life, Elisabeth finally took over her personal responsibility.

Her life provides a story for reflection. It shows that a child in her situation and state does not need more than a five-minute conversation with an adult who is willing to accept her own personal responsibility. An adult who supports the child to take over responsibility for their own life rather than death, by acknowledging her fight for integrity.

Elisabeth is representative of many children (and adults) who feel reduced to objects of their parents' and experts' loving and well-meaning and sometimes relevant (social) responsibility because of an illness, handicap, mental retardation or deviant behavior. People are often too preoccupied with finding out what is best for the child to see what consequences their overprotection may have on the child's existence. If children like Elisabeth signal existential discomfort by adding a psycho-social dimension to their problems, they are often overlooked. Instead of taking these troubled children seriously, even more experts are consulted and the adults become increasingly worried and helpless.

Children always cooperate as long as they possibly can. But if their caregivers are only concerned how pedagogical assistance could improve their child's life without being aware of the price the child is paying for adapting, they are left with two options:
1. The child can choose to give up their personal integrity entirely. Usually, children who do so are easy to handle, which is why adults appreciate them especially as long as they are small. But once puberty arrives and adults challenge them to act independently, as well as to make their own decisions in everyday life, the situation becomes difficult.
2. The child can also choose to vigorously fight for his-/her integrity and personal responsibility. But in doing so, they rarely achieve a satisfying

outcome. This is not due to the fight per se, but due to the fact that their caregivers are not aware that they need to support the children's personal responsibility and leave room for growth. Consequently, the child's fight *for* him-/herself becomes a fight *against* adults and their assistance.

Regardless of the child's reaction, all require awareness of the fact that loving or pedagogical responsibility can also be experienced as insulting or oppressive.

Often, we have to remind parents of the fact, that they are equally as cooperative as their children. In light of the situation they feel dependent and take specialists serious. Because of this they tend to understand the expectation of specialists wanting their cooperation, as the necessity to comply to the experts' opinion even in their own home. Many parents suffer nagging feelings of guilt and compensate this by taking on the role of the *helper*. In doing so, they limit the children's existential space. What often adds to the difficult situation is that the relationship between father and mother is strained. Children sense this and, consequently, increasingly feel like a burden to the family. Usually this additionally inhibits their ability to integrate pedagogical support.

Adults Personal Responsibility

We already looked at the personal responsibility of teachers in the chapters about professional integrity, authenticity, and peer interaction. Here, we want add another dimension: the willingness to assume responsibility for personal expectations, limitations and behavior patterns. This is a dimension in which adults play an important role as models in both good and bad ways

For a long time, it was taken for granted that pedagogues had relational competence. The idea though was very contrary to what we are talking about in this book. The culture of obedience fostered attitudes, which can be summarized as follows:

- My expectations are justified.
- My behavior is infallible, and if it exceptionally is not, it is because the children provoked me. And that is not my responsibility.
- My boundaries are formulated in institutional rules. If they are violated, it is not my responsibility but the fault of children or parents that violate these rules.

Today, only few teachers would presumably agree to the above statements. And yet, they still shape institutional cultures and norms as well as teachers' daily work.

The relevance of these statements is interesting and important especially when it comes to the topic of responsibility. With these obsolete attitudes in mind, experts get stuck in continuous frustration about violations and disappointments and simultaneously are unable to draw on means and methods which once were so successful. Even if their approach to education seems old-fashioned, the violations and disappointments they experience are none the less serious.

Adults' personal responsibility and children's social responsibility conflict each other in these situations. With good reason, children feel treated unjustly if adults make them responsible for their own destructive behavior. Children understand the adults' behavior as not taking their responsibility for others (children) seriously. Children are thus not only confronted with adults denying their personal responsibility, but also with adults who treat them unjustly. But at the same time on a daily basis, these children have to cope with the experience of being held responsible for their own behavior towards adults and other children. If they dare to defend themselves or try to deny responsibility with words like '*I didn't start it! or It was her fault!*' adults usually remind them of their (personal) responsibility for their own actions. A generation ago, children knew that this simply was a fact. Different moral standards applied depending on whether you were an adult or a child. It was useless to protest against this. Today, however, the situation is different. Children unmask adult double standards and object them. Usually by irresponsible behavior along the line of '*If adults can do so, I can too*'.

Fortunately, on the contrary the above mechanisms can also lead to positive outcomes. If teachers assume responsibility for their own behavior, the personal and social responsibility of children increases. Children's sense of responsibility develops best when confronted with adults who actually practice, and not only talk about responsibility, and know how to keep it apart from blame.

Over generations, adults have blamed children. So, it does make sense that many only think in opposites. Someone has to be to blame. If it is not the children, it must be me, or vice versa. Of course, we all share responsibility and are, therefore, sometimes jointly responsible for certain developments in life, but blame is not a helpful approach.

If, for example, Erik's teacher gets angry and makes a mean, sarcastic remark, it does not mean that all that happens from there on can be blamed on the teacher. But the teacher has a greater responsibility. The teacher can repair damage done to Erik, to their mutual relationship, as well as to the teacher's image of himself by taking full responsibility for what he said *'Listen, Erik, I am sorry about what I said to you yesterday. I was angry and got carried away. Please, forgive me! ... Is there anything that you would like to tell me?'*

Almost without exception, kindergarten children *feel* responsible for adult failures, even if they think the teacher behaved unjustly. From school age onwards, this sense decreases. Yet, they all show similar reactions to violations by adults. They mentally and emotionally distance themselves from the adult concerned. This, in turn makes it difficult for him or her to establish a fruitful cooperation on a pedagogical level. This pattern of interaction is easy to explain. A teacher's job is to guide and form children, and aid their personal, intellectual, and social development. But they are also dependent on the children's willingness and openness. This willingness and openness decreases with every emotional violation they experience along the way. This reaction towards teachers is essentially different, to situations where children are confronted with parental violations. In these cases children generally tend to submit and feel guilty.

Personal responsibility can be summarized in one sentence: *Everything I say – and do is part of myself and, consequently, lies within my own responsibility.*

This obvious fact does not mean that teachers can always act responsibly and balanced. But it shows why it doesn't make sense to give the children a *telling-off* and passing on their responsibility, by explaining why they overreacted or justifying their behavior whenever they feel provoked, angry, unhappy or dissatisfied.

EXAMPLE

The sixth-grade had prepared a small party that was going to take place on Friday. On Monday, they were already restless, laughing all the time and chatting about what the party will be like, who might fall in love, etc. The class teacher was with them in the morning and also taught the last lesson on Monday. Suddenly, she had enough: "Now, shut up and listen! I'm done with your chatting and I don't want to hear another word about the party. I'm here to do my job, and my job is to teach you, which hasn't been possible today at all. Now, I want you to pull yourselves together and focus on the test you are going to write next Thursday. And I want you to do that RIGHT NOW!"

The teacher was yelling as loud as she could. Her neck was showing red spots and her eyes were sparkling with anger. There was no doubt that the fuss in class exceeded her limits.

Some children got scared, others were shocked and others felt sorry – and that is ok. Somewhat older children are not harmed by an adult's feelings like this, regardless of how responsible or irresponsible these may appear on the outside. But if the teacher's anger humiliates, ridicules, or hurts children in any other way, it weakens her position as a teacher. If she marks her boundaries by violating the children's needs she loses her credibility.

On the other hand, there is no doubt that the teacher would not have achieved the desired effect if she had masked her authentic frustration in an appealing, regretful, and sweet expression. This would affect her credibility to the same degree as violations would.

As we will explain in detail, the teacher's personal responsibility does not only include respecting children's needs and limitations but also one's own personal needs and limitations in an authentic way.

Authenticity and Authority

Teachers who aren't comfortable in their professional relationships to children likely suffer from this inner conflict. Previously, their status as adults and role as an expert gave them almost unlimited power to define contents, processes, conditions and consequences of their professional relationships. That is, as long as they did not cross legal boundaries. It was a *role-based* authority that built the basis for their interactions with children and parents. It isn't helpful to try and understand this kind of authority, because it is part of the past and not relevant interacting with parents and children nowadays.

There are many reasons though to take a closer look at what is developing now; the need for *personal authority*. Personal authority is based on the ability and willingness to keep a maximum of authenticity in professional relationships. This means to act in accordance with professional and personal moral values, professional commitment, self-esteem and inner responsibility.[3]

To demand a *maximum* of authenticity in this context might, however, be misleading. The focus lies more on the quality than on the quantity. The degree to which an individual teacher is able to show their authenticity and feel comfortable showing it differs greatly and is a personal process. But experience shows that it does not suffice to act authentically and feel comfortable in work relationships only ten percent of the time. But on the other hand, it would be wrong to demand that teachers must be fully aware of their moral concepts and expectations all the time, possess a high level of self-esteem, and be in touch with their inner responsibility 95 percent of the time.

Authenticity and authority interact closely. Over the course of their career, every teacher goes through phases in which doubt replaces determination, feelings of insecurity surpass feelings of security, deficiency turns into surplus, and the need for introspection and reflection is bigger than the desire to be responsible and outgoing. Situations where we feel like self-esteem is something we once knew. All of these experiences are not alien to educational practice. They are actually an integral part of every teacher's work. In the past, professionals considered them an obstacle and tried to hide these experiences because they feared that would interfere with their professional authority. But denial is only one of many ways to deal with facts.

The reality, including feelings and emotions, is rarely a problem in itself. Our way of dealing with them can, however, create difficulties.

One of the most common things that adults try to hide or compensate is professional, and in particular, personal insecurity. Interestingly enough though, these attempts to hide or compensate always weaken one's personal authority. *Closeness* gets lost when we exclude personal issues from relationships. At first glance, one might be tempted to think that it is the feeling of insecurity per se which weakens the relationship and not the way of dealing with it.

But *it makes a big difference if we feel insecure or know that we are insecure*. The feeling of insecurity is the same starting point. But every individual copes differently with this feeling. Some are overwhelmed and allow their insecurity to affect their entire awareness. They respond with motoric restlessness, seem helpless and can no longer think clearly. It gives the impression, they have *become* their insecurity. Others react with passivity, and some actively withdraw from relationships. These personal patterns reflect what helped gain security in previous relationships. Allowing feelings of insecurity to take over and become victimized by them often stirs confusion and discomfort in adult-child relationships. If the teacher concerned is very close to individual children or even several children at once, like in daycare centers, they are likely to react with empathy and care. Other children react indirectly by withdrawing at least a little from the relationship in order to grant the adult some time alone. Some children also take the insecure adult by the hand, sit on their lap or simply ask: *Are you sad?* Children sense their own lack of security in this process actively and react to it (take care of themselves and the adult). In larger groups, however, children have less opportunities to demand and give individual attention. A collective feeling of insecurity impairs the relationship though to a large extent. In groups, children express their insecurity in a variety of ways, which depends on the age and the general culture of the group or class.

Instead of allowing their own feeling of insecurity to take over, we can see it as an important signal to take a break and a closer look at what the signal might mean in the concrete situation.

A simple example is when we are confronted with the objective insecurity of not knowing how to answer a question. We can either allow the insecurity to take over and *feel stupid* or admit that we do not know the answer but are interested in finding it out. In other words, we are insecure how to answer the question, but we are still secure about how to deal with this insecurity.

This way of approaching personal insecurities we encounter in professional as well as private areas affects our relationships with children in a positive way. Children have the chance to experience adults who struggle with the same insecurities they have, but in addition, they know how to handle these insecurities. This relaxes children and reassures them.

Moreover, this approach also fosters and reinforces other qualities that support personal authority:

- The approach is *authentic* and in line with our inner voice telling us: *I'm feeling insecure, and I wish this feeling would stop.* The paralyzing effect of insecurity is not actually an authentic feeling, but rather the expression of a learned defense strategy. Insecurity itself does not make us passive. Rather, passivity is an acquired method of dealing with insecurity.
- Acknowledging insecurity as authentic also facilitates *developing self-esteem*. Discovering new aspects of our own insecurity (e.g. what makes us insecure) supports the quantitative dimension. And acceptance and interaction with the insecurity instead of self-criticism enhances the qualitative dimension of self-esteem.
- It also *enhances interpersonal relationships and improves group dynamics* by showing that it is a natural thing to not always be sure about oneself or one's actions.
- Last but not least, it shows children that they can interact with adults as people they can identify with. This increases the quality of the relationships as well as the children's self-esteem. (e.g. if insecurity arises from a factual question, it teaches children the significance of seeking answers).

This authentic approach to personal insecurity does not depend on how insecurity shows. There is not *one* specific method how to react to insecurity, how to deal with nervousness and another how to cope with low self-esteem, etc. We have to find our own way, but to put it plain and simple: we own our feelings, and not vice versa.

Many adults are afraid that by showing their personal *weak spots*, they become more vulnerable. This, only happens if we distance ourselves from our insecurities or create a gap between ourselves and our professional roles. At the same time, accepting our insecurity does not mean invulnerability. Children, parents, superiors or colleagues can always react in insulting ways, either accidentally or deliberately. This is a fact, we have to decide how to deal with. We can see it as a challenge and part of our continuous professional development or as something to be avoided. And in the same way, we can try to strengthen our personal authority or maintain what is left of it.

Many people mistake authenticity for *staying true to one's feelings*. From our point of view, authenticity is more complex. Of course, taking our feelings seriously can help us establish a foundation in search for authenticity, but we have to be aware of the fact that not all feelings are per se *authentic*, like in the above-cited case of insecurity. Some feelings are representations, some derive from our life approaches, and others are reflections of basic emotions acquired culturally or in course of our upbringing. Moreover, as pointed out by Murray Bowen[4] (more to his ideas about the differentiation of self page 164) it is not a good idea to allow feelings alone to determine behavior.

Only few people come to see clearly how to show authentic reactions in the course of their lives. And even experts who are aware of this fact react spontaneously on the basis of their current feelings and thus allow these to influence professional relationships. If you get angry, if you regret or fear something, you cannot simply change that fact. You simply feel the way you feel and act accordingly at a given point in time and in a specific relationship. The way the feelings are expressed may not be authentic, but it is still an actual product within the given relationship. This possibly destructive influence of spontaneous emotional outbursts can be worked on directly within the relationship, or as part of a supervisory process.

However, there is an important difference between *destructive* influence and *negative* influence. Destructive influence means another person's personal integrity is violated and/or the process of teaching is diverted from the educational goal. Negative influences are reactions of anger, regret or rejection. The latter is an unavoidable but constructive part of every kind of relationship. Which feelings a person classifies as *negative* depends on personal experience. Yet, all feelings considered negative have the power to temporarily cause imbalance, discord or fear of the consequences. Negative feelings are not negative in the sense of *bad* for an individual or a group of people. Rather, they are smoke signals, which draw attention to circumstances that need to be recognized and processed.

For a long time, these negative feelings have been experienced as inconvenient or downright inappropriate, particularly in the professional world. A place where adults were only allowed to show negative feelings if the children's behavior *objectively* justified their reaction. But selective control, in this context, only increases resistance and fear on the one side but not authority on the other side.

This means that it does not require comprehensive training or fully developed personalities to successfully combine authenticity and personal authority. If anything, it requires professionals to be in an ongoing process of development. In the course of our childhood, some of us encountered teachers who seemed to have natural authority. Natural authority was long thought of as innate, but it is actually the combination of special conditions growing up, as well as passionate professional commitment. Building on the rich experience we have today, we now know that personal authority can be learned by most. People have always known the vigorous effect of combined authenticity and professional authority. Especially, the world of art appreciates this combination as an art and clearly distinguished it from mere practice. Even if education is more like a *handcraft*, it is also an *art*.

Integrity and Educational Ethics

Personal integrity is the key element of professional relational ethics. The personal integrity of a child always is more important than the actual educational goal. Educational approaches, rules or methods should never violate a child's personal integrity or consciously transgress personal boundaries. And if existing relationships to children or adults violate their personal integrity teachers must ask for help and support in developing their relational competence. Both staffing policy and co-workers are obliged to offer this help and support.

As the examples below demonstrate, a child's integrity can be violated in very differing ways, some of which are even condoned in pedagogical settings.

EXAMPLE

A seventh-grade math class: The kids wanted to tease the teacher because they often felt like he treated them badly so they hid all the blackboard chalk. The teacher recognized the prank immediately and summoned Elisabeth to the blackboard to solve an arithmetic problem. Elisabeth wasn't very self-confident and very vulnerable at the moment because her parents recently had gotten divorced. Desperately, she turned to the teacher and said that she couldn't write because there was no chalk left. The teacher got angry and scolded her. Shaking with fear, Elisabeth wet the tip of her finger with her sweaty palms and started writing on the board. She was able to solve the task correctly, but once she got to the end, half of her calculations had already disappeared. Triumphantly, the teacher gave her a bad mark and sent her back to her place remarking how exceptionally stupid and ugly she was. (Please, note that this is not an example of 1952 but an actual incident in 2002.)

Elisabeth was devastated. Her best friend knew that she would never dare to tell her mother about what happened. So, she told her own mother about the incident, who immediately contacted the headmaster. After a brief evasive conversation, he sent the concerned mother away with the blunt statement 'that it was a rather unfortunate incident, but we are talking about an otherwise very competent teacher'.

Now, let us move from the above example of conscious child abuse to two examples which we title the 'tyranny of reason'.

EXAMPLE

Frederik was five years old and went to kindergarten. He was generally known as a cheerful and healthy little boy who got along well with everyone and always found a way to keep himself busy. But one day, he acted differently. He withdrew from the group and declined other children's invitations to play with them. He sat down at the table where Camilla was absorbed in drawing a picture. Suddenly, Frederik seemed to need exactly the same purple crayon Camilla was using and aggressively snapped it from her hand. The girl tried to get the crayon back, but Frederik was stronger. Camilla started crying while Frederik just sat there with his head hanging. Grimly, he drew on a piece of paper and then threw the crayon on the table so it broke. Alarmed by Camilla's loud protest, the teacher came to see what happened:

Teacher: Camilla, what's wrong?
Camilla: He took away the crayon that I wanted to draw something with.
Teacher: Is that true, Frederik? Did you take away Camilla's crayon?
Frederik: I wanna draw with that crayon! Camilla's just a stupid girl!
Teacher: But, Frederik, what's wrong with you today? You know that we don't say things like that here in kindergarten.
Frederik: You're stupid too, 'cause this is my crayon and I wanna draw with it now!
Teacher: Now, I want you to be nice, Frederik. You're usually not that mean ... have you forgotten our nice Frederik at home? You know that we always share toys and that we don't yell at each other. Now, please give the crayon to Camilla. You can use it afterwards, right, Camilla?
Frederik: You're stupid, you're all stupid!
Teacher: No, Frederik, nobody's stupid in here. We want to be nice to each other. Camilla's just promised to give you the crayon afterwards.

Frederik got up from the table and went outside to the playground and ran around restlessly. Two days later, his mother explained in tears that on the respective morning she had lost her temper and slapped her son in the face because she was angry and mad at him for refusing to put on his slicker. Frederik had a lot of reasons that day to believe that the entire world was 'stupid', and his teacher's sweet instruction on how to solve conflicts really was the last thing he needed. The teacher's observation that their 'nice Frederik' was absent and replaced by somebody else was correct. Yet she allowed her moral ideas to prevail over her empathy. This makes the result of her approach ethically doubtful.

EXAMPLE

Søren was going to preschool. Occasionally, they had a substitute teacher who obviously had difficulty handling this class. Søren was a friendly and talkative boy full of energy. One day, the substitute teacher was unable to stop Søren from talking and threw him out. He literally pulled the boy from his seat and dragged him in front of the classroom. This was a traumatic experience for Søren, who felt humiliated and was really unhappy afterwards. He was also the first one in class that had been thrown out of the classroom.

At home, he was able to tell his parents about what happened and what it was like for him to be thrown out of class. At school, however, he told his classmates that he would jump out of the window if the substitute teacher came back to class. Luckily, Søren's class teacher reacted very competent. When, one day Søren actually jumped out of the window, she was able to figure out what was going on. Søren did not see a choice, "I said that I would jump, which is why I had to, although I knew that we are not allowed to do that. But if I hadn't, the other children wouldn't have believed me anymore."

Probably, most people can understand the helplessness of the substitute teacher. But his behavior shows that he is in a deadlock and needs help.

He does not need to be judged, but treated him with the same relational qualities that he needs to acquire for his relationship with children like Søren.

One of the few possibilities for children - especially preschool age – is to express their integrity and enhance their *visibility* and to openly show their spontaneous reaction to present interactions. This is why *we do not recommend talking to children about how to behave. Not during a conflict nor afterwards.* The only message children receive through these lectures is that they as a person and their behavior are out of place. Consequently, this reinforces and prolongs irrational behavior. Just the same as for adults in similar situations.

Part Three
RELATIONAL ASPECTS

CHAPTER 5:
Interpersonal Relationships

Although psychological research moved away from the official cause and effect model as explanation for interpersonal behavior 70 years ago, it still influences general every-day considerations and educational practice to this day. One explanation might be that interpersonal realities clash with moral conceptions in many ways.

If an alcoholic husband physically abuses his wife, who becomes unhappy and decides to get a divorce, our moral conceptions tempt us to think that his behavior was the cause of her unhappiness and the divorce. We identify him as the culprit because we generally condemn alcoholism and violence and take the wife's side. But if, upon closer look, she turns out to be a true vixen, who had one affair after another, we may also put part of the blame on her. The common conclusion then is that both partners are equally *guilty*. If we, furthermore, find out that both individuals grew up in dysfunctional families with alcoholic fathers, we may raise the number of culprits to four. With increasing insight into the behavior and personalities of the mothers, we are likely to sooner or later add them in too.

In the moral world, the above reasoning is fully justified provided that it is based on the *right* moral conceptions. But the problem with moral conclusions is that they only result in self-righteousness. From an interpersonal or relational psychological perspective, the situation is much more complex and requires a thorough clinical examination of the interaction of the parties involved. Then we can determine some of the factors, which over the course of time, caused physical and psychological violence, alcoholism and infidelity to shape their marriage and divorce.

The numerous every-day *projections*[1] that happen between individuals also tend to affect objective professional analysis. If we look at a project team that consists of four students A, B, C, and D, who currently attend a seminar together, we can describe the group dynamics as follows: If A thinks the cooperation with B problematic because A feels insecure in his interaction with B, and C finds the cooperation with B difficult because C feels provoked by B's political ideas, and D thinks that the cooperation with B is problematic because D has a different understanding of the project objective than B, B's alleged 'dominance' is quickly established as the cause for the groups low productivity and becomes an accepted 'truth' of the group. Summed up, the interpersonal reality of their way of cooperating causes three team members to feel dominated, albeit in different ways, and the fourth member to be forced into role of the most dominant.

By analyzing the reciprocal actions within the framework of traditional individual psychology, we can unearth different realities about the parties involved. B is an only child who lacks the experience of cooperating with people the same age and same position. A grew up in a family with a dominant father and a weak mother and has learned how to avoid any kind of conflict. C grew up as the youngest of two siblings who constantly had to fight for what they needed. D's mother always fell in love with dominant men but was never able to establish an equal relationship.

There are four obvious reasons why the project team could have difficulty fulfilling their task. But it is problematic intervening on the basis of the individual *intrapsychological* profiles. Individual explanations do not necessarily change the relational quality within the group despite fostering insight on behalf of the members. Our experience shows that groups like this will always have problems cooperating. Insight into their individual background can raise their understanding of the problems and help them find ways to reduce projecting the major responsibility on B. A qualitative change of interaction within the group depends on the individual maturation processes of its members, which, in turn, might or might not also lead to qualitative changes in the individuals' relationships to their own family members. Anyway, developments in both areas require time and, therefore, hardly ever benefit the current work in the respective group.

The crucial discovery of group and family theory[2] and practice is that analyzing and intervening in the *current* interaction can achieve qualitative changes in the group process *and* in the individual behavior of group members at the same time. None of these theories deny the constructive or destructive influence of an individual on interpersonal processes. But they understand these dynamics as a result of earlier relational experiences and trust new experiences to bring changes into relevant current (and sometimes even old) relationships.

Individual, personal and relational development is a reciprocal, dialectical process, where changes in interaction go hand in hand with individual change. These individual changes, in turn, cause changes in the mutual exchange, which again induces changes on the individual level, and so on.[3]

There is no objective evidence to prove that B is the cause for A's, C's, and D's negative feelings in the group or that B is to be blamed for the reduced efficiency of their work. In the cosmos of the group, all four individuals are both cause and effect. In the present situation, as a so-called peer group, they are a group of equals, and are, therefore, equally responsible for the dynamics of the group. From a psychological perspective, the tendency to *blame* (or not blame) others in the group shows the individuals' personal insight and willingness to take over their own *internal responsibility.*

Although, awareness of the significance of relationships is growing, moral judgements and the denial of responsibility, are still daily practice in schools. The belief that this will eventually disappear may be unrealistic, but from an ethical point of view and our personal experience there are a lot of reasons to at least try to elevate the current standard. The personal and social price is substantial for both sides, and even higher where one side has power over the other.

Levels of Interaction: Content and Process

A graphical representation of the systemic processes at work in larger groups would be very complex and confusing. And since this book is primarily concerned with relationships between two individuals or two parties, including the implications for culture and the *atmosphere* in specific groups and institutions, we have opted for a simplified representation.

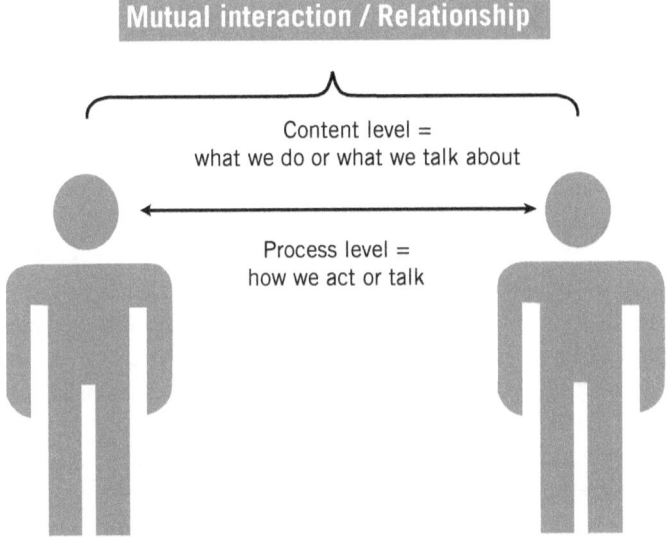

The content level describes what we do, what we talk about and what we teach.
The interest for topics and contents varies from person to person, from acquittal to engaged interest, from passion to reluctance or even aversion. Academic contents are usually defined in advance. But the differing levels of interest for specific topics also are relevant in other relationships as well as in families.

The process level describes the way we do things. It encompasses all various phenomena that influence the general tone, mood, atmosphere of life, cooperation in relationships and our pedagogical methods. These phenomena include body language, indirect communication, expressed as well as suppressed emotions, openly stated or secret attitudes and daily routines.

Simply put, it's the sum of our conscious and unconscious external and internal behavior.

In schools, e.g. external conditions play a major role. It can make a huge difference if we talk to a child or parents in the middle of a crowded hallway or a calm separate room. In addition, the quantity of cubic meters available in a room per person has an impact on the quality of interaction. A high relational quality, however, can reduce the influences of bad conditions to a certain extent.

Usually, the content dimension influences the process dimension less than vice versa. This is especially relevant in private love relationships of adults or parents and children. Moreover, it also plays an important role in teacher-child relationships. Different activities in schools make different demands on children and adults, which obviously influence the quality of the professional work and ways of cooperating. Content-related professional processes have always played a major role in teaching. They have their own well-established professional disciplines and methodological, didactical, and motivational concepts.

The significance of interpersonal process level, however, has more or less been neglected.[4]

The study of these interpersonal processes puts the focus on what is going on between the parties involved at a specific moment in time rather than on the individual background of the individuals. The quality of interpersonal processes determines the extent to which individuals involved repeat constructive and destructive patterns of behavior, which become manifest as an integral part of this relationship. In therapeutic practice, we distinguish three basic patterns of interpersonal processes between family or group members[5]:
- *Creating symptoms*: One of the individuals develops (self-) destructive behavior which is new to the present relationship, and possibly not visible in other relationships.
- *Maintaining symptoms*: the (self-)destructive behavior of an individual involved stays stable.
- *Healing symptoms*: the (self-)destructive behavior disappears both in the

present relationship as well as in other relationships in which the individual is involved.

All interpersonal processes (and long-term communities) show different combinations of the above patterns. All of us are to some extent potentially violent and thoughtful, egocentric and cooperative, open and withdrawn, stubborn and flexible. The quality of what takes place between us and others is crucial for the way these characteristics develop, independent of our awareness, intelligence, or ability to get in touch with other people. But infants, senile old people, mentally handicapped persons and psychotic individuals always show distinct reactions to the relational quality in personal and professional settings.

But we want to emphasize that the current interpersonal process is never the cause of specific symptoms. There are always several influences at work at once, depending on the individuals and their history. The significant role of this quality of the relational processes, however, places a major responsibility on the *person in charge* of the process.

We have used three overlapping terms: interpersonal relationship, interpersonal process, and reciprocity or reciprocal action. Psychological language distinguishes between *relationship* and *interaction*. Relationships are long-term and personally relevant contacts, while the term interaction tends to refer to short-term and less personal exchanges. Everyday life in schools include a variety of interactions that do not always lead to relationships. In this sense, a kindergarten teacher may have a good relationship with one parent but minimal interactions with another. Similarly, there may be children with whom teachers are unable to establish a true relationship, although they interact with each other on a regular basis. The *personal* quality of the interaction is relevant in either situation and contributes to defining the relationship.

Our experience gives rise to the assumption that children up to the age of twelve largely experience interactions with teachers or other adults the same as relationships. They do not differentiate in this way. Due to the children's openness, dependence and hierarchical position, every contact with an adult influences them. Of course, there are differences in the intensity and length of the effect of a conversation depending how close the relationship between a teacher and the child is. But usually, children cannot consciously protect themselves from infringements in every day interactions with adults until they are much older (or already very disturbed).

Adult-Child Relationships

- In reciprocal interactions between equal adults - in symmetric relationships - both sides are equally responsible for the quality of the interpersonal process and for the individual or the group.
- In reciprocal interactions between adults of whom one has, or at least represents more power than the other, - asymmetric relationships - the one with more power has more responsibility for the quality of their relationship and its consequences.
- In reciprocal interactions between children and adults, the responsibility for the quality of the interpersonal process and its consequences lies exclusively in the hands of the adults.

There are two reasons for this:
For one, children are simply not able to shoulder the responsibility for the quality of their relationships with adults. They can express opinions, provide proposals, and request changes, but they cannot assume full responsibility. This is a main reason why democratic values do not work as basis for adult-child relationships. Every time we directly or indirectly hold children responsible for their interactions with adults, their wellbeing and, in further consequence, the relational quality decreases. This can be seen in families where parents are not capable of leading as well as in institutions where adults approach children with a defensive attitude or have destructive conflicts. The problem is that children still cooperate and automatically try to fill the vacuum, which adults have left.

It is important to repeatedly draw attention to this inevitable reaction of children, especially when talking about families or school classes where conflicts arise from the feeling that children have *taken over*. In fact, children never take over, even when it looks like they have. Rather, adults have been unable or unwilling to accept their processual responsibility. Of course, children are interested in influencing the content of a discussion within the limits of a democratic process. But situations in which children seem to have *control over everything* are destructive adult-child interactions. Just like many adults, the children are unable to find words to describe the destructiveness of interpersonal processes and, instead, express them indirectly through their behavior.

Secondly, the relationship is asymmetric due to the actual power, experience and insight of adults (and the emotional dependency in families) as well as their processual influence.

For many generations, adults have refused to accept this responsibility, especially in conflicts. In schools, this happens on a daily basis. On the whole, official institutions name children (and their parents) as *the* main cause for unsatisfying professional interactions. In our opinion, this fact is an ethical stain in pedagogy and it needs specific relational training to counter this.

A few simple and personal expressions actually are the basis for a new approach. At first, the teachers' use of a new language may appear somewhat unusual. Professionals have learned that instructing, criticizing and blaming children and, thus, holding them responsible is a way of pedagogical conduct and expression. They may not always be convinced of the children's respective responsibility, but the language used stems from a time in which the ideal adult-child relationship was a subject-object relationship.

The lack of a suitable linguistic tradition is an essential problem. Very often, language interferes with the otherwise child-centered attitude and expertise. The same is true for many parents.

A common comment might sound like this, *Peter appears to be isolated and distracted.*

Alternatively, the teacher could also frame their observation this way, *when Peter is with me, he does not seem to be interested in contact. I find it difficult to gain his attention. We should observe his behavior in other relationships as well.*

While the first statement put all responsibility on the child and *excludes* the reality of the teacher, the second example shows two important qualities: first, it confirms the responsibility of the adult and, second, it *includes* the child's reality. Based on these two qualities, pedagogical interventions can acknowledge and improve the relational quality and contribute to reducing or even ending the child's alarming behavior. In this context, it is not relevant if the teacher-child relationship is the cause for the behavior or merely another destructive component in the child's life situation. Children (as well as adults) who are not doing well need to feel seen, heard and taken seriously in their essential relationships. There is no good reason these qualities cannot be integrated in professional behavior. No existing educational settings, objectives or resources are in conflict with this.

Situations in which the alarming behavior of children does not get better or stop need psycho-social exploration. This should include all relevant people working with the child, as well as the parents. Even if a closer analysis reveals that the child concerned struggles with serious familial problems and/or shows symptoms of psychological or child psychiatric disorders, it does not change the fact that the child has both a general and a current specific need for trustworthy and responsible relationships to his teachers.

We use the word *trustworthy* in this context because we are convinced that relational competence depends on the adults' absolute sincerity. It does not suffice to replace educational jargon with another type of jargon, which objectifies children merely in a different way.

A child's behavior influences interpersonal processes as much as interpersonal processes influence the child's behavior. But even if the child's influence seems overpowering, adults are responsible for the general relational quality. Children have a share in creating the relationship, but they do not share the responsibility for it. In the same way adults need to be seen, heard and taken seriously. But this need can only be fulfilled to the extent to which they assume and act according to their responsibility - both on the content and process level.

EXAMPLE

Getting back to the kindergarten we mentioned above, we can see it follows the general principle that children can decide for themselves how they want to spend their time. Every day, a group of twelve children spend the day in the woods. This is essential for the children's comfort, for there is simply not enough space for all children to remain inside all day. But since the children decide for themselves, it sometimes happens that all children want to go outside at once or that none of them want to leave the kindergarten. This has caused a lot of chaos in the institution.

The problem in this example is interesting because it involves use of language, responsibility and leadership.

From the language point of view, the kindergarten has decided to work with a leadership concept based on *self-organization*. This term, which originally was a well-meant attempt to democratize education is used very differently and inconsistently. Yet, as experience has shown, this attempt does not meet the children's real needs, for it does not take the process level into account. While we can democratize the content level, we cannot democratize the process level. *Democracy* is a political concept which determines the distribution of power. In the same way, the word to *decide* is about power. So, if kindergarten teachers urge the children to *make their own decisions* about what they want to do and what they do not want to do, they give them power over their own activities in kindergarten. Undoubtedly, it is good and reasonable for children (as well as the future society) for them to participate and be able to co-create their own lives. Yet, there is good reason to doubt that they benefit from having the power to decide. This is because children may be aware of what they currently want, but they are not fully aware of what their superior needs are.

Playing in general is pleasure-oriented but children's playful activities only make up a fraction of their lives, for which adults are responsible. At the beginning of the 1960s, a whole generation became obsessed with *pleasure* because it represented *freedom*. Today's parents and teachers, however, consider pleasure a key concept, that doesn't violate a child's integrity.

The underlying assumption is that we can secure both the political rights as well as the psycho-social development if we give children what they want. This, however, is not the case.

Ensuring that children get whatever they want most, will be sure to fail providing them with what they need most. What they need is adult guidance, which assumes responsibility for the entirety of children's lives. Children need adults who are willing to take their desires seriously, to listen to them, to acknowledge them and to include them as far as this is feasible and responsible.

In this kindergarten, the teachers do not take superior responsibility for the relational conditions and atmosphere. The shortage of space requires that twelve children play outside each day. It will contribute to a good atmosphere if the teachers try to find out which children want to go to the wood and take it seriously if children who do not want to go. Yet, to take wishes seriously does not entail the obligation to comply with these wishes. But these kinds of conversations, that take the other person seriously without being able to comply are new to most adults and need practice. Adults in charge are tempted to avoid these conversations by resorting to old rules and general conventions.

This brings us to the aspect of leadership: the central and superior aspect is the adults' willingness and ability to take over responsibility for the quality of the relationship and to acknowledge if they fail to fulfill their responsibility. This applies to both pedagogical and personal adult-child relationships. Beyond this, relationships include several further partial qualities, which we will deal with later in the book.

Peer Relationships

In reciprocal relationships between equal adults (symmetric relationships) both sides are responsible to the same extent for the quality of the interpersonal process and its consequences, both negative and positive, on the individual and the community.

Early-care teachers have always cooperated closely. They have usually had plenty of opportunity for mutual exchanges. But in schools, teamwork is a novelty. It breaks up the isolation of teachers and makes new demands on their abilities to cooperate. From a moral perspective, most teachers believe that the ability to cooperate comes naturally by growing-up and being well raised. In reality, most adults find it difficult to cooperate closely with (specific) other people. This leads to regular crises in which we tend to scapegoat others and trigger more serious conflicts.

We have already touched the main responsibility of the heads of an institution for the atmosphere and general tone of the respective facility. Each teacher, however, has a share in the responsibility for emerging conflicts and problems. The first thing we need to be aware of is that it is a myth that a good workplace is one without conflicts. This idea is a product of the culture of obedience, which cannot handle disagreement and diversity and therefore oppressed emerging conflicts.

From time to time, conflicts arise in every cooperation of committed, autonomous, and independent people. Some of these conflicts relate to work, others relate to personal matters, and again others are an obscure combination of both professional and personal issues. In most cases we have limited possibilities to decide for ourselves with whom we want to work. And only few people work together with others easily. There are always children and parents with whom we are unable to establish a fruitful cooperation. The price of our autonomy and freedom is that our essential relationships confront us with who we really are and with the necessity to take over responsibility for ourselves.

In schools, the quality of collegial cooperation influences way beyond the individual interaction. It both positively and negatively influences all colleagues, children, and parents. The situation is similar to production companies, where peer relationships influence the quality of the final product, or in the service industry, where it directly influences customer relationships.

It is useless to *demand* that peer relationships (just like any other relationships mentioned in this book) should not have an adverse effect on other relationships (e.g. children and parents). We cannot prevent negative influences, not even in the best of institutions with exemplary leadership. But we can expect that the parties involved in a conflict or the head of the respective institution take the initiative and assume responsibility to clear problems and provide those concerned with an appropriate explanation.

Collegial cooperation is like any other kind of cooperation between humans It is no big deal as long as everything is going fine. But it becomes an art to act right when things do not work out. There are a lot of excellent books about teamwork, conflict management, reconciliation and group psychology[6]. In this book, however, we want to place focus on two possibilities of action which can help prevent chronic frustration in the first place. These are
1. to take stock of cooperation and
2. meetings on the work climate and team days.

1. Taking stock - Regular reflection

We advise teams and reflection groups to regularly take stock of their cooperation. In most cases, it makes sense and promotes cooperative processes and group dynamics, if participants are invited to asks their colleagues, "What is it about me that makes it difficult or easy for you to work with me?" Apart from important information and problems of communication this question provides training how to evaluate other professional relationships. The professional relational qualities colleagues like or have difficulties with are most commonly the same children and parents find constructive or destructive.

EXAMPLE

A group of Danish ninth grade teachers had to work in a team. Four of them jointly planed the Danish lessons. They already worked together in the eighth grade. Kirsten had the impression that she previously withheld a lot of her ideas to give the other teachers more room for action. This is why she wanted to push her own proposal this time. In her opinion, the others owed her something because she so often yiel-

ded to their wishes. The rest of the teachers, however, saw the situation differently. They always found it difficult to know what Kristin really wanted. She never had clearly stated her expectations. Therefore, they had assumed that she simply didn't have any ideas and they secretly were even annoyed with her jumping on to their suggestions.

Now Kristen had an idea, which she really wanted to put into practice, and was convinced that she would only have to state her idea and it would meet her colleagues' approval. She thought they knew that it was her turn to decide. Yet, her plan didn't work out. The others energetically discussed their own ideas as usual. Kirsten felt overlooked and hurt. She gave up on her plan and the others agreed on another topic. Kirsten participated in the discussion of the new topic, but she didn't show commitment and enthusiasm.

On a professional level, Kirsten's and her colleagues' difficulties are about assuming personal responsibility and, thus, social responsibility. Obviously, Kirsten has problems taking over personal responsibility – the responsibility for herself as a part of the group. She does not take herself or her wishes seriously. She cooperates without taking a stand and verbalizing what she wants. If she talked to her co-workers about last year's situation, and if they had taken over social responsibility (that is the responsibility for the entire group) they would have been able to help Kirsten clearly state what she wants.

The interpersonal team process is not about Kirsten getting her way by convincing the others of her idea. It is about Kirsten becoming an equal team member by taking her seriously and helping her find a place in the group.

The more each team member is able to take over personal responsibility, the easier cooperation gets for the entire group. Kirsten could take both personal and social responsibility by telling the group, *"I'm not really happy with this and I actually feel embarrassed about not knowing how to make myself heard and understood. So, I'd appreciate your help"*. This way, Kirsten could express responsibility for the group, using the energy of the cooperation instead of just sitting there and being quiet. In addition, the others would know more about who Kirsten is and be able to take over their responsibility by openly stating what they observe. Kirsten is in a situation in which she feels pressured and has difficulty getting the others' attention. She might need assistance, e.g. by direct invitations, "Kirsten, you haven't said anything in a while. I'd like to know what you think about this last suggestion." By incorporating this new language into peer relationships, both sides also prepare for interactions with children and other adults.

Personal responsibility is not the same as egoism or self-centeredness, although they are often confused. The ability to take over personal responsibility is a precondition for relationships based on equal dignity and sharing responsibility for the community.

As long as teams work well, the groups themselves can organize regular self-evaluations once or twice a year. But if the cooperation isn't working well, the group should get help from outside. That is, from someone we refer to as a conflict advisor. This could be a colleague from another group, an expert who is familiar with the system, or an independent counselor. In no case, however, should the principal help as a *conflict advisor*. Even the most popular and respected leader primarily represents power. This power can destabilize a relationship which is unstable already.

From time to time, conflicts arise in any teamwork. For different reasons, we sometimes allow these conflicts to escalate and to eventually destroy any possibility to restore a fruitful cooperation. In most cases, solutions can best be achieved if the institution is willing to shift the focus from the content of the conflict to providing *process*-oriented support. Otherwise, the conflict usually takes a destructive direction for both persons directly involved and the entire institution. Since institutions have the duty to protect the *rights* of all parties involved, they all too often neglect important *needs*. Therefore, legal interventions should always go hand in hand with at least one meeting that allows the parties involved to discuss the consequences at a personal level. An independent advisor should always moderate these meetings to prevent personal offence.

2. Work climate - Team days and meetings

Usually there are policy based official meetings and structures that primarily focus on the institution's *content* level. In addition, we suggest team meetings focusing on the work climate once a year (or every two years) that give each staff member an opportunity to express their feelings about their working conditions, the actual pedagogical work, working as a team and about the leadership. Experience shows that it makes a big difference how regularly these meetings take place. Most schools are too large to enable regular contact with the whole staff otherwise. Moreover, regular meetings facilitate a culture in which communication and exchange does only take place once there are problems. The principal should participate on these days just like any other staff member. In order to guarantee that these days are as effective as possible, they should be accompanied by an external advisor. The major purpose of these team days and other meetings is to reveal the various feelings and team phenomena which cannot be planed, but for which both the principal and the staff can take over responsibility and find solutions once they appear. The goal is not to have a conflict free institution or team. Processes like this rather keep institutions alive and improve both the professional quality and work relationships.

Teacher-Parent Relationships

In interactions between adults of whom one holds or represents more power than the other, the more powerful party has more responsibility for the quality of interpersonal processes and its consequences. We call these relationships asymmetric.

When we talk about *power* in relationships between experts and laypeople, we do not only refer to the formal or actual power which the experts have legally (e.g. the obligation to report to welfare authorities.) We also use the word to include non-formal aspects of power. Non-formal power arises from the experts' professional knowledge, the fact that they have specific know-how. But it also arises from the fact that some parents (and especially socially disadvantaged) tend to ascribe power to their children's teachers. Generally, this is in contrast with the experts' feelings of powerlessness, especially in imbalanced relationships. But still, parents all too often feel manipulated and overlooked in contact with teachers and school.

Unlike a child, parents can influence the reciprocity if they consider it necessary and put a little effort in it. They may interfere by saying: *Wait! There must be a better way to discuss this!* But in reality, parents rarely feel confident to interfere and their attempts often aren't appreciated. In conflicts between parents and teachers, the latter generally tend to consciously draw on their processual power to get their will. *In fact, all relationship-centered professions bear the risk of processual abuse of power by the expert.* This risk increases if feelings of insecurity and fear rise. Similarly, the tendency to abuse power decreases with heightened relational competence.

When interacting with parents, teachers have the role of hosts. They are responsible for the general tone, mood and the atmosphere of the conversation. This responsibility also includes the obligation to end conversations and seek help from outside if they do not succeed in establishing a largely positive atmosphere. We used the word *largely* here because conversations between humans are hardly ever entirely balanced, reasonable, and purposeful. There always must be space for unbalanced emotions and disagreement. Teachers have always had a major responsibility for the content and objective of the conversations. Now it is time to expand this responsibility to include the process level of interaction.

Paradoxically, the failure to take the process level into account arises from the high responsibility to ensure the content. Processual responsibility does not mean including small talk about the weather or allowing parents to take control of the conversation. Processual responsibility means to heighten the awareness for interpersonal processes and their influence on content and goals. Destructive processes sooner or later undermine the objective contents and goals of any conversation.

Conversation and Communication

Johannes Sløk[7], Professor of Philosophy, describes conversation as follows:

> *Conversation – or dialogue – can be described as two people's journey through language, through questions and answers, through careful mutual examination. Very often, conversation is a long way to a distant goal, an as yet unknown 'truth'.*
>
> *Whenever the partners successfully complete their journey and reach their goal. They come to a point in which they cannot get any farther. They reach 'the truth' about a topic, which has been the subject of the conversation. The travelers, however, did not discover a 'truth' which existed throughout.*
>
> *The 'truth' is the result that these two partners obtain. They obtained a specific result only because there were no more options to continue their journey. This means that they did not discover a predefined 'truth'. Rather, they determined a 'truth' simply because they could not get any farther.*

Johannes Sløk was strongly influenced by the Danish philosopher Søren Kierkegaard. In this quotation, he adapts existentialist tradition to a postmodern understanding of the significance of language as well as the nature of conversation. His approach is different from modernist tradition, in which there is a distance (duality) between reality and objective observation and description. It is not based on the assumption that there is a predefined hidden truth to be discovered. He thus puts an end to the expert role. The quality of the process determines the quality of *truth*. The difference between Sløk's conception of conversation and our delimitation below is that Sløk primarily refers to *intellectually equal* dialogues. But he also considers equal dignity - the mutual respect for each other's conception of reality - an important prerequisite.

Later in this book (in Chapter 8), we will revisit the experts' that see themselves as the ones who know the truth on a issue and the goal of a conversation in advance. This attitude threatens establishing contact, mutuality and dynamics in conversations with parents and children alike. One of the central educational concepts *motivation*, is, actually very often the teachers' attempt to sell their own truth to other parties if they do not show enough interest or respect for the truth. Instead of trying to balance the asymmetric character of the relationship, teachers often stick to their position. Ironically, this does not motivate at all.

In this context, we use the term conversation to refer to each dialogue which between teachers and children or their parents in schools or early child care. They can be compulsory, spontaneous, arranged or necessary. Successful conversations in educational context correspond to Sløk's above definition, but because of our focus on asymmetric relationships we want to replace his idea of *equality* with *equal dignity*. His understanding of a valuable dialogue makes equal demands on both sides. But, of course, teachers cannot simply expect children and parents to be able to fulfill these demands. It is in the nature of asymmetric relationships that each party involved can only do its best to meet these basic demands and to set a basic tone that is inspiring and encouraging. Moreover, all valuable qualities in interpersonal interaction, first develop in the process of building relationships. They are not a priori but have to be created through stability and renewed again and again.

Communication is the technical part of conversation. It is about providing information, which is central to teaching. The ability to communicate in writing and speech also plays an important role in providing parents with necessary information. Communicative qualities such as clarity and understandability contribute to creating a stable foundation for increasing personal contact, while the lack creates a rather instable basis.

Conversation and communication are not clear-cut categories. They share qualities such as the ability and willingness to take account of another person's way of understanding and self-conception. Yet, we think it is helpful to keep the terms distinct. If, for example, Christian's teacher states that he and the boy had *communicative difficulties*, it would be helpful to know what he means exactly. Does he want to say: *I don't think Christian understands my way of teaching mathematics* or *Whenever I talk to Christian, I feel like I don't really know him.*

What we describe as conversation is also known as dialogue. The theoretical physicist David Bohm[8], who researched the nature of dialogue all his life, explains the difference between communication and dialogue as follows:

It may be useful to begin to discuss this question by considering the meaning of the word communication. This is based on the Latin communicare meaning 'to make or do something together' but also 'to share'. Which can mean to convey information or knowledge from one person to another as accurate as possible. This meaning is appropriate in a wide range of contexts. Thus, one person may communicate a set of directions on to how to carry out a certain operation to another. Clearly, a great deal of our industry and technology depends on this kind of communication.

Nevertheless, this meaning does not cover all that is part of communication. For example, consider a dialogue. In a dialogue, when one person says something, the other person does not in general respond with exactly the same meaning as the first person expected. Rather, the meanings are only similar and not identical. Thus, when the second person replies, the first person sees a difference between what he meant to say and what the other person understood. After considering this difference, he may then be able to see something new, which is relevant both to his own views and to those of the other person. And so, it can go back and forth, with the continual emergence of a new content that then becomes common to both participants. Thus, in a dialogue, each person does not attempt to make certain ideas or items of information that are already known to him common. Rather, it means that the two people are making something in common, i.e., creating something new together.

But of course, such communication can only lead to the creation of something new, if people are able to listen freely to each other, without prejudice, and without trying to influence each other.

This concept of dialogue or conversation does not fit traditional pedagogical thinking and practice, where the idea is to reach a goal or result at the content level that was defined in advance. If this didn't work out, one of them would say, "Now, we need to have a serious talk." The following conversation, however, was usually more a lecture than a dialogue between equals.

Sløk and Bohm focused on intellectually stimulating dialogues. But their basic principles equally apply to conversations meant to reveal processual *truths* and aid personal development. For the essential characteristic of subject-subject relationships is exactly their subjective quality. If a teacher feels threatened by a child or vice versa, their feelings are a truth in his own reality, yet not necessarily in the reality of the other.

Chapter 6:
Relational Competence

In our opinion, the term relational competence should be used exclusively in the context of professional relationships. These are relationships between professionals and non-professionals. The main reason for this is that the decisive quality of private relationships between parents or grandparents and children or grandchildren is characterized by irrationality and emotionality. In a way, this is also true for professionals. Yet, we demand different and higher standards from professionals' rationality, reason and knowledge.

The urge us to establish relational competence as a separate interdisciplinary field of knowledge, stems from recent findings concerning the competences and development of children as well as today's insights on specific relational details and their significance for well-being on both sides.

Said simply, we deal with three *parties* instead of two.

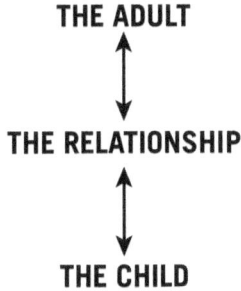

Traditionally, relationships are seen, having two sides – e.g. the adult and the child – and pedagogues and other professionals have been interested in what is good and necessary for each side. In addition, both parenting and pedagogy have treated the two as opposing parties. If something is good for the child, it probably is bad or difficult for the adult, or the other way around. In light of our experience with interpersonal relationships, we confidently state that this polarization is irrelevant. The same social and existential qualities are equally beneficial for both children and adults and enable intact and dynamic relationships characterized by equal dignity. Therefore, it does not suffice that teachers have specialized knowledge about children and teaching, no matter how valuable. They also need relational knowledge and competences to establish, correct and improve relations.

Modern Infant and Attachment Research

Since the 1950s, infant researchers and researchers on bonding and attachment around the globe have collected a wealth of material in form of video recordings, particularly of the mother-child relationship. This research has brought forth three major findings, which strongly differ from previous assumptions about child development and their competences.[1]

Today, we know that infants are born with the following natural competencies:
- *A child is born inherently social.*
  This insight is based on the finding that they have the ability and need to establish social (interpersonal) relationships from the very first moment.
- *A child's reactions are always meaningful.*
  Research has shown that a child is capable of intersubjectivity. They adapt to the mood of adults by receiving, interpreting and reacting to their signals.
- *A child can assume personal responsibility.*
  Children are also able to take over responsibility for personal issues such as hunger, taste and closeness from the very beginning on. From preschool age onwards, this competence rapidly develops further. (compare Chapter 4 – children's personal responsibility, page 87)

Another result concerns basic relational quality. Research has shown that subject-subject relationships provide the most fruitful basis for a child's development and wellbeing. These are relationships in which adults consider and treat children as independent subjects (persons) and, thus, grant them space to actively participate in the relationship from the very beginning. Traditional educational science and practice treated children as objects, meaning adults did something *with* and about children. This is called a subject-object relationship. In this book, we use the term *mutuality* to describe the specific relational quality of subject-subject relationships**.

Sigmund Freud's work influenced educational science through the assumption that children are born *asocial* and potentially *antisocial*. In line with this idea, pedagogy primarily pursued the goal of *making* children into social beings. Another basic assumption was that children lacked compassion. This meant that the pedagogical goal was to teach children how to be emphatic and compassionate. It is easy to recognize that previous attempts to turn children into social and emphatic people were not only redundant but also contraindicated, since children are born with both the competence and need to socialize, as well as basic empathy. It is not an adult's achievement that a child grows up to be an emphatic adult. Actually, it is an achievement that children's innate emphatic ability largely survives pedagogical mistreatments.

In a similar way, pedagogues and parents were not aware of a child's capability of intersubjectivity. And only to a limited degree did they recognize their ability to understand and interpret signals. In most cases, this ability was accredited to a competent environment rather than the child. The significance of a child's spontaneous reactions in specific relational moments, however, was neglected almost entirely, just the same as their role in conveying essential information about *who* the child is and about the relational qualities which it is comfortable with or not. Adults interpreted a child's reactions almost exclusively as characteristics of *what* they are (independent of relational qualities). They understood a child's reactions as obedient or disobedient, spoilt, hysteric, overtired or bossy.

** The mentioned competencies are a summary of Daniel Stern's research, our own clinical experience, as well as interviews with Stern, etc..

The Swedish psychologist Margaretha Brodén[2] research and clinical examination of mothers with early-childhood traumas and their newborn babies revolutionized our knowledge and provided the necessary foundation for discovering how we can understand children's competence. Brodén showed that even emotionally neglected mothers are able to acquire the necessary parental competence by developing and training their awareness of the babies' reactions and signals. This, in turn, had a *therapeutic* effect on the mothers' self-destructive tendencies. Simply put, infants can teach their parents how to treat and care for them.

Professional pedagogical relationships have a lot of different qualities than a mother-child or a father-child relationship. But we refer to these findings because they shed light on basic relational phenomena which are helpful to understand other essential relationships.

The insight that children are competent in certain areas might seem to contradict another *new* concept that was also discovered within the framework of attachment theory: the resilient child. As Dion Sommer describes the *resilient* child has an almost incredible resistance and ability to survive most terrible circumstances and relationships.[3] This seems to be in contrast to the existential vulnerability of a child many readers connect to when reading about the *competent* child. But this *vulnerability* must be seen in relation to a child's ability to *cooperate*, which is an inherent way to adapt and survive. Vulnerability and survivability do not oppose each other. They are two components of one and the same phenomena, of being a child.

This combination of a child's existential vulnerability and adaptability is one of the central challenges of education. Due to this, children can seem and even be comfortable over an extended period of time and, apparently, under very different educational settings. In a way, this means that all educational theories and methods *are effective*, as long as they are implemented convincingly and systematically within a rather isolated educational setting. *This is why, we are convinced that, all educational theories and practices must answer the ethical question of why their method is effective and how it influences the children.*

Adult-Child Relationships between Now and Then

Teachers do not go to work every day pondering over basic research. Even if they did, they could not simply deduce answers to daily challenges. Pedagogical practice has its own history, tradition and moments of indolence which combined with the disposition of the individual teacher (their personality and values), uniquely form professional behavior.

As described above, new demands on educational thinking and action have been arising consistently since the post-war era. In specific, this concerns following areas
- democratic and humanistic values
- learning psychology
- educational psychology
- child and youth culture
- modern infant and attachment research.

Children change their behavior more quickly than adults do. This has always been the case, but the current accumulation of knowledge and social changes may well be more substantial than in any other historic period.

A long time has passed since schools had the power to define family values. Concerning the relational quality of adult-child relationships, families represent the vanguard, while schools are usually more in a defensive position, and daycare centers seek a constructive dialogue with parents. Today's children are no different from the children of previous generations. The difference lies in our knowledge about the nature of children and thus, the nature of us all, regardless of age.

From our perspective, there are only a few key factors of major educational relevance that currently need to be focused on. Most aspects discussed publicly and energetically by the media and politics are not much more than hot air.

The decisive factors are:
- the end of pedagogy built on obedience and the widespread insecurity about successful alternatives
- the children's open protest against being objectified by adults as well as evidence for heightened wellbeing and development potential in subject-subject relationships
- the decreasing tendency to scapegoat children for every discord in adult-child relationships

These factors show that adult's knowledge and ideas progress faster than their behavior and that behavior generally changes faster in harmonious, rather than in unharmonious interdependency. This is a general human truth. But a difficult fact is that all *pedagogical language* emerged from the knowledge and moral concepts which objectified children and expected obedience.[4]

The relationship between words/language on one hand and consciousness/behavior on the other hand is dialectical. This means our way of expression does not only reflect who we are but also shapes who we become. *The way we use language in relationships establishes contact to others but also to ourselves.* Thus, language is more dynamic if we *express* rather than *describe* ourselves.

There is a big difference for oneself between
Nowadays, it is difficult to raise children.
and
I find it difficult to include our middle child.

We can use either of the statements to describe one and the same frustration. The same applies when describing others:
Jakob is in his terrible twos.
or
Jakob wants to be independent now and do everything on his own.

In educational settings, the problem is no less complex, for it requires mastery of at least three different languages.

- The terminology used in the specific discipline (mathematics, language, creative subjects, ...) and differentiates it from others
- The partially adapted jargon that is used for communication with peers
- The language adults use relating to children.

The fewer values these three types of language share, the larger the everyday discrepancy between pedagogical behavior and the individual teacher's consciousness.

Making children the object of pedagogy had its own language. This language is most evident in questions like the following:

- What do you do with children who refuse to eat vegetables?
- What do you do with children who do not want to listen?
- What do you do with a three-year-old child who does not want to sleep in their own bed?

All of these ways of speaking objectify children and reflect the illusion of a universally applicable answer. Over the course of time, answers to similar questions were found based on two different perspectives. Either, there was a *correct* answer to each question, or the one interested had to gradually find an answer by *experimenting*. There is no objective answer to questions like these. A relevant answer requires in depth knowledge of who the parties involved are, how their relationship is and what specific changes they desire or need. The success of an intervention depends on the adults' commitment, the child's experience of being included and taken seriously and the ethical approach that doesn't build on strategies and moralizing.

This development goes hand in hand with both a new way of talking as well a new professional identity and role. These necessary changes are the same for parents and pedagogues. Such fundamental changes in a short period of time, however, tend to stir insecurity, fear and chaos on all sides, which a lot of pedagogues and parents are experiencing. While some focus more on striving away from familiar and secure grounds, others seek new approaches of which they have a more or less clear idea. We no longer live in the 1960s or 70s when we had the choice between a limited number of defined attitudes that provided security. We now find ourselves in transition between two essentially different paradigms.

Public and professional discussions about education and parenting stirred by this insecurity often simplify the issue strongly, because they still rely on outdated concepts such as *external conditions, pedagogical consequence,* and *permissiveness*. A tiring and polarizing debate develops with two sides arguing about what is right and what is wrong about specific approaches. In fact, parenting and teaching are currently in a phase, which we can mostly aptly describe as an experimental state lacking a greater context. A polarization we see is between adults who rely on what seems effective day by day without questioning and those who are inactive out of fear they could do something wrong. Neither attitudes help children or adults. But to complete the full picture more and more schools and families are working together to connect their values and actions.

Defining Relational Competence

Our concept of relational competence as outlined below includes all necessary components and applies to all *professional adult-child relationships.*

We use the term competence, because it implies both *knowledge* and *power* and is more precise than e.g. quality. Quality is a smooth word, that leaves too much up in the open for every day issues in pedagogical contexts. In this book, we talk about moral concepts in everyday use. We use this term according to the concept of the author and thinker Ole Ravn Jørgensen. *In Tænk fremtiden*, which literally translates to *Think future*, Jørgensen suggests defining quality as *moral concepts realized*[6].

Relational competence, thus, is a way to realize fundamental moral concepts of building healthy relationships. Our experience shows that the realization of moral concepts enables a high level of quality in adult-child interactions which benefits both the humans involved as well as the academic goal of educating children.

Definition:
Relational competence is the teachers' ability to see each child on their own terms and to adapt the personal behavior accordingly without giving up the leadership. It is also the ability to remain in contact authentically and the ability and willingness to take on full responsibility for the quality of the interaction.

Relational competence is both a matter of pedagogical trade/craft as well as a matter of ethics.

The sum of a teacher's *teaching* competence and *relational* competence determines their *professional* competence.

Relevant Moral Concepts

The above definition includes several key concepts, which relate closely to the moral concepts discussed in this book.

Seeing
The ability to *see* children depends primarily on four factors and their different possible combinations.
- The adult's *willingness* to see.
- The adult's *personal perception* of being seen or unseen. Adults who experienced relationships in which they were seen in their childhood and/or adulthood are usually equipped with the ability to see others. The same applies to people who consciously didn't experienced being seen, but were able to retain their inner intactness and openness and thus developed the capacity.
- The adult's overall *experience* with children and thus resulting personal *image of human kind*. There is a lot of truth in the old saying, we *see what we want to see*. And more than most of us would believe possible in everyday life. Whether we see mankind positively or negatively determines our interpretation of everything we experience.
- The adult's *professional development*; the more we interpret other

people's behavior as a reaction to our own behavior, the less we are able to see the other.

If we want to *see* children comprehensively, we have to develop a descriptive language. The experience of being *seen* as the person you are is distinct from the experience of being looked at, watched, observed, exposed or eyed. Beautiful or ugly people, as well as people with physical and mental handicaps, very often feel looked at but not *seen*. The feeling of being seen can either confirm what you know about yourself already, or it can lead you to a new spontaneous (liberating or upsetting) insight about who you are. Often, the feeling of being *unseen* is expressed as the feeling of not being heard, even if we know the other person was listening to us. The other may have just heard the content of our expression but not gotten the entire message.

To *see* children entails more than considering their immediate and most outstanding behavior. It means to look *beyond* their behavior, but not in the psychological sense trying to find explanations or analyze the behavior. It means to see the subtle expression of sorrow in a child's eyes rather than focusing on their hyperactivity and anger. It means to see the reluctance in their body language, even if the child agrees. It means to see the frown while trying to make themselves understood in a conversation with its parents. It means to see the loneliness of 'everybody's darling'. It is, primarily about the adults' ability to collect this subtle information and modify their image of an individual child accordingly, time and time again, until they achieve both a deeper understanding and an acknowledging language to express it. Acknowledgement gives children the feeling of being seen, while normative and evaluative language conveys the feeling of being unveiled, exposed, and criticized.

Above all, the value of an adults' ability to *see* the individual child lies in the opportunity to strengthen the child's self-esteem as well as their inner responsibility. The contact between the child and the adult becomes more tangible and, thus, creates a stronger foundation for the professional part of reciprocal action. This also means that children who are *seen* take adults more seriously and show a greater deal of respect and empathy for them.

Leadership
We use the term leadership to refer to adults' ability to plan and implement processes necessary to achieve specific educational goals, without violating a child's personal integrity and losing personal authority.

Adult guidance is valuable for it confirms and develops the teacher's professional self, creates a secure environment for children and provides an ideal adult example with whom they can identify and in relation to whom they can discover themselves.

Authenticity
Authenticity is the ability to be fully present and sincere in relation to another person, child or adult.

It is valuable in two ways. For one it provides the necessary framework for developing personal authority and for continuous professional development. At the same time, adult authenticity enables children to discover and express their own authenticity. This paves the way to developing their own inner responsibility and social understanding.

Responsibility
In this context, responsibility describes the adults' responsibility for the relational quality of interactions with a child or a group of children.

The adults' ability to assume this responsibility is necessary to reinforce personal authority and prevent violations of personal integrity on either of the sides.

This quote from, Søs Bayer puts words to this aspect in a different way. She talks about three competencies, which teachers of today and tomorrow need to be equipped with:[6]

The competence to build relationships with children.

When we look at modern childhood (the way children live today away from the close relations in the family many hours every day, spending the day in kindergarten, daycare, school) we see how important it is to build relationships to other persons than the parents. And we know that human society builds relationships because they represent the basic logic of human society.

The next two competencies are nuances of the first and build on it:

The competence to take a place in children's lives, despite not being their parent.

This refers, with a hint of cultural criticism, to adults who – for primarily cultural and ideological reasons – are unwilling, unable or afraid to gain a significant role in children's lives unless they are their parents. The most common explanation for this is the ideological view of family as the primary and sovereign relationship between adults and children. By pointing to this as a future competence, I want to draw attention to the importance of challenging established conceptions in one's own culture and to the fact that there are, indeed, (many) children who depend on this. In other cultures, it is more acceptable to take on both professional and private importance in children's lives.

The competence to bear that educational reality is just like life itself.

This competence includes considering reality as the connecting link between institutions and teaching. I mean to focus on the fact that educational reality (what an expression!) is a reality constructed by teachers. If teachers wouldn't construct this reality, it would be closer to life and other realities. They are forced to arrange an educational reality, because otherwise, they would have to act on the basis of human dignity, which undoubtedly requires other competences, and these cannot be acquired in practice or through formal training.

In other words, this competence means refraining from constructing a reality for themselves and children, and allowing institutional reality to resemble real life. It is the competence to accept human society as it is.

We ask our readers to keep this last thought in mind, it is beyond the scope of this book to point out the numerous parallels between life and work in educational institutions and their immediate environment.

CHAPTER 7:
Professional Development

Personal development plays an essential role in being a teacher. As experience shows, the most important *tools* a teacher, and all other professionals working with children, have are their *character*, their *methods* (ways of working) and their *knowledge*. This first became apparent in child and adolescent psychiatry and children's homes. Looking how to train the personal character these institutions turned to psychoanalysis first because of the many overlapping topics. Building up on the experience that each prospective psychoanalyst has to pass through a training analysis to qualify for clinical practice, this made sense for other professionals as well. Similarly, other body- and psychotherapy training methods require practitioners to go through personal processes before working with clients.

In the 1980s, these personal developmental aspects found their way into broader educational circles. Some professionals started participating in workshops on personal development and started individual therapy. Regardless of whether their motivation was personal or professional, most of them soon recognized personal advancements in their daily work. It improved their range and depth of professional relationships, and they experienced a stronger inner balance between themselves as a *person* and their *function*. It became easier to integrate these two parts of themselves as a person. The most obvious conclusion was that in order to be a competent teacher, you have to go to therapy.

As we will explain later in this chapter, there are several reasons why we are skeptical about this conclusion despite its underlying sensible reasoning. The alternative we offer here is based on our long-term work at the Kempler Institute[***], where we developed the principles and methods of what we call *professional-personal development*. Professional-personal development includes a range of activities based on psychotherapeutic experience but without using psychotherapeutic methods.

[***] Now called DFTI – Danish Institute for Family therapy

The starting point for our approach are following thoughts.

The quality of each professional interaction is strongly influenced by the charisma, character, and assertiveness of the person involved.

Professional-personal development is an ongoing, structured process in which personal patterns of thinking and action are examined, recognized, and processed to find new relevant ways of interaction. This is helpful for both the teacher and the child. This examination is especially helpful to uncover patterns that seem to inhibit our commitment, goals and potentials in professional relationships.

The term *'professional-personal'*, highlights the necessary integration of both professional and personal aspects. And we want to emphasize that professional educational tasks are the basis for this process. But they develop in a dialectical process, because both aspects of being human are interdependent.

In the following, we want to take a closer look at the aspects of professional-personal development and the relevance in educational settings.

Professional-Personal Development

For a long time, personal behavior in professional relationships was considered to be a private matter – as long as it wasn't criminal behavior. The professional ideal was a clear-cut separation between the personal and the professional role. Today, only few share this understanding. More commonly, people believe that this kind of objectivity is unrealistic, and for different reasons, also undesirable. In fact, personal behavior is so closely tied to professional behavior, it seems illogical to try and separate one from the other.

In studies of related disciplines such as social-pedagogy and psychotherapy[1], the clients and students emphasize the significance of experts' *personal* presence and *personal* commitment, as well as experiencing *meaningful* personal contact in supporting professional relationships. In other studies,[2] the lack of the above qualities is named as the reason for holding on to self-destructive patterns. Clients and students also show very little interest in an experts' formal qualifications and current professional status. These studies correspond with our own experience and demonstrate that there are good reasons to give *structured professional-personal* development a high priority, because it contributes to stabilizing pedagogical values and improving teacher's relational competence.

These are all good reasons for professional-personal development, but the four questions *why, when, how* and *what is the goal* remain and need good answers to be implemented in everyday professional life.

Why is personal development an important component of teacher's relational competence?

The most concise and general answer possible is that we all cooperate with both constructive and destructive elements of our childhood. We develop unique combinations of healthy and self-destructive behavior. Self-destructive behavior is always also destructive to important relationships and hurts people who love or depend on us.

survival strategy - new relevant relationships - possible life strategy

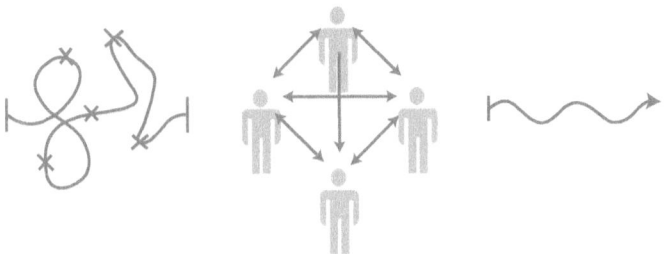

The first part of the graphic illustrates A's behavior pattern. 'x' marks the moments in A's life in which his integrity was violated or ignored and where he had to give up on himself to maintain contact to people close to him. Some of the violating phenomena, such as violence or emotional failure, were one time occurrences during A's childhood and adolescence. Other phenomena happened recurring, e.g. not being allowed to show personal emotions, fear of being ridiculed, physical and psychological assaults or neglect. Due to these experiences A developed his personal and unique *survival strategy*. Over the course of time most people typically develop cognitive attitudes that support this emotionally necessary behavior. A survival strategy is largely the sum of a long list of unconscious adjustments and attempts to adapt to the reactions and feedback a child received from parents and other important adults.

The middle part of the graphic illustrates how other important and relevant relationships replace or complement A's relational patterns (unless the patterns are highly self-destructive such as addiction, eating disorders, suicide attempts, etc.). Usually other people especially partners and children as they are the most important people in our lives see reckless tendencies in our behavior before we do. This has two reasons. On one hand, we get used to the self-destructive elements in our own behavior, because they serve us well over the years and encapsulated the pain to which they were once related. This enables remembering things without connecting to the pain. On the other hand, we tend to open up in love relationships and become more vulnerable.

A father, for example, may think that he is in full control of the alcohol he consumes that consists of four to seven glasses of wine or beer between five and nine o'clock every evening. His wife and children, however, are affected by his decreasing presence and make their own (very often self-critical) conclusions. It is especially children who do not question an adult's behavior, but rather feel guilty about their own behavior. Therefore, in many cases, others have to show severe reactions, before we recognize the self-destructive nature of our own behavior.

These inter-relational dynamics do not only apply to close and personal relationships. Similar processes, albeit often delayed, also happen in professional relationships with children (who are very dependent and thus most vulnerable), colleagues and superiors or employees. Generally, self-destructive behavior on one side triggers self-destructive behavior on the other. Rarely does the counterpart of A. e.g. then take on the responsibility for his or her own behavior. It is usually blamed on A. This mutual effect is not a symptom of a bad relationship it just shows how we continuously and actively contribute to the interactive processes, which can also bring forth mutual insight and maturation.

The third part of the graphic represents the goal, which most of us have in one way or another. This goal is to gradually transform our survival strategy into a *life strategy*. *A life strategy* that corresponds with our need for individual wellbeing and fruitful relationships. Some self-destructive tendencies disappear if we consciously change our interaction for a short period of time, but we and our environment have to combat other patterns for years until the first results become visible.

Another important aspect of conscious, structured professional-personal development is in the strengthening of the awareness of an individual's constructive potential, as well as encouraging using these potentials in professional relationships. Sometimes, our self-destructive tendencies obstruct the realization of this fruitful potential. But most experts possess a *treasure chest* of valuable qualities that only have to be *seen* and supported by others to unfold. In most cases, the frustration and exhaustion many of us experience in our daily work is not due to problems but to the fact that much of our energy is wasted in suppressing our valuable qualities.

The motivation of most teachers is predominantly based on one of the most basic human needs: the need to experience that we are valuable (professionally and/or personally) to people we work with. The experience of losing energy in professional relationships is largely connected to the experience of not being of value to the ones we would like most to be of value for. Often, this means that we, in fact, are not of the value we could be of. The feeling of *not being good enough* is the more self-critical version of the same message.

The triggers for professional-personal development are often conflicts that arise with children, parents and colleagues. These conflicts in general have just as many resources as problems. The term *survival strategy* also includes *existential* aspects in the broader sense of the word. Besides the existential issues such as death, loneliness, freedom and meaninglessness, there are also internal and external behavior patterns that developed in the individual's attempt to be seen and loved by their closest relatives.[3]

All important relationships can confront us with existential issues, whether we want them to or not. In this case, there are only two sources we can draw from for energy and inspiration. These are our inner responsibility and our closest relationships. Most other conflicts and problems can be solved by means of *tools* and methods. But existential conflicts and problems require introspective, reflective and interpersonal processes, which can be supported by methods to a certain degree but not solved by one method in specific. Personal access to one's own inner responsibility is one of the most important mental health factors we know of. For this reason, it is vital to create a culture in schools and day care centers that take the inner responsibility serious for both children and adults.

It is often difficult to give feedback to friends or colleagues that is both supportive and challenging. It can be equally difficult to find a balance between exaggerated self-criticism and non-reflective self-satisfaction. One problem is our habit to mix up psychological issues with morals: which turns incompetent mothers or inept teachers into bad people.

When should conscious, structured professional-personal development take place?

The answer to this question depends entirely on the individual's motivation and personal decision. A conscious, self-regulated process cannot be forced. Schools and persons responsible should offer and support professional-personal development as an opportunity rather than a requirement that only leads to conformity and new evasive actions.

One of the fundamental experiences in psychotherapy and counseling when dealing with conscious, structured personal development and therapy is that the individual's inner *timing* is decisive for the quality of the process and its result. There are numerous factors that collectively contribute to the *right moment*. One factor can be discomfort with the status quo, in connection with other emotions, that play an important role in the quality of their private and social relationships. We have seen many who got seriously and responsibly involved in the process, without achieving any effect or change at first. Then, only a few months or years later, the same persons showed quick progress. This shows that professional-personal development cannot be *switched* on spontaneously when we feel a need for it. We rather achieve the best results when actively involved in the process for an extended period of time without interruption. This is true concerning the quality of these processes. But from an ethical perspective, we are convinced that the individual must make a conscious decision. Human beings also often need the opportunity to say *no* and experience the acceptance of their refusal before they can say a wholehearted *yes*.

In the past few years, many teachers have struggled with situations that led to burnout and personal breakdown. In some cases, the long-ongoing experience of being forced into a defensive position goes beyond the personal capacities. In other cases, the reason can be found in singular traumatizing events related to physical violence or other severe violations of their own personal integrity. When such breakdowns first occurred, the teachers concerned were often left to themselves and had to content themselves with the passive sympathy of superiors and colleagues. Respect for staff's privacy and lacking the practice in how to handle strong personal reactions caused personal breakdowns and their progression to be kept private and individual. This tendency still dominates – even if the willingness to help individual teachers has increased.

We know from other professions that subtle exhaustion and occasional or cumulative traumatic experiences often lead to existential crises or similar situations which force people to face the self-destructive side of their survival strategy and personal life values[4]. Teachers in such critical situations definitely need sufficient individual help and support.

General signals for needing support
The individual range and ways feelings show are too vast to make a complete list of signals when support is needed.
Common signals though, are

- a low frustration tolerance
- a low tolerance for conflicts
- a low level of physical and mental energy
- fear showing in nervousness or physical tension
- the feeling of having to pull oneself together to be able to go to work
- self-accusation and continuous self-doubt
- a tendency to scapegoat others
- a tendency to complain
- addiction
- …

Mental exhaustion and traumatizing experiences do no only arise from the individual psychological profile and history. They are also *socio-psychological* phenomena that have both collective and individual causes and effects. Moral ideas and legal regulations assign guilt and legal responsibility. This, however, is not enough for either of the persons involved.

According to our experience structured professional-personal development has proved very valuable in preventing long-term consequences for teachers as well as treating issues that have already arisen. In addition, it also enhances a healthy culture in institutions.

We know from experience that most teachers like participating in these processes. Conflicts and resistance are rarely due to a lack of individual motivation. Usually they are a consequence of the low quality of previous processes or of a general climate of insecurity in the institution.

The specific opportunities available for professional-personal development vary from institution to institution. Rarely schools organize *child-free workdays* that allow the staff to work together. Sadly, teachers are the most neglected professional group when it comes to opportunities of interdisciplinary exchange and professional-personal development. In the light of teachers' comprehensive responsibility and the significance of their work, the situation is hardly appropriate.

What is the goal of professional-personal development?

Why professional-personal development makes sense can be seen from different perspectives. To better understand the underlying goals, we refer here to two different models, to help understand personal and professional development and mastery.

One is Murray Bowen's concept of *differentiation-of-self* and the other Dreyfus & Dreyfus' *model for the human learning process.*

Below, we summarize Bowen's model of *self-differentiation*, which is one of six key concepts of his family systems theory[5]. The concept refers to the individual's ability to stay connected to one's own personal needs, limitations, emotions and values in close relationships, as well as the ability to differentiate emotions from thoughts.

Bowen developed a scale of differentiation, which defines all stages or phases in the transition to full differentiation:

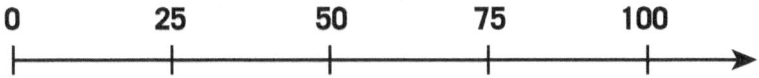

The higher the ability to differentiate the higher emotional tolerance. That is the ability to cope with emotional tension, conflict and intensity. Reactivity describes the other end of the scale. This is the tendency to feel dependent on others which manifests itself in self-sacrifice, victim mentality or submission. The ability to differentiate develops by first seeking consensus, over self-assertion to a balanced ability to recognize nuances and assume self-responsibility in full recognition of one's realistic dependency on others.

The following key words describe the stages of Bowen's scale of differentiation:

0–25: People with the lowest level of *self-differentiation* show a high degree of fusion. Their thoughts are controlled by feelings. They have difficulty feeling separate from others and are dominated by the feelings in their close relationships. Their main focus is on preventing discomfort and conflicts by entering dependent relationships to others.

25–50: People with a low *self-differentiation* are predominantly controlled by feelings and dependent on harmony or disharmony. They often lack energy for self-organization and focused behavior. They have a tendency to submit to external authorities and systems characterized by a simple and clearly laid out worldview: either authoritarian or submissive.

50–75: People with a relatively high *self-differentiation* show a low degree of fusion. To a degree they have adequately defined and nuanced personal opinions and values, as well as a low level of projections. But fear to express themselves on highly controversial matters.

75–100: People with a high level of *self-differentiation* are controlled by internal factors, independent and un-dogmatic. They have a very nuanced emotional life, clear life values and a high level of tolerance. They demonstrate a strong interest in, and responsibility for, society and the ability to enter into intense relationships.

The lower a person's level of *self-differentiation*, the more fear starting a personal development process will cause. The underlying feeling on the lowest level mainly consists of fear. And the self that is looking for development is highly dependent on the social environment. Higher levels are characterized by greater confidence and self-determination.

Any new step in a developmental process is a step into the unknown. This can be either frightening or tempting but does not change anything about the fact that there is always a risk of regression to immature patterns of behavior. It seems self-induced processes pass with more harmony than externally provoked developments, which are more likely to cause short-term or long-term phases of regression.

Examining one's own relational competence is, however, only possible if there is a willingness to work with externally provoked developments, because they always involve other people. When we meet highly differentiated people, most of us are either fascinated or react with timidity and by distancing. There is a risk for teachers to replace their own low integrity with official authority and exertion of power when dealing with children who are highly differentiated or have a high personal integration in specific areas.

Personal development is inevitable. For most of us, personal development is partially a conscious process, often interrupted (and sometimes also determined) by life crises and/or traumas. *Professional-personal development* describes a conscious, structured developmental process that takes its starting point in professional issues. We are convinced that conscious, self-regulated personal development is a private matter, which no one else but the individual concerned should be able and allowed to determine. But a lot of reasons speak for professional-personal development becoming an essential component of professional development.

While Bowen's concept of *self-differentiation* focuses on personality, Stuart Dreyfus and Hubert Dreyfus developed a model of the human learning process that, more or less explicitly describes the professional dimension.

Model for the human learning process

(freely adapted from Dreyfus & Dreyfus)[6]

Expertise	Beyond rules and guidelines. Action and decisions are made intuitively, holistically and synchronal.
Proficiency	Beyond analytical rationality. They understand and organize intuitively. They approach decisions analytically.
Competence	Behavior can be adapted to specific situations. They can set and analyze priorities and make conscious decisions about plans and goals. Interpretation and judgment are part of their action. They have an internal relationship to their own actions and results.
Advanced beginner	The level of an advanced beginner is characterized by context dependency. Relevant aspects in relevant situations are recognized, provided they show similarities. The preferred method is based on trial and error.
Novice	Bound to textbooks/guidelines. Action does not arise from specific situations – context is not seen. Action and result are not part of oneself.

Level of expertise   personal development

It may be helpful to locate yourself in the above scale if you do not want to drown in overwhelming demands on yourself or feel inferior in comparison to other more experienced colleagues. This model offers subsidiary goals for each stage and important main goals in supervision and collegial reflection.

How can professional-personal development be structured and supported?
In the following we describe different ways of supporting and enabling professional-personal development within pedagogical settings. First, we explain our model of collegial reflection, then how supervision can support individuals and teams and in the following we show in depth how everyday professional relationships with superiors and children can support and enable development.

Collegial Reflection
or how to obtain a constructive relationship to your own limitations

The following model was first developed and formulated by our colleague: the psychologist Peter Mortensen. For many years, Mortensen has worked with school staff and he developed a working method that is compatible with both the structure of schools and official teaching procedures and can be implemented with a minimum of external help. Other pedagogical institutions use his model modified for their context.

Our experience with the collegial reflection as a method for professional-personal development has been very positive.

As outlined above, voluntary participation is very important. This has caused astonishment in some schools, due to their culture that is oriented collectively. Our experience is that, more than half of the staff register for voluntary reflection sessions within the first year. By the second year, a considerable majority takes part.

In addition to supervision (see p. 177), which is defined by an expert with special competency and a specific role leading the process, experts have introduced different forms of group work around the globe that are sometimes called *peer group supervision*. We use the term *collegial reflection* for a specific structured work situation among colleagues on the same hierarchical level and who are equally qualified. The long-term objectives are to improve the participants' professional competence, to foster cooperation and to increase the individual's professional self-esteem and personal wellbeing at work. In short, collegial reflection is how to interact with one's own professional limitations in a constructive way.

A starting point is to accompany a colleague's own thoughts beyond their own perspective by showing thoughtfulness and empathy with a good sense for critique and responsiveness. As we will see later on, collegial reflection can be adapted as a concrete tool for developing professional relational competence. But before looking into this, we will examine some necessities and challenges of introducing collegial reflection.

Goals and requirements
What is compelling and good about the exchange among peers is that it draws on existing commitment and expertise. The shared daily routine offers detailed insight into the working conditions and institutional goals, into the expertise and character of staff, as well as students/children. This is, without a doubt, a great resource for the structured work. The difficulty, however, is that the group depends entirely on itself and is must assume a responsibility that otherwise lies in the hands of the supervisor.

Within the framework defined by the work place, self-regulatory groups have to determine their own structures and forms of cooperation. The timeframe, content, responsibility and roles within the group need to be clarified and arranged at the beginning. The participants themselves have to mutually react to appearance, work discipline, group changes and experienced outcome. These structures provide the boundaries of the collaboration and ensure the continuity of the shared work.
The decisive aspect is the individual participant's ability to maintain their motivation. The work of the group depends on the individual's willingness

to share their present need for reflection as well as on their colleagues' ability to create an atmosphere that encourages trust, exchange and reflection.

Mutual relationships and the working climate are the core of the group. The group members should have a basic trust in each other and handle the content confidentially. At the same time, it is only natural that there are reservations and uncertainties when starting a group like this. Trust in the working platform is generated by the work itself and the willingness of the individuals to give it a chance.

It takes will-power to question ourselves and it is difficult to accept challenging and confronting responses. Usually, cooperativeness is closely tied to loyalty. Responses need to be both empathic and supporting as well as thought-provoking and challenging.

Every issue also contains personal aspects. This is obvious if the problems arise from a lack of inspiration and ideas. Yet, finding a solution can be difficult if the person concerned shows a lack of understanding or sensitivity, and refuses to recognize their own destructive behavior patterns or assumptions.

It can be helpful to divide the issues according to the ways they show:
- *Practical/professional:* the individual's conception of their job and skills, as well as professional knowledge.
- *Personal*: the individual's sensitivity, empathy, self-awareness, self-knowledge – in other words their way of relating to their own actions and reactions.
- *Relational:* the way of interacting with the people concerned. The processes and reciprocal qualities between the professional and the individuals they are in relation with.

Usually, peer groups deal with practical and professional aspects of a problem. But in order to achieve a both humane and pedagogical approach to a difficult pupil, for instance, the teacher involved has to first develop a nuanced understanding of the pupil's behavior and difficulty. At the same time it isn't hard to see that a possible approach will be coming from the teacher, and therefore must also take the teachers resources into consideration as well as how difficult or stable the teacher-child relationship currently is.

By incorporating these aspects, the participants strengthen and expand their collegial relationships.

Nuanced reflection is a true balancing act. It balances between the learning process that the collegial reflection seeks and the daily routine in which this learning process takes place. But it also balances between keeping up trust and understanding, while at the same time both showing vulnerability and personal flaws, as well as being confronted.

Phases of conversation in collegial reflection

Collegial reflection is a professional exchange between equals. The site of the exchange is the relationship between a person presenting a problem and a supportive and co-reflecting counterpart. Usually, these two dialogue partners are embedded in a group whose members can participate if desired. Later on, we will explain this possibility in detail.[7]

This specific type of dialogue has three phases: the *static*, the *reflective*, and the *dynamic* phase.

The static phase at the onset of discussion allows the person presenting the problem to describe the situation as he or she perceives and experiences it. The way the issue is expressed very often reflects their frustration with the current situation. Their use of language is often passive and presents the problem as not being part of him- or herself. This often is like a documentation of what is going on, or a justification of personal failure. (Video recording can be a helpful to see the underlying structures in this phase). Besides listening actively, the main task of the co-reflector is focusing on the question: *What do you need my help for?* This way the co-reflector achieves a clearer picture of the concrete needs of this person. By interacting, the dialogue partners establish contact and gain clarity. It is essential that the helper tries to gain both insight into the problem described, as well as an understanding of the other person's experience. In summarizing their understanding of the situation, the topic or current focus of the following dialogue becomes clear. In formulating where he or she needs help the focus is turned to the professional involved.

The next phase - the reflective phase - is the working phase. The dialogue partners seek a professional approach. This is comparable to the situation of an adult showing a child how to play cards. The adult and the child look at the cards dealt to organize them and see how they could be used. On the basis of the shared information, they develop different approaches to and different ways of conceiving the situation. The purpose of this is to find an approach that makes enough sense to both of them to be discussed in more detail. In doing so, the focus shifts from the personal experience to the question of how the situation can be understood. In this phase, it is not about finding solutions, but about getting an in-depth view of how the person understands and sees the issue. This is where both professional, personal and relational aspects come into play. What can the person concerned say about the problem him- or herself? What were their initial considerations? What are their current doubts? Examining the individual's capacity, both strengthens their confidence in personal abilities, and gives insight to thoughts and attitudes, which can be supported or challenged later on in the process. This process is a conversation between equals, in which different perspectives are exchanged to ensure they are talking about the *right* problem. By showing interest in well-developed abilities, the helper gets the opportunity to *intervene* and offer ideas, as well as to test whether their help really corresponds with the recipient's need or their own ideals.

The conversation will naturally pass into the third dynamic, activity-oriented phase, if phase two is accomplished successfully.

In many cases, there is no need for extra advice. This is true especially if the person concerned is reassured of their competence, has regained confidence and energy and has a satisfying personal conclusion.

If not, the last phase needs to focus on the personal need formulated in the first phase. The way of finding a solution for a satisfactory next step has to integrate both what the person knows about themself and the professional view on the issue developed through the common dialogue. Commonly, the conversation includes a number of *ifs and buts*. This is an indicator for deficiencies in the previous phases. Often, *but* starts a sentence that expresses the need to explain oneself more thoroughly, and shows insecurity concerning the degree to which the person sees themself understood.

Integrating the group
These different phases of the conversation can also be used as a helpful framework to integrate the other colleagues not participating in the direct dialogue. This enhances all participants' reflective abilities and adds additional perspectives and ways of understanding.

Working this way challenges the dialogue partners to complete the static phase in five to ten minutes. While the rest of the group listens carefully, the dialogue partners examine the underlying problem of the specific questions. Then the dialogue is opened. And the person seeking help just listens to the reflections of other group members. It is very important that each contribution directly relates to what the person seeking help previously said. In doing so, the group can stick to the facts, and does not allow space for subjective interpretations. Their contributions reveal each group members' individual conception and understanding of the central problem. At this point, no solutions should be offered. The task is simply to find a broadened professional perspective of the problem presented. *What do I hear the issue is about and what is my reasoning?* The contributions of the individual group members are equal and should remain uncommented by others. It is not about finding a common understanding in the group.

Depending on the complexity of the topic, there may be a need for comments from different perspectives. Once this need is satisfied (it should not turn into a discussion within the group), the two dialogue partners turn their focus away from the group and back to their dialogue. Now their task is to find an approach they both consider feasible, but focusing stronger on what seems relevant for the one presenting the problem. The co-reflector either supports, modifies or questions.

In this way, the group reflection happens between the first and the second, and the second and the third phase. The dialogue phases each take about five to 10 minutes, depending on the group's agreement beforehand. The dialogue is always concluded at the end of the predefined timeframe after three dialogue phases. The process is finalized irrespective of the perceived satisfaction with the solution. The main criteria of the success is how thought-provoking and inspirational the progression of the conversation was.

It can be tempting to go for a solution that comes up at any point in the conversation, without deepening on doubts and without getting a nuanced picture of the *other* perspectives. In the same way, it can also be difficult to move on, if the group is still analyzing and developing an understanding of the central problem. But it is important to take serious that the solution has to develop within the person concerned. It has to be relevant for themself personally, so they can implement it. In the same way, it is also important to keep in mind, that complex issues sometimes need time to unfold and cannot be solved at once (or in one single session). For these reasons, it is very wise to take the predefined time structure seriously and thus also keep personal boundaries protected.

Establishing collegial reflection groups
As stated above, *collegial reflection* only works if the participants are willing to contribute personal issues. Therefore, we recommend clearing following relevant questions before the group starts.
- What can I contribute?
- What do I want to give to the group - As the one seeking help, the one offering help or as group member?
- Which aspects of my professional life do I want to show?
- How do I balance the professional, the personal and the relational parts of work?

Once the participants have considered and found personal answers they can enter into a meaningful interaction about what the group can be, and which needs it can fulfill. This conversation is not about finding a consensus but about creating space for differences and nuances.

The following step examines the present level of trust among group members: *How secure do I feel and where do I experience these colleagues supportive or challenging?* This does not mean evaluating colleagues' character traits. It is about becoming aware of one's own natural reservations that are related to the fact of sharing vulnerable personal aspects about oneself with a random group of co-workers.

It can be helpful to inform the others about
- how you see yourself as a group member
- possible behavior patterns you would like to change
- personal patterns you would like the group to support
- personal reactions you find inappropriate and you want help to get rid of.

Questions concerning the expectations of superiors should be clarified. These can be about which resources the group can expect. Or how far the principal trusts the group and respects the discretion. Generally, superiors are not involved in collegial reflection groups. Collegial reflection should always take place among equals. Even in cases where staff are treated as equals, the participation of the superior will be an obstacle unless the superior presents individual's issues in the same way as all other participants. Specific topics and questions in relation to this role must be discussed in a separate forum with equals of the same hierarchical level. And last but not least, the participants' needs for support like an introduction of the method, additional workshops or opportunities to consult an independent advisor if the group work gets difficult, need to be clarified.

The group is *neither* a therapy session *nor* an encounter group. It does not replace nor expand staff meetings. It is an independent forum whose content is the work of its participants with other individuals who require their support. It is relevant that the forum does not address private issues, but it can take personal circumstances into account, as far as they influence work. Similarly, problems with colleagues, superiors and cooperation should be the subject of other platforms. All of these restrictions protect the collegial working situation.

It makes sense to give a *weather* report in the beginning of each meeting: *How am I here today as part of this group?*

Also, it can be useful if each participant thinks of a possible topic beforehand and presents it an introduction round. This helps gain experience in determining topics which may not be fraught with problems but are still worthy of consideration. This way, there are always plenty of topics available, and the group dynamic does not tempt more outgoing people to work, because others don't speak up.

As mentioned previously, there are different ways of integrating the entire group in the collegial reflection. In the beginning, it makes sense to pursue a clear approach: the person presenting a problem should enter a dialogue with one colleague as a co-reflector. This ensures that his/her needs are in focus. The group's need to comment on the situation comes second. Once all participants are familiar with this approach, other group members can be involved, if the co-reflector wants support. He or she can ask individual group members to comment on specific topics at a specific point in time to support their progress. Later on, the group can also use additional empathy exercises and/or role plays.

This form of professional development benefits intensely from continuity. Continuous personal reflection, receiving feedback and response, as well as acknowledgement and empathy, strengthen relational competence and personal development.

But we do want to say that collegial reflection groups also experience failure. There may be situations, problems or relationships in the group that require further help. In this sense, collegial reflection can be seen as a preliminary stage to supervision. Collegial reflection can successfully handle a considerable number of topics, discover new perspectives, test approaches, and enable new experience. But the range of topics discussed can also increase the desire for expert knowledge by a professional supervisor.

To conclude, we want to emphasize that collegial reflection does not only have to focus on *problems*. Collegial reflection also has an essential professional and mental health function if the participants regularly present and analyze their successes.

This aspect draws attention to a controversial issue in collegial reflection, counseling and supervision: how do you give feedback without saying what you think the person did wrong? Without focusing on mistakes? And if you mention the mistakes, do you not become part of the *error culture* which the collegial intervention seeks to resist? There are many experts who would immediately affirm this last question.[8] From our point of view, the situation is more complex. We agree that counseling and supervision must primarily pursue a supportive function. In other words, counseling and supervision must reinforce the constructive aspects of professional action. Yet, we also think that supervision should challenge and, therefore, should refer to and discuss problematic professional behavior. Our reasoning is an ethical one. There are children, adolescents and adults who experience violations in their relationships with professionals. Not always do they have enough time to wait for the teacher to discover and eliminate the *stumbling block* on their own. Moreover, we have experienced that not all problematic behavior is due to personal reasons. Often, it is due to a lack of expertise and insight. And a detailed behavioral analysis can reveal the manifold reasons behind problematic interactions. We are aware that many people might disagree with us on this point. Therefore, it is necessary to clarify this aspect within the group before starting collegial reflection and supervision.

Supervision

Supervision, as opposed to collegial reflection is based on formally as well as factually different levels of competence and roles. The supervisor is an experienced person appointed to be responsible for the process of supervision. This role and relationship is maintained throughout the process.[9]

Over the past years, the concept of supervision has increasingly entered discussions about professionality and psychological health in health, social, and educational sectors. This reflects a heightened understanding of the need to provide staff with professional and human resources to fulfill the growing demands for assistance, advice, knowledge, care and therapy. Work in the social field does not only depend on professional and methodological know-how. It mostly relies on human properties and qualities like personality, life experience, charisma and the ability to treat people with respect and to inspire.

Personal qualities cannot be taught once and for all in formal education and or training. We have to continuously activate and work on these qualities just like on our expert knowledge. This can be provided by offering structures and meetings, where the staff's need for development, inspiration, relief and self-care are supported.

Generally, social facilities draw on supervision to support complex and emotionally challenging tasks. Parallel to the increasing demand for individual counseling, action plans and training, there is also the longing to revise professional perspectives and find solutions within a forum of attentive, structured and committed cooperation of professionals. In addition, there is an increasing need to experience empathy and self-knowledge to support personal and professional understanding of life situations and behavior patterns that may be outside one's own experience or relate to personal experiences in a difficult way.

In Denmark, we introduced supervision to several daycare centers and special schools with great success, despite the fact that supervision seemed to be incompatible with the self-concept and working conditions. Several psychologists, educational advisors and other persons qualified as supervisors volunteered to take on this position. In the beginning, we focused on the relationships which the participants considered the most problematic. But in the long run, regular supervision makes sense so that it can also focus on general aspects and on the fact that professionals tend to *put their foot in it* in relationships they personally find unproblematic. What adds to this pitfall is that parents and children often have difficulty giving teachers honest critical feedback. Therefore, teachers can miss essential opportunities for development if they only evaluate relational qualities on their own.

Another difference between collegial reflection and supervision is that the latter also includes a quality control. Supervision in an institution is thus the only ethically founded opportunity available to ensure that parents and children do not fall victim to internal problems of a group of teachers and superiors or idiosyncratic behavior patterns of individual professionals. This is also why it is makes sense to replace the supervisor regularly, about every two to three years, even if this can be emotionally difficult or exhausting. The change of a supervisor puts staff in a similar situation as children and parents when they are confronted with the replacement of the head of an institution or a change in staff.

The Role of Superiors

What characterizes educational institutions is that the staff have a large number of distinct relationships which always include people in leading positions. The relational competence necessary of superiors and leaders is in large part the same as for others described in this book. Below, we summarize the significance of these qualities for superiors. And specifically look at the roles of superiors as human resource managers and leaders, who are responsible for the working atmosphere and the institutional culture.

Process-oriented Leadership

In a relationship between two adults in which one side has more power than the other, the more powerful carries the main responsibility for the quality of the relationship. In educational institutions, this applies to the relationship between a principal and the staff. In both good times and bad, the head of an institution is responsible for the general atmosphere and for the quality with which other staff members fulfill their role as leaders. This responsibility entails a rather frightening kind of power that is difficult to define. It is often not explicitly referred to or defined in official statements, although it makes up one of the most important competences in institutions that have the purpose of educating, teaching, treating or caring for people. The wellbeing of the staff, the quality of professional work, as well as the profit, directly depend on the ability and competence of the leadership. People in charge cannot simply transfer their responsibility to others or democratize it. They are responsible regardless of whether they are aware of this or not.

The dilemma is how to prioritize this function over growing administrative requirements. Yet, administrative and relational responsibilities are not as incompatible as they might seem at first sight. In fact, educational institutions whose heads are capable and appreciative of their own procedural responsibility and relational competence have less trouble with bureaucratic issues than institutions where the heads are less competent and aware of this responsibility. In order to realize institutional goals and values, educational facilities must create a balance between administrative and human values, or better still place more value on the human side. The conflict between the different types of values is ongoing by nature. Therefore, superiors and teachers together have to consciously provide human values as professionals.

The relational competence of a superior includes all components previously described. But, adult employees are not at the mercy of superiors to the extent that children and adolescents are at the mercy of their teachers. Adults have ways to directly express agreement or rejection, to distance themselves and to exert a certain degree of influence. Adult cooperation is often regulated by a set of rules and agreements. Working together with one and the same superior over a longer period influences teachers' behavior and collaboration with children and parents, both negatively and the positively. There is no way of preventing this. It is impossible to work or live with others over an extended period of time without also experiencing destructive issues. Therefore, *relational competence does not depend on constructive or destructive qualities in the inner and outer behavior as much as it depends on the ability and willingness to accept responsibility for the consequences* of destructive behavior patterns. That is, to the extent that one is aware of them.

Educational leadership may build on a specific educational philosophy and approach. In this case, the head of the institution appears as a *figurehead* for the ideology. But a leader can also understand him-/herself as a person whose concern is to create synergy in an environment characterized by different personalities and visions. It is vital for superiors to behave in line with their personal and professional values even in difficult times. If unchecked, inconsistent behavior can quickly manifest itself in other areas.

EXAMPLE

In the past decade, Scandinavian schools have focused on preventing mobbing by means of campaigns. Schools where the headmasters value administrative rules highly, carried out these campaigns with commitment and responsibility. They indeed achieved a decrease in the number of mobbing incidents. But these campaigns are based on the assumption that adults have the 'correct' moral understanding and behavior

> and thus know what to do, and children are incompetent and unsocial. Other schools where the headmasters had a strong tendency to support human values took a different approach. Instead of organizing campaigns, these schools decided to discuss and question their own school's values and behavior patterns. They looked into all interpersonal relationships and, thus, were able to improve the quality of the behavior of all parties involved.

It doesn't take an expert to predict that there will be a decrease in mobbing in the first schools initially (the first two to three years), only to be followed by an increase afterwards. The number of incidents may even be higher than before the campaign. In the other schools, the occurrence of mobbing will decline continually until the desired minimum is achieved after two to three years. The reason for this is simple: to a certain degree, the children's behavior is always a result of the school's culture. Schools that place adults above children and pursue a one-sided campaign against children are, actually, mobbing children themselves. The adults' behavior does not correspond to their message. As a consequence, their behavior will *outpace* their message in the long run.

At schools where everyone concerned is equally invited to reflect on shared values and induce possible changes, the process and content correspond with one another. As a result, such schools can maintain desired improvements in the long run, provided that there are no substantial or unexpected changes in the leadership or staff constellations, that bring in a new culture.

These different approaches provide an example how the entire institutional culture depends on the values of the leader and his/her ability to realize them. Imagine, for example, a school in which the majority of teachers support the campaign, while a handful of teachers decide to take a more balanced approach to the issue. Individual groups of children who have a strong relationship with the latter teachers will cooperate with the adults. This, however, cannot effect a change in the overall culture of the school.

The same applies to campaigns against eating disorders and alcohol or drug abuse. As long as principals, teachers and parents enthusiastically work together, they will be able achieve results. These results, however, only last as long as the synergy is maintained and no longer. Only in very few exceptional cases can actual anti-campaigns achieve a sustainable effect, regardless of whether the target group are children, adolescents or adults. The reason for this is simple: if you want to eliminate self-destructive behavior patterns, you do not need anti-campaigns but *campaigns-for-life*. Anti-campaigns either not work or appear partially to fully non-credible. Instead of producing slogans and handing out information material, *we should introduce values that individuals can thrive on and that maintain everybody's individuality in daily relationships.* Self-destructive behavior is always the result of both destructive relationships and individual and personal decisions. This is why collective campaigns can neither prevent nor reduce it.

Campaigns against specific symptoms may be a useful political tool, but from an educational and psychological perspective they are unprofessional, especially if the goal is beyond mere moralization.

Political systems and authorities define the tasks of educational institutions. Of course, such political entities do not primarily follow educational and psychological reasoning. Therefore, it is important for institutional heads to be courageous enough to disobey specific instructions to the extent necessary for their professional work.

Individual or Relational

Most professional workplaces (not only in the world of education) have an utterly unprofessional tradition of experts protecting each other and justifying that this is best for those who call on their services. Our experience is that there are big differences between schools and daycare centers concerning this. This may be because schools have had a long authoritarian tradition. Consequently, many headmasters believe that they have a certain kind of loyalty towards their staff that, in effect, only undermines the institutions' ethical integrity.

We are convinced that his misunderstood loyalty needs to be traded in for purposeful relational interventions.

EXAMPLE

Inger was a class teacher in fifth-grade. She had taught this class from first grade on. She was experienced and taught Danish from first to seventh grade. At the regular parent-teacher meeting in the fall, Inger told Daniel's parents about her observation of his learning difficulties in Danish. She suggested Daniel should visit an educational psychologist. This was not the first time Inger addressed Daniel's difficulties. Yet, until then, Daniel was able to 'get the most out of his abilities' with Inger's assistance. Therefore, she had not suggested remedial classes or psychological examinations in earlier conversations.

The parents were caught by surprise by the teacher's suggestion. And they were unable to recall having talked about this issue before. The mother started crying, while the father fell silent. Inger was astonished. She was convinced she had informed the parents about Daniel's difficulties before. She felt at a loss and unsure about how to react to the parents' behavior. Therefore, she suggested meeting the following week so they would have enough time to talk the issue over. Daniel's parents were angry and found it difficult to accept that their son might have problems. They felt mistreated and blamed everything on Inger. They told several parents of Daniel's classmates about their encounter. This led to some of them developing serious doubts about Inger's approach to teaching. They decided to contact the headmaster. Both the headmaster and the head of the school board received a letter, upon which the headmaster informed Inger, who was completely shocked.

The headmaster called for an unscheduled parent-teacher meeting, where he explained the Danish curriculum to convince the parents that Inger's teaching was in line with official regulations. Since the teacher was not only shocked but also hurt by the parents' action, she felt unable to take part in the meeting. The fact that the headmaster hosted the meeting instead of the teacher, however, raised even more suspicion on the part of the parents.

In the above example, all of the parties involved, only saw their own issues. Professional standards were ignored, because people felt personally offended or compelled to act correctly (according to what they considered as bureaucratically correct). In the end, all parties involved lost more than they won.

In fact, the headmaster had two options:

1. He could have had a talk, or several talks, *together* with the class teacher and Daniel's parents to renew their cooperative relationship. In the process, he could have also found out whether the parents' reaction was emotional and/or objectively founded. To do so, he would have had to

take both sides seriously. The progression of the conversations might have shown that the relationship between the teacher and the parents hadn't been the best before the incident. In this case the teacher-parent relationship would have needed attention as well, while the headmaster would have had to take on the role of an advisor and mediator.

2. He could have organized a platform for the teacher and the parents involved to discuss the parents' complaints about the Danish lessons, in which he also would have had to assume a role as mediator. The teacher would have had to participate. However, she could have asked for individual support before, during or after the discussion. It would have been the responsibility of the headmaster to create an appropriate atmosphere during the discussion. He could have achieved this best with openness: *"I have invited you all because some of you expressed a certain dissatisfaction with the Danish lessons your children attend. We will not take a vote on this. If the parents of only one child are unhappy, we take this seriously. All of this started with a conversation between the Danish teacher and Daniel's parents. The conversation did not run smoothly and left both parties with hard feelings. I am not sure how many of you have been unsatisfied with the Danish classes over a longer period of time and simply not stated this. Now, you have the chance to bring your dissatisfaction forward. It can concern the way of cooperating, the teacher's approach to teaching, her relationship to you as parents or other possible causes. But we need to be aware not mix all of these causes up in our discussion. I will try and keep professional and personal issues separate. It is very important to me that the parents as well as the children and teachers involved at this school are treated appropriately. This is why I organized this meeting tonight."*

It is important, that the subsequent discussion gives all parents the opportunity to express their opinion about both aspects of the conflict. This is necessary for two reasons: first of all, the opinions of the parents who signed the letter diverge from one another and listening to the different nuances can prevent collective mobbing of the class teacher. Second of all, the teacher and headmaster have the opportunity to gain insight into the different issues the individual parents grapple with. This provides a basis for the teacher's further personal and professional development. As far as she is able to take the parents' issues seriously, their anger with her teaching will disappear.

A parent-teacher meeting like this illustrates that democratic approaches do not suffice to solve relational conflicts. No majority is able to decide whether the style and behavior of the teacher is *right* or *wrong*, or whether her Danish classes have the expected level of quality or not. The fact that maybe only a few parents want to take personal revenge and go through all the formalities to reach their goal should not tempt the headmaster to do the *correct thing* at the cost of the *right thing*. As the person in charge of the institution's culture, the headmaster is responsible for preventing the lowest common denominator to determine the tone. This applies to conflicts between the children, the staff or other relationships involved.

EXAMPLE

Hanne was one of five teachers in a team. The other four team members agreed that the cooperation with Hanne was becoming more and more difficult. They often had to fill in for her when she had difficulties with parents or children. All four of them have been part of the team since the first grade and have tried to solve the team issues in a variety of ways. Yet, none of them ever openly addressed the problem. In the annual staff appraisals with the single teachers, the headmaster sensed the difficulty in Hanne's team. Consequently, she decided to put Hanne in a different team. Together with a strong teacher, Hanne was asked to teach the new first graders. She knew the new partner would not be affected by Hanne's tendency to expound the problems of daily situations easily. The children respected him for his natural authority and he was on good terms with their parents. The headmaster chose him to team up with Hanne, because he would unlikely be quickly discouraged by Hanne's issues. In addition, this would prevent parental complaints, which may arise from Hanne's behavior.

Hanne was one of those few people at school whom the other teachers try to avoid. They have a lot of good explanations why they cannot talk to her about this and what they find problematic about working with her. They think, for example, that Hanne would not strong enough to deal with criticism or that it would not possible to talk to her without the situation getting even worse, or that it is simply not their responsibility.

In the example above, the colleagues' ideas about Hanne provide the lowest common denominator. The headmaster allows these ideas to determine the daily work. Obviously, the team's problems cannot be clarified or solved as long as Hanne is not involved. The headmaster's message is as definite as it is destructive to the institutional culture: *If you are difficult or unpopular, you will be isolated, and I will delegate the responsibility to the colleague whom I consider strong.*

Appropriate personnel management includes that the persons concerned analyze and solve problems together. If the headmaster decides to transfer Hanne to another team, she must make her decision transparent. In addition, she must provide the new team with the support necessary. As soon as the headmaster develops doubt about her ability to act as advisor and mediator in the process, she needs help from outside.

EXAMPLE

Jens was a math and German teacher of in his fifties. He was not an exceptionally good teacher and, his relational competence in dealing with his pupils, their parents and colleagues left a lot to be desired. This was an open secret which none of the colleagues had even dared to talk about with Jens himself. Another open secret was that Jens had a bottle of port wine in his closet, and that he regularly drank from it.

Jens was responsible for a class of sixth graders. He had great difficulty with his pupils and the pupils with him. The children knew of his drinking problem, as did their parents. Still, nobody stepped in. Instead, everybody participated in one and the same story at every single parent-teacher meeting. 'Jens was unable to attend, and the class teacher delivered Jens' dissatisfaction with the children's school and social performance and asked the parents to rebuke their children.'

After a year, a parent got in touch with the headmaster and demanded that something was done about the situation. As a consequence, a different teacher took over Jens' lessons. In an official statement, the reason given was the unacceptable behavior of the class. Unfortunately, not only the headmaster and teachers, but also the parents failed to take responsibility in this situation and in the end, the children had to pay for it.

The above examples do not represent extreme cases. We have selected them because of their unambiguity. They illustrate the urgent need that relational values are integrated in leadership and teamwork processes. On the one hand, this is necessary to support the wellbeing of teachers. On the other hand, this is necessary because the values can only take effect if they are consistently implemented. And above all, we finally have to stop passing the buck to the children.

Equal dignity among adults relies on respect of differences. Therefore, it is important not to reduce values to uniformity and to avoid creating a new type of conformity. Unity is good, but difference is better (and the reality). Interpersonal conflicts are an unavoidable and necessary component of life in every institution. *The leader is largely responsible for not allowing these conflicts to develop into obstacles, which drain the institution's energy.*

Professional-Personal Development of Superiors

Since professional development is one of the most important moral concepts in education, it is vital for superiors themselves to show active commitment. General professional development needs to be developed together with the staff and kept up to date. Yet, it is also important for superiors to be aware of their own specific needs. While there is an overall more general responsibility for organizations, individual leaders need to take personal initiative when it comes to more specific issues.

Ideally, regular personal supervision or coaching is a minimal requirement for the head of an institution. Monthly supervision provides superiors with the opportunity to reverse the situation for a few hours. That is to lay off their leading role and reflect on their own actions and behavior with the help of a professional with know-how on leadership, organizations and interpersonal relationships. This can be a simple and inexpensive method to assure the quality of institutional culture and optimize personnel management.

Moreover, major specific personal developmental processes take place by acting as advisors and moderators in daily interpersonal conflicts at all levels of the organization.

The list of managerial requirements, which push a leader to participate in trainings and go through personal developmental processes is long. Our experience is, that by strengthening relational competence the sum of these requirements becomes more transparent and less daunting. But, we are also aware that superiors differ from one another and have different needs at different points in their careers. And thus, don't want to fall victim to the *law of the instrument*[****]. That is: if all you have is a hammer, everything looks like a nail.

The Children's Role

The traditional subject-object view on educational relationships sees adults responsible for essentially contributing to the life and development of children. In return, they expect children to behave well, develop a good character and show respect.

[****] The law of the instrument (also known as the law of the hammer) refers to the cognitive bias of over-reliance on a familiar tool. (Maslow, 1966, The Psychology of Science)

Teachers have always experienced rewarding and enriching aspects of working with children: their spontaneity, their zest for life and their ability to wonder about realities, which adults find trivial until a fascinated child inspires them to reconsider the matter. In other words, teachers have always appreciated the child's *nature* more than their competences.

The more experience we gather looking at adult-child relationships as a *subject-subject relationship*, the clearer it becomes that children have much more to offer. Personal development is mutual to a large extent. The mutuality is obvious in cases where the relationship is successful in the sense that the educational interaction confirms the plans, methods and goals, and the children therefore strengthen the personal professional security. The situation, however, becomes more complex when there are at least one or two children whose reactions are not in line with the expectations. They force teachers to reconsider the approach and to determine whether it is their plan, method or the interpersonal process that failed.

Children react very differently depending on the situation. Therefore, we have to pay close attention to situations in which different adults describe their relationships to one and the same child or their behavior in differing ways. And usually we cannot take over the *methods* for a specific child from our colleagues. It makes more sense, to take a closer look at one's own attitudes, expectations and concrete ways of interacting. The more experience a teacher has, the more nuanced the resources available become. But even experienced teachers encounter relationships, which bring new learning experiences.

The children with whom adults have difficulty establishing a fruitful relationship and who obviously have a difficult life are probably the biggest and most important challenge to the traditional professional identity. This professional identity consists, among other things, of a fundamental obligation to aid children. That is to support them in becoming something they are not yet able to be socially, personally or intellectually. On a very basic level this often leads to a series of attempts to change the child or at least the external behavior of the child. In this context, it is not relevant whether the experts' motivation is to calm the group, to reduce conflicts between the child and the adult or to act *on behalf of the child*. What is crucial is that the adults' attempts are condemned to fail as long as their goal is to change the child.

The explanation is obvious; actions aiming to change children reduce them to an object in the relationship. A child is thus prevented from getting the opportunity to develop in line with their own need. Instead they feel the demand to change in line with the expectations of the social environment. Most likely the same expectations in earlier and other relationships caused the problem in the first place. The same problematic treatment thus reinforces the self-destructive behavior of the child. Similar phenomena can be seen in private adult relationships. If you start a relationship with the goal of changing the other, it will fail.

Often, teachers are left alone with unbearable situations and their professional duty *to do something*. Nonetheless, the pedagogical responsibility is to reflect and analyze how they can change their behavior and how that can be worthwhile for oneself. A change of behavior makes sense if it is in line with one's personal professional integrity and related moral concepts, limitations, strengths and potentials. The art is, then, to change their own way of interacting out of personal respect for oneself. Through this the child involved is also offered a new experience and can regain trust in the relationship. Hence, professional development can also enable necessary development of the child.

For many experts, this process is the end of a firmly established and familiar professional identity, based on mainstream knowledge. For good reason, it can therefore feel like a loss of values and status. But from our experience, this loss is quickly compensated by the new satisfaction of fruitful and dynamic relationships in which development is mutual.

Supervision, collegial reflection and similar professional methods are invaluable in difficult relationships. But children themselves provide us with a resource, which we are not yet used to drawing on. We are used to describing children's behavior and talking to other adults about our observations or to sending children to specialists in hopes they can determine the reasons for their behavior and at best, try to change it. *We draw on secondary relationships in the hope of being able to change primary relationships. In most cases this utterly makes no sense.*

According to our experience, children can provide a lot of inspiration for professional-personal development, if adults are open, personal and responsible:

"Listen Thomas, I am not happy with our way of working together. I don't know exactly why or what we could do about it, but I assume you're unhappy about it too. So, I'd like to know if you could help me? I suspect there are things you don't like about me, and it'd be very helpful for me if you just told me whenever I do something you think is stupid."

Usually, acquired survival strategies also show in professional relationships, sometimes more obviously and sometimes less obviously. And this also applies to the interactions with children. The underlying cause of the behavior is not necessarily relevant in the current relationships. What is relevant though, is that strong *present* relationships can reduce or even reverse negative consequences of *past* relationships. They can also reduce or reverse destructive phenomena in a shared history.

EXAMPLE

Kirsten was a kindergarten teacher. For personal reasons, she found it difficult to express her wishes and needs and to show her limits so others understood and respected her. Her attitude towards other adults was reflected in thoughts such as 'They must know when to stop on their own!' or 'One need not tell an adult person to clean up their own mess!', when she shared the same room with other colleagues.

Kirsten got along best with children who acted independently and understood her expectations and boundaries the first time she mentioned them. However, she found it more and more difficult to handle children who needed clear instructions. And also had less sympathy for these children. She did not recognize that the core of her relational conflicts was of an existential nature. Instead, she talked about deficient parenting, of bad education, of planned children or little princes and princesses. All of these facts certainly had some significance. But as long as she focused exclusively on these aspects without taking her own role into account, her relationship with part of the children remained difficult. And neither the children's nor her own self-esteem had an opportunity to grow.

Kirsten's way of communicating tended to be characterized by a hint of resignation: "Aaaaanton, you gotta listen to me! I've told you that ten times." In some cases, however, she also came over moralizing: "Christian, you know that if you don't stop talking, there's no time for the others. But they'd like to say something too."

Often, Kirsten's statements gave the children the feeling of being out of place, and when this was the case, their survival strategies, even if inappropriate, were activated. Thus, both sides got trapped in a destructive relational pattern.

Kirsten's situation is common. In many respects, it is typical of her time. Discord has arisen between several generations of adults who learned to take themselves back (and to idealize the past) and younger generations of children and adolescents who have been taught to express themselves openly. Neither Kirsten nor many of her colleagues are pleased with the situation or the habit of backing down and therefore blame the other parties. But if Kirsten received help and support in developing her professional authenticity, her way of cooperating with children could improve on the professional, social and personal level.

In the example below, the teacher gains professionally from the conflict indirectly (this depends on her personal story, self-recognition and sensitivity). Primarily, it is about obtaining a balance between *product*-oriented and *process*-oriented teaching.

EXAMPLE

A fifth grade, where children were working in groups: the teacher tried to divide the children into groups that would raise their productivity.

> *There are always children who have difficulties working in teams and/ or whom other children do not like to work with.*
>
> *Niklas was one of these children. He was in a group with four others. They started working, but Niklas wanted to sharpen his pencil, get a drink of water, borrow an eraser and go to the toilet. He was setting clear signals showing his difficulty working in the group. The teacher tried to support him: "Niklas, just get to work now. Have you found the book you need to work with? Then just get started. Here, look at page 37." After a couple of minutes, she intervened again: "Niklas, you won't get anything done if you keep getting up. Could you just stop interrupting the others!"*
>
> *Niklas restlessness increased. Shortly before the end of class, he wanted to leave the room. The teacher stopped him and told him to wait for the break. Niklas was desperate and reacted by threatening to beat her up. The teacher was frightened. Immediately, she sent him to the principal's office to have a talk. In hindsight, she was appalled about the idea that Niklas would even think about threatening her with physical violence.*
>
> *In a following reflection, she realized that Niklas was under pressure more than he could bear. She saw his difficulty working in teams and that his fellow students did not want to work with him either. Niklas was unable to talk about his situation. He would have needed the teachers help for this. But since he did not get any help, his restlessness, frustration and pain escalated as did his behavior, which made it so difficult to work with him.*

In this case, we do not know what prevented the teacher from seeing Niklas and his need for help. Maybe she was too focused on the goal that children need to learn to work in groups, and that groups should provide output. Maybe she had had only had good experiences with groupwork and could, not imagine how difficult it would be for a boy like Niklas to get involved. Maybe the contrary is true. She knows isolation and loneliness herself and ignored this pain until she finally repressed it and became immune to the pain of others. Professional supervision and reflection with good colleagues can revealed this in the interest of both parties involved.

We do not know the entire story why Niklas has difficulty working in groups. His behavior seems to show: *It is difficult to be here. I hate groupwork because it makes it obvious that the other children only talk to me because the teacher wants them to. I can't stand this. I'll do just about anything to get out of this situation. I have no idea what's wrong with me, but it's got to be something about me. I can't ask anyone, so I'll just say group work is stupid and boring!* We do not know why Niklas' self-esteem is so low. And in this context, this is not important. We know that he needs a teacher, who is aware that children usually like to work together, and realizes that they may need support when they do not.

What is or was going on in Niklas' family or what violations the boy had to put up with in earlier relationships with teachers is not relevant to the current situation. Both the teacher, as well as the other children would benefit from taking Niklas' behavior seriously instead of judging and categorizing it.

Speaking in current educational jargon, Niklas could be described as a child lacking social competence. But if a concept of social competence fails to incorporate the willingness to treat people who are hurt or different, or fails to build a community where everyone is welcome, the concept is nothing more than a useless euphemism for *functioning*. In fact, Niklas has one of the most important competences required in any community: the competence to express one's feelings about being part of the group. The fact that his expression is distorted and needs empathy from his personal environment may be the reason we need teachers. As long as the teacher does not become aware of her role, Niklas takes up the courage to carry his behavior to extremes by even threatening to hurt her. This actually invites possibilities for professional-personal development.

Without doubt, Niklas lacks at least one vital component of social competence, and his teacher has reached the limits of her relational competence. This makes up a learning community. The following example shows the same, in which the teacher neither lacks empathy, nor the intention to use it.

EXAMPLE

Michael was in sixth grade. He was talented and did not have learning difficulties. He was the oldest of four children. The father was mentally ill and was hospitalized often. The mother made a living as an unskilled worker. Michael carried a great responsibility at home. For one, he was the oldest boy and picked up his younger brothers and sisters from school. He looked after them and did the shopping. But he also reacted like many children in these situations: he felt responsible for his father's health, his mother's wellbeing, the family's financial situation, etc.

At home Michael was a great model of (social) competence, but at school and after school he had great difficulties. At school, he had a lot of conflicts with his teachers and other children – disputes in which he appeared very cold. During his leisure time, he hung out with a group of children who stole from supermarkets, made illegal graffiti and drank alcohol.

Michael's class teacher liked him and took extra time for him. She organized additional remedial lessons for Michael; both creative and practical subjects in which she taught Michael. She was the only adult at school which Michael was able to connect with. The teacher thought a lot about him and was worried if she and the school were doing enough to help him. She took a lot of time to talk to colleagues, the psychologist and the community advisor. Often, she found herself in situations in which she felt like she had to defend his provocative behavior.

Michael was a child who found it difficult to establish close and stable relationships without destroying them immediately again. One day, the class had domestic education, and the class teacher participated to support Michael. The lessons passed without incidents. The children cooked and Michael talked to his teacher and the other children in a friendly way. It was one of these days where she could take a deep breath and was convinced that the boy was finally making progress. She was happy to have supported Michael's place at school.

Towards the end of class, Michael approached her with a lemon dessert which he prepared especially for her: "This is for you." The teacher was delighted and interpreted Michael's gesture as a sign that he had had a good time as well. But when she took a bite of the dessert, it was inedible. It was spicy and way too salty. Thinking about having to mobilize all of her energy to continue working with Michael, she suddenly felt exhausted and helpless.

This teacher has worked with Michael over an extended period of time. She has commitment, understanding, empathy, flexibility, endurance, etc., all qualities we consider positive. She has given Michael a place in her heart. What more can you ask of her? What can she learn in this situation, if she does not want to come out hurt, disappointed and turn into a cynical teacher?

She needs support. And she needs to talk about herself with her colleagues, a supervisor or a psychologist. She needs understanding and acknowledgement while talking about her reactions and experiences. In a first step, she needs the opportunity to openly state what she would like to tell Michael. This can create a new foundation to continue their relationship.

This will take time: *she first needs to find a way of expressing herself which protects her own and Michael's integrity.* For many it is difficult, to really comprehend and process what this kind of experience means to the person involved. Some find it unprofessional to be emotionally affected by a child's behavior. *Not being affected* would be unprofessional. Her professionalism shows in the way she processes her reactions

In the next step, the teacher needs to look at what her contribution might have been that caused Michael to damage the otherwise mutually positive contact: Did she forget her own feelings and standards and become a willing *victim* of his need for care and attention? Was she too preoccupied fighting *for* him that she forgot to fight *with* him and depersonalized her interaction with him? She will need time to consult her *inner* responsibility to gain insight into her relationship with Michael. But the process will strengthen her self-esteem and personal authority as well as provide new nuances to her wealth of professional experience.

Once she is ready to confront Michael with her new insights, the boy needs to go through a parallel process. If the teacher is able to express her sadness, her anger or helplessness, Michael will get an idea how his behavior affects others. This personal interaction can help Michael gain access to his inner responsibility and the emotions that cause specific behavior. More than anything children like Michael who are burdened with a load of social responsibility, need an adult who is capable of showing them the way to inner responsibility, and can help create a space for their own personal emotions and needs. Ideally, Michael's entire family needs regular counseling. The teacher is not responsible for the child's future alone. The teacher is only responsible for the relationship between the two of them and, maybe, for making the social system aware of the fact that the boy needs more support.

EXAMPLE

Ida was four years old. Three months before, her beloved grandmother had died suddenly. Her parents tried to comfort her as best they could. But Ida's mother was developing a depression and had started to withdraw. Therefore, she was not a model in dealing with sadness and loss. In kindergarten, Ida's behavior was gradually changing. She was oversensitive and burst out in tears with every little frustration. One month after her grandmother's death, a new teacher started in the kindergarten. The staff informed the new teacher about Ida's situation and behavior. The teacher immediately showed sympathy and empathy for Ida. But a few days later, he was annoyed with Ida's 'arbitrary and childish' reactions.

The teacher seized the occasion to discuss Ida's behavior with the kindergarten's supervisor, convinced that he must take action to help Ida 'function'. In the process, he discovered – to his own surprise – that he had suppressed a whole lot of his own feelings after his father died several years ago. He was the oldest child in his family and took on the responsibility of helping his mother over the difficult times following his father's death. Ida's obvious grief had connected the teacher with his unresolved feelings. But just like the little girl, he was unable to express his emotions more than as a vague discomfort.

His new insights enabled interacting with Ida in a whole new way. He talked to her about his own grief and the loneliness he experienced after his father's death. Soon, the kindergarten became a place where Ida was allowed to play and 'function'. A place where she experienced existential reciprocity that enabled her to mourn openly. Her previous behavior had been the expression of neither having a place to mourn in her family nor having had enough trust in the teachers to mourn in kindergarten.

If adults get *annoyed* with a child, it is very often because the child's behavior draws attention to unresolved issues (emotions and/or attitudes) in the lives of the adults. The adults' willingness to reflect and share this with the children decides for them all if it the environment enhances personal growth or categorizes a child as problematic.

We want to emphasize that the main goal of this perspective is not to solve conflicts effectively. As mentioned above conflicts are a normal part of personal interactions. Mutual growth and development are vital for everyone, but the most important aspect is experiencing mutuality as a relational quality.

The Parent's Role

Equally, working with parents offers plenty of opportunities for professional-personal development. But since these interactions only take place irregularly, the results are rarely as spectacular as in adult-child relationships. Training family counselors and family therapists includes the experience that everyone learns most, when the professional realizes their own prejudices. This is regardless of whether they are cultural, religious or social, and if they have affected the relationship positively or negatively.

Some teachers have difficulty dealing with parents who are clergy. Others have difficulty dealing with business people who appear in suits. Some are very sympathetic and flexible to parents who are teachers themselves, and others are more rigid. Some react with reservations when confronted with single mothers. Others become sentimental and even clingy. Some try to indoctrinate Muslim parents. Others tend to become inappropriately reserved. Some become aggressive in the presence of homosexual couples, and others put a lot of effort in demonstrating just how tolerant they are.

Among qualified professionals it is generally not acceptable to have prejudices. Yet, all of us have prejudices. Our prejudices are closely connected to our own cultural and educational background as well as the degree to which we are capable of self-differentiation (see p. 164). But again, how we deal with our prejudices is more relevant than the fact that we have them. The more we try to hide or suppress prejudices, the more destructive they become. Of course, the lesser prejudices we have, the better. The most effective way of resolving them is to handle them openly in the presence of those they are directed at:

- I have difficulty with parents who are teachers themselves. Often, these situations turn into power struggles. Should you realize that this is also the case in our discussion, please let me know immediately.
- I know very little about what life is like for a manager in the private sector, so I might be biased …
- I am afraid you might call me racist, which is why I use all of my energy on my own image rather than the topic of our discussion …
- The few conversations we have had since Maria is in kindergarten have always left me with a negative aftertaste. Only after I talked to my colleague, I realized that I obviously have prejudice against adoptive parents. It would be very helpful, if we could talk about this before we proceed …

Sometimes, only a few sentences suffice to pave the way for a professional conversation. If you realize your own prejudices during the conversation, you are well-advised to react with humor and self-irony to limit the damage and offer new perspectives.

It may happen that a teacher feels so provoked by parents that he or she completely loses their composure and professional distance. As a consequence, he or she is forced deal with personal aspects in more detail than he or she might have wanted to. In this case, the ongoing conversation is rarely the appropriate way to address the issue. A collegial reflection or supervision is more appropriate to find out whether the teacher concerned should transfer the contact to another colleague or return to the parents involved with a new perspective and an apology for their prejudices.

According to an old saying, we learn most about ourselves from people for which we have the least sympathy. Not only do they confront us with our prejudices, but they also confront us with unlikable aspects about our own personality. Aspects we do not like to identify ourselves with. Conversely, we feel most secure with people for whom we feel immediate sympathy because they confirm those parts of our personality which we like most about ourselves. In the working world, we do not often have the opportunity to choose relationships. *Consequently, it is essential for professional development to sacrifice the feeling of security for the sake of relational quality.*

In Chapter 8, we propose a new approach, taking us from a modern to a postmodern concept of communication between teachers and parents in which the experiences and perspectives of parents receive more space and significance. If teachers give parents more attention, they recognize that parents can contribute valuable experiences from which teachers can profit and draw inspiration.

EXAMPLE
The kindergarten teachers often had intense conflicts with Mads. The boy consistently fought with any attempt of others to make decisions for him. Mads was an only child. Thus, the teachers thought that he had just never learned how to integrate into a larger group and accept that there were different rules than at home.

The parents just nodded smilingly and knowingly whenever the teachers told them about a conflict. They confirmed that Mads had always been like that. They took lengthy time talking to their son and giving him thorough educational explanations why he needed to put

> on his rubber boots, brush his teeth or eat, but without succeeding. When Mads had turned two, they had realized that they needed to give clear instructions like 'I want you to come in and eat, now!', accept his refusal, and leave him alone for a couple of minutes. If they did so, Mads would appear at the table after some time and act as if nothing had happened.
>
> The kindergarten teachers adopted this approach and, ever since, their relationship with Mads was less fraught with problems and characterized more by mutual respect.

This helpful foundation could be summarized as follows: *We are a group of adults who are committed to the life and wellbeing of this child. All of us want him to have the best opportunities. But at the moment, some of us have more success with the boy than others. So, let us see what we can learn from one another.*

There are parents who may feel forced into a corner when consulted by their children's teachers. They are not able to react with openness. Yet, if experts develop a good routine in working with parents who are more open, the interaction with the other parents will become easier and allow change over time.

Part Four

BUILDING RELATIONSHIPS

CHAPTER 8:
Teaming up with Parents

This chapter is not about organizational, political or administrative things, that are also part of school-home cooperation and require other competences. Instead, the following is devoted to the everyday *problem-oriented* and *regular* interaction. But before going into detail, we want to bring up some general thoughts.

For one, we believe that understanding the teacher-parent relationship as a relationship between an expert and a non-expert needs a revision. This is also true for other professional relationships with parents.

For another our experience is that parents also interact very differently with schools and daycare centers. As we understand, this has both historical as well as cultural reasons. Daycare centers are a product of the social and political discussions that arose from anti-authoritarian pedagogy, the liberation of women and the collapse of patriarchal family structures. In a way daycare centers were born with democracy. Daycare centers are smaller systems than schools and are also more transparent. There are more and easier possibilities for unofficial and personal contact between teachers and parents. Consequently, daycare centers often have a good basis if acute and problematic things require close cooperation. Often parents have good memories of their own time in nursery or kindergarten and therefore are open towards the caregivers.

The image of school is burdened with authoritarian culture and historical norms. The institutions and all who have a say are usually much less transparent. The legal framework dictates both the daily structure of lessons and of teachers and limits informal contact between teachers and parents.

But regardless of these different background issues the dynamics are the same if the relationship with a child is difficult and the teacher does not know what to do. In this context, it is secondary if the cause is psychosocial, family-related or functional (motor, speech or learning disorders).

According to our experience, similar to other social areas, about 75 percent of the important and *necessary conversations* fail. That is, they do not lead to increased contact, intensified cooperation and serious changes. Instead they often leave both sides not knowing what to do and/or in greater resistance to each other than before. But even if studies revealed that the number of failing conversations between teachers and parents were only 50 or 40 percent, the number is higher than it should be.

It is difficult to talk and write about failing interactions without using a language which assigns guilt or scapegoats individuals at least in some way. To avoid this, we want to offer a theoretical framework for our new understanding. The American family therapist and theoretician Harlene Anderson[1] offers a theoretical framework that supports our practical experience of 20 years for *moving from a modern to a postmodern conception and practice of conversation.* Her ideas go beyond narrow professional discourses and differing methodological approaches.

We do not want to *therapeuticize* conversations between teachers and parents or children. But there are important parallels to dialogues in education and teaching, because they are all interpersonal processes. Therapeutic dialogues are the most intense and professional form of conversation and their goal is to uncover and change behavior that is perceived as afflicted. Over the past decades, a lot of research and experiments have been done about therapeutic conversations[2] that we can draw on to better understand difficult conversations.

Approaches to Conversations

According to modernistic thinking, there is a *truth* about the world – a truth which we can unearth by thinking and researching. We call people who know the truth experts. The relationship between experts and non-experts is asymmetric, where the experts having the dominant role due to their greater knowledge. On the contrary, postmodern thinking sees no universal or predefined truth but *only isolated truths*, which are negotiated and formulated by the participants in a conversation. As Flemming Andersen, a Danish educational expert put it: *In education, there is no truth, only locally negotiable terms and texts, which last until we have agreed on another concept. The concepts we draw on for orientation are not objective; they are something invented to bring order into the chaos*[3].

A further change is the transition from the role of an expert to a reflective practitioner, described by Donald A. Schön[4].

Knowledge expert	Reflective practitioner
I am expected to know, and must claim to do so, regardless of my own uncertainty.	I am expected to know, but I am not the only one in the situation that has relevant and important knowledge. My uncertainties may be a source of learning for me and others.
Keep my distance to the client, and hold onto the expert role. Give the client a sense of my expertise, but convey a feeling of warmth and sympathy as a sweetener.	Seek connections to the client's thoughts and feelings. Allow his respect for my knowledge to emerge from his discovery of it in the situation.
Look for deference and status in the client's response to my professional demeanor.	Look for the sense of freedom and of real connection to the client, as a consequence of no longer needing to maintain a professional façade.

Sadly, since social and educational fields have recognized the significance of family and started to incorporate it into their work, the relationship between experts and families has developed in a negative direction. Initially, working with families was based on the insight that, in order to help a person, both a child or an adult, one needs the support from the closest relatives. One needed the thoughts, experiences and reflections of other family members. By consulting them, experts learned just how valuable it is to *personally* experience the reciprocal processes within a family. This is necessary to detect possible causes for the child's issue and to activate the unique healing potential of the family.

This way of cooperation is built on the idea that the expert needs family members to be able to aid both the individual and from there the entire family. In the meantime, professionals have become family experts. This has turned the situation around: the family needs the expert. One of the most obvious, and also most destructive results of this way of thinking is that parents often come out of conversations with professionals without feeling of value (neither for their child *nor* for the expert). Often, parents feel worse after the conversation than they felt before. Teachers cannot avoid this by simply calling parents experts or by praising them for their commitment to their child. The parents' feeling of being valuable just because they are parents, regardless of how much they *make fools of themselves*, can only arise if the expert fully realizes that he needs the parents more than they need him.

If parents and teachers meet for a problem-oriented conversation, neither of them is a true expert on the issue, which brought them here. The child's inner life is the issue.

Teachers know a lot about education, teaching, the social and intellectual performance level of a child and general aspects about child development. However, parents know much more about the development of their own child and about their character. They know how they act in the family and during leisure time. Naturally, the child itself is the one person who knows most. Yet, they lack the language to express their inner life in a way which adults can understand or accept as valid.

The well-meant idea that was pursued in the professional world for a while to give parents the status *experts on their child* is basically meaningless. It was an idea to integrate the parents and weaken the professional dominance. Parents, for sure, possess unique knowledge about their children. Experts are well-advised to consider and use this knowledge. But parents tend to be *blind in one eye* when looking at their children. Some parents romanticize the personality of their children. Other parents are too preoccupied with their child's problems to even recognize the qualities, which are obvious for others. The same applies to experts. Ideally, the teacher is *blind in the other eye* and together they can construct a common *truth* about the child. Instead of engaging in a pointless power struggle about who is right.

EXAMPLE

Jonas was in seventh grade. His class teacher had invited his parents because Jonas consistently didn't bring his homework. The parents were invited to find out the 'truth' why Jonas didn't do his homework – a truth which was true for all involved and which could offer an opportunity for change.

After a brief introduction, the teacher began:

Teacher: I am glad that all of you were able to come, because I'd like to talk to you about something I just can't understand and, therefore, need your help with. Jonas does not do his homework. He's never done his homework, and I've not yet been able to find out what's wrong.

Mother: But that's not possible. He doesn't do his homework? ... Is that true, Jonas?

Jonas: Well, ... at least not often.

Father: But Jonas, I thought we'd agreed that ... last year, when we received a letter ... that you would do your homework, and that we will help you, if necessary. Don't you remember?

Jonas: Yes I do, but I just can't get myself to do it ... I don't care about it.

Mother: Well, we don't really have much time, although we of course would like to help him ... We have to take care of the gas station. You know, somebody's always got to be there. We are *open until late, everyday ... We've already been robbed several times, which is why we like to be there ourselves, instead of giving the responsibility to the young people there. Can you tell me: does he have difficulty keeping up at school?*

Teacher: Jonas is intelligent and talented. But, as a matter of fact, he does not keep up the way he could if he did his homework. We are wondering if you will be able to stay at this school, Jonas.

Mother: But that's terrible. We're really surprised that there are such big problems. You've never told us anything, Jonas.

Teacher: Well, let's get to the point. Like I told you, I can't understand why an intelligent and talented young boy like Jonas won't do his homework. Anything you can tell me about Jonas' life that could be of help?

Father: Well, there was a time when he went to a lot of parties and drank a lot. But we got a grip on that, right, Jonas? *(Jonas nods.)*

Mother: We've always had problems. When Jonas was born, our business was going well. But ever since Jonas started school, he has refused a nanny. He's always been very independent. He's always found a way to keep himself busy on his own ... maybe, we've left him alone too often?

Father: Nonsense, I'm sure that's not it. My parents were self-employed too, and I was always happy when they left me alone for a while. After all, we have to get the meals on the table, and with everything that is going on – with all the fast-food places and supermarkets and all that stuff – we gotta be around ourselves.

Mother: Well, but maybe exactly because of this Jonas could think ... do you think we've left you alone too much, Jonas?

Jonas: No, I don't know ... there's nothing that could help. I like to play on the computer and to be with my friends.

Father: But, for God's sake, you have to do your homework. You just have to do your homework when you go to school! What can you do with such a rascal? You sure know what other parents

>*do in such a case. These brats nowadays are so damn independent. They won't listen to us anyway.*

Teacher: Well, I don't know ... it's not always useful to draw on the experience of other parents ... And I don't pride myself that we will find a solution now and today. I don't know if I have already told you why this is such a mystery to me, but I have thought about it carefully. I'd like to share some of my thoughts with you, if you are interested in the opinion of an outsider.

Father: Sure, just spit it out – we'll be able to handle it!

Teacher: As you mentioned, you were always forced to work hard to make things work. This is why I wonder if you have always had enough time for each other in the family. Most thirteen-year-olds are happy when their parents aren't around all of the time, but a seven- or eight-year-old is not. The problem is that only Jonas could answer this question, but, as far as I can tell, he's as loyal to his parents as any other kid. Children find it easy to criticize their parents and be angry with them in minor things – but it's difficult for them in serious issues.

Father: Are you trying to say that we haven't cared for him properly?

Teacher: No, I would never say anything like that. I don't know you enough to know. All I am saying is the impression I have. I suggest you talk about this at home, and we'll meet again in a couple of weeks – we need to find a solution soon.

The teacher's approach has two essential qualities: he does not talk about the importance of homework and, thus, avoids humiliating Jonas. You cannot call a child intelligent and talented and, at the same time, tell him obvious facts without making them feel stupid and inferior. Secondly, the teacher avoids *talking about responsibility* and leaves the responsibility with those who have it: Jonas and his parents. This way the teacher adopted the role of a dialogue partner. As a result, the parents can leave the conversation feeling responsible, instead of feeling indirectly guilty for having neglected their responsibility.

It is not actually relevant if the teacher's hypothesis is *true* or not. The main thing is that he shared his professional reflection and challenged the parents' *truth* about their family. Most families hold on to the image they have of themselves until it starts to crumble for different reasons. The teacher's approach also avoids criticizing or humiliating the parents. He merely asks them to reconsider their position. The reflections and hypothesis of the teacher, however, are not based on fleeting or incoherent thoughts. They have to have a quality which Erik Erikson, referred to as d*isciplined subjectivity*[5]. They have to be factually justified and expressed in a way, which also makes sense in the world of the parents.

Should the hypothesis prove *true*, in the sense that it reflects Jonas' actual experience, the teacher has helped Jonas with something he could have never achieved on his own. He has drawn attention to his loneliness. This feeling of being seen might give Jonas the energy he needs to turn his situation at school around. In addition to his existential loneliness, failing at school will isolate Jonas socially as well.

Teachers often find it hard to accept that it is also possible that the *truth* will never be found, because, they are used finding certainty and support in knowledge. In situations like the above the ability to initiate and guide a fruitful conversation (a relational quality) gives inner security. Yet, this requires a shift in one's professional identity and self-concept. And the transitional phase entails a certain degree of uncertainty.

Most institutions want to work together with parents and have relationships shaped by mutual respect, trust, openness, security, equal dignity and tolerance for difference. And it is up to the institution whether its fundamental values are values in *action* or values on *display*.[6]

It is rarely difficult, if there are only good things to say, but an approach that can be helpful to not have to *say the same every year* or to *not have anything to talk about* can be to look at specific actions in the child's daily routine, be it at home, during leisure time or at school/daycare. This makes the dialogue concrete and relevant and enhances the understanding of one another. The builds a good foundation in case parents or teachers really need it further on.

Cooperating on a Regular Basis

Some institutions offer regular conversations. To help focus on the relevant issues it can be helpful if the institution sends out a letter prior to the annual meeting, providing some key topics for input:

'We would like to offer a few ideas, which we think deserve attention in our upcoming meeting. Please, feel free to add any issues, which are of importance to you.

We would like to tell you what we think Kristoffer feels like in kindergarten. We are interested in your opinion about Kristoffer's situation and development, both at home and in kindergarten.

Should you have any concerns, we would like to hear about them too. Of course, we will let you know any concerns we might have.

We look forward to talking to you ...'

Often, parents find it difficult to criticize institutions and teachers, particularly teachers, which they personally like, or ones they feel dependent on. It can be helpful to invite parents as concrete as possible: *"Since we have agreed that everything is working out well so far, we would like to know if there is anything in your opinion we could improve – anything we should pay more attention to."*

These regular conversations give teachers the opportunity to address issues which may not be very serious or urgent but still do not fit into the brief moments of everyday contact. They offer parents important information and teachers an opportunity to practice talking about difficult topics in a constructive way:

"I realized that when you pick up Johannes, you immediately ask him if he has eaten his lunch. I'd like to know whether this is really important to you or just a standard question which you don't even think about."

"I'm not sure ... maybe it's just ridiculous ... but it's important that he eats ... right?"

"Yes, of course, but if you ask him that every single day, he might get the feeling that it is the only thing you are interested in and the only thing he should do to make you happy."

If teachers decide to wait for the annual conversation to address a serious problem they need to state this clearly. It is appropriate to prepare the parents for what is awaiting them and to give them time to prepare themselves: *"There is something we would call serious that we want to discuss with you. We needed some time to figure out how best to tell you. Now we are clear. We would like to take the time and talk this over with you today, even though we didn't have the possibility to prepare you earlier. Are you okay with this ...?"*

The main goal of regular conversations is to tackle the root of possible problems and to strengthen the daily contact so that everyone involved, particularly the child, gets the feeling that everything is in order. It is important that the most important adults in their life talk to one another. We also suggest including children in these conversations and asking them to describe their current life experience. Often, children mention surprising aspects in the presence of adults who show an honest interest in their joy and sorrow. It is of great value if the child's viewpoints are taken serious as an essential component of the truth about their time in school.

If time is limited it can be helpful for the teacher to conclude the conversation by stating: *"Unfortunately, the time for today is up. But before we leave, I'd like to know, if there is anything on your mind which we should talk about at our next meeting?"*

Parent-Teacher Meetings

In the following, we will look at the situation in schools. The principles described and the fundamental needs of everyone involved, however, are the same in other types of institutions.

Many teachers feel highly uncertain and anxious preparing for parent-teacher meetings. It is tempting to blame this on the unsocial, complacent and demanding mentality of some modern parents. However, in reality, the situation is more complex.

To make it clear, these meetings are *teacher meetings* for parents. The teachers invite parents to their workplace, to discuss with one another, to listen to each other, to provide mutual advice, to correct each other and to make plans together. The parent-teacher meetings are not a democratic forum in which parents take votes on the professional quality of teachers and their methods. It is an opportunity for the most important adults in the child's life to take responsibility for their wellbeing, development and education by clarifying organizational things. And the teacher hosts the meeting.

The individual teacher's character, insight and experience determine the agenda, structure and way of guidance. In order to give parents, the feeling of being taken seriously, teachers must always schedule time for unforeseeable events.

It also makes sense to include the class in the planning and implementation of parent-teacher meetings as early as possible. It can be very beneficial for children to contribute topics, to sometimes participate and to even to guide some meetings later on. If the pedagogical and social atmosphere in the classroom develops into a negative direction, the participation of children is a necessity from our experience.

There are countless examples of unfortunate parent-teacher meetings and at least as many attempts of blaming someone. The responsibility for the general tone and atmosphere as well as the content of the meetings lies with the teacher. They are, however, often caught between two contradictory approaches. One is goal-oriented focused on adequacy and efficiency. The other is primarily concerned with the process and synergy effects. Both approaches are not necessarily incompatible. Yet, it is essential to know when to use which one. A further influencing factor is the procedure and general culture of meetings in the institution.

EXAMPLE

"So, good evening, I want to welcome you all to this meeting. My name is Marianne Madsen and I'll be the class teacher in first grade. I'm sure you agree with me that it is very important that your children have a good start at school. Today, society places great importance on grade point average and life-long learning, yet, it is probably even more important for children to experience school as something meaningful in their everyday lives.

As I've mentioned, I'll be your children's class teacher, at least in first grade, and it's always a challenge to enable a good start ... So, here at this school, we appreciate close cooperation with the children's parents – by the way, we must not forget to vote two parent representatives today. Should anyone of you like to volunteer, please let me know before we start voting. Anyway, just like I said, we appreciate positive cooperation with parents and, therefore, I hope that you'll agree with me ... So, let's take a look at your children's curriculum ..."

The teacher in the example above does her best to appear friendly, informative, accommodating, and correct and, thus, seems to have established a comfortable atmosphere for future parent-teacher conferences. The problem is, however, that her *welcoming* consists of empty phrases and social clichés, if we look closer. It makes a huge difference, if you are greeted by a person who actually says *welcome* and looks like he or she also means it than by a person who says *I want to welcome you* but never actually does so. The teacher's promise to establish a good relationship and cooperation is not credible since it lacks substance.

The teacher personally is likely to feel a certain relief about having fulfilled her duty and role without having publicly embarrassed herself or revealed her nervousness. The parents are likely to leave the conference with the idea that it is best to keep their relationship with the teacher impersonal and to fulfill their role as parents correctly, and not allow irrelevant and irrational feelings to touch the world of school. They surely read the dominant moral concept between the lines: be friendly, do not interrupt each other while talking, be aware of your large responsibility for the children, etc. These messages are correct, but boring and predictable.

Alternative:

"Good evening and welcome! I'm Marianne Madsen and I am your children's new class teacher. I'll give my best to make you feel welcome here at our first parent-teacher conference. But before we start, I'd like to know your names and whose parents you are and maybe who's also part of your family ...

Thank you! It's always helpful to me, if everybody says something – then I'm not quite so nervous. Now, I'd like to try to tell you more about me to give you an impression of who I am and what I do. Like I said, my name's Marianne Madsen, I'm married, my husband's called Claus and he works in the technical management of the city hall. We have two children. Our daughter is 20 and no longer lives at home, our son Kristoffer is thirteen and in seventh grade.

I thought I'd also tell you more about what it is like to be a teacher and tell you about my two most important jobs. One of my jobs is teaching children and trying to make them feel secure and learn something, and the other is to cooperate with you on different matters.

Let's start with the latter. Here at this school, we have organized school-home cooperation. This means that we will select two parent representatives today who are willing to help me and other teachers organize parent-teacher meetings and other joint activities. I assume some of you are interested and active, while others may need some more time to get to know each other. Obviously, it is important that we choose somebody who is interested in this task.

It is most difficult for me to work with parents whose children feel uncomfortable or do not learn enough – or where both is true. And I know from experience that I will have these situations with one or the other of you in the next ten years. Therefore, I'd like to try and prepare us for it. Of course, we all hope that the children will be fine and that we'll all get along well – that goes without saying. I think teachers are in a similar situation as parents: You raise your children, spend time with them, and want them to feel comfortable, to develop, and be successful at school and later in life. I love teaching, at least most of the time, and I try to do my best. In return, I expect children to learn what they should and to treat me with respect. I expect this, although I am aware that this will not always be the case.

There's almost always a child or two in the class whom I have difficulty with but treat just like any other child, because that is my job. Children are different and I'm not a robot! Just like parents feel like it is a huge success to see children happy, well-educated and cooperative, it is also easier for me to work with children who like to go to school. Just like parents dislike when they are called bad parents, we also find it difficult as teachers to deal with criticism. I'm not saying this because I hope you won't dare to say your opinion after this but just to remind you that teachers are humans with strengths and weaknesses. We also make mistakes and embarrass ourselves.

Should you experience that your child or you yourself are treated badly or unjustly, please get in touch with me or the respective teacher. We may know a lot about how to teach children, but as parents you are in touch with the rest of their lives. Therefore, we may need your knowledge, particularly in the first couple of years, more than you need our knowledge ..."

In this example, the parents encounter a teacher who finds it more important to appear as a human being of flesh and blood rather than *nice* and correct. By acting as host and informing about the rules and values which provide the basis for a fruitful cooperation with her in the following ten years, she also asked the parents to contribute as the humans they are. In this way, the parents are not confronted with the unrealistic expectation that they should fulfill their social role as parents with pretentious perfection.

In the example above, a mature and experienced teacher spoke. Of course, the same words would sound very different if they were coming from a young and less experienced colleague introducing herself to the parents. The quality of the contact develops both through the words chosen and the tone of the speaker. The more nuanced and honest both words and tone represent him or her the greater the quality of the contact.

But why is this the case? What speaks against emphasizing the other part of reality? Emphasizing the fact that the teacher has a formal role as public employee to implement local rules and regulations? Let us take a closer look at the diverging values that build the basis for one's personal understanding of leadership.

A teacher's leadership must show in exemplary behavior by being a good example. If a teacher tries to lead by appearing as correct as possible, the following inevitably occurs:

Correctness and friendliness create a façade which make a person appear unassailable on the formal level. For some this form of correctness is a lifestyle. But for most experts, it is a protective mechanism compensating for a lack of self-worth, insecurity and vulnerability. The result is an ambiguous message. I am vulnerable and unassailable. This message is always provocative. Some parents are considerate of the teacher's vulnerability, while others feel provoked by the lacking congruence and can become aggressive.

Correctness and friendliness are transparent protective mechanisms. The environment can clearly see a person's character hidden beneath the façade. But since the teacher determines the tone of communication, she only lays a basis for cooperation in the smooth part of the journey. She will also try to act as if she were only existent in her expert role and hide her actual person and character.

This role play leads to everyone being frustrated because both sides are involved with very personal things. While parents interact on the basis of their irrational and personal love for their children, the teacher interacts on the basis of her profession. However, also on a professional level the relevant and primary effects come from the teacher's personal qualities.

This brings us back to the point, that the success and significance of parent-teacher meetings depends on the ability of the teacher to get into contact as a person. Their willingness to share the responsibility for the children's behavior with parents, even in difficult situations enables relevant possibilities of interaction. If experts fail to do so, they run the risk of being the scapegoats in the end.

Daily Interactions

Today's parents are not only sensitive, but they are also committed, demanding and discerning. They also expect to be involved. Only a generation ago, parents were convinced of not having to have a say. Daily cooperation is not about democracy, participation and consumer rights. It is much rather about establishing of meaningful relationships that benefit everyone.

Institutions for infants and toddlers have always tended towards more informal exchanges. Many parents want to make use of the advice teachers may have to offer. Since the parents come to the institutions daily, the teachers have an opportunity to advise them on the basis of their everyday observations. For example, when Asger's mother wants to say goodbye to her son, the teachers are watching and receive an opportunity to provide advice. It takes a while until his mother is ready to leave. After three attempts to put Asger's lunch into the fridge so they are both satisfied, Asger wants to wave goodbye from three different windows. The more time passes, the more stressed his mother is getting. She has tried hard to find a way of saying goodbye in a more relaxed way.

Observing these scenes provide the teachers with the possibility to offer help. They could say: *I see that you have difficulty saying goodbye to your son in a satisfying way. I think it might help, if we talk about what you and Asger need in this moment. Would you be okay with this?*

It only takes a brief conversation for the mother to realize her needs and to find a way of giving clearer signals to her son. Consequently, the boy is more relaxed and able to let his mother go more easily. In addition to providing concrete assistance, the teachers also managed to create a positive atmosphere in the institution. An atmosphere where advice does not expose but rather provides a welcome opportunity to learn more about what it means to be a parent.

This way of concrete cooperation is valuable for all parties involved. It provides parents with a feeling of security and conveys respect for the professional qualification of teachers.

EXAMPLE

Kathrine was nine months old and had just been admitted to a daycare center. Her mother devoted the last 14 days of maternity leave to make the transition as smooth as possible. She was committed to being a good mother and therefore watched Kathrine's reactions constantly.

Before Kathrine started going to daycare, her mother spent a lot of energy on trying to assess the quality of daycare centers in her district. She discussed extensively with other mothers and argued with authorities to get a place in one of the institutions she considered most suitable for her daughter. Still, she was not able to get a place in the institution she had preferred the most. Therefore, she used the first contact with the institution to find out whether it would fulfill her expectations and whether she could rely on it to take good care of her daughter. The mother's priority was that her daughter is seen, understood and taken seriously the way she is.

For Kathrine's mother, this meant that her daughter's wishes and needs were answered the moment they were recognizable. Yet, from the teachers' perspective, taking Kathrine's needs seriously did not always entail instant satisfaction.

Although the institution was actually very good, the mother started to doubt her decision and to worry that her daughter may be overlooked and her needs for contact and care may not get satisfied. Kathrine cooperated with her mother's uncertainty and cried every time her mother dropped her off at daycare. She did not cry though when her father took her there. When the mother brought her to daycare, she said things like: "Now look, Kathrine, you can go over to Birthe and Mette – they are already waiting for you. Don't you want to wave goodbye to your mom?" At the same time, however, there was nothing she would have rather done than take her child with her. Since the girl was crying, she was convinced that she did not like going to daycare.

The behavior between mother and daughter is on the verge of developing into a destructive game in which Kathrine's needs, wishes, and cravings and the mother's abilities to fulfill them take over. It is the mother's way of loving her daughter. Therefore, it is important that the teachers react specifically to this approach, instead of starting an exhausting power struggle or theoretical discussion about the child's needs. The teachers should invite to a dialogue with the entire family as a starting point. In the process, they should address specific issues where they feel like they can contribute to an improvement or give the parents advice if they ask for it themselves.

Cooperating on Problematic Issues

Problem-oriented conversations between experts, parents and children are a central part of school relationships. Many people refer to these as *difficult conversations*. We, however, prefer to consider them necessary conversations. They are the conversations which are *necessary* as soon as anyone involved perceives the interaction as unsuccessful, inappropriate or dissatisfying, - or when the relationship is meaningless and out of balance. Whether these conversations are *difficult* depends mainly on whether teachers accept conflicts and problems as a natural and necessary part of life or have a more romantic attitude.

These *necessary conversations* need to be differentiated from cases where the teacher is forced to switch their role from a dialogue partner to an authority to address very serious issues. This is the case if suspicious facts arise or there is evidence of failing care, of sexual abuse, etc. the kind of things that must be reported because the need clarifying and counseling that goes beyond the responsibility of schools.

Concern about the general wellbeing of a child in connection with the parents' social situation, their health condition or their ability to care for the child are reasons to invite parents to *necessary conversations*. The concern may relate to specific aspects of a child's psychological, social, intellectual or physical development, which can include behavioral problems, growth failure, language disorders, tendencies of self-isolation, general passivity or aggression.

On the other side, the parents' concern about their child's situation in school or daycare is also a natural need. Questions which may arise can be *'why is my child not able to read yet?'* *'What if we do not want our daughter to participate in mixed swimming lessons?'* or the like. But problem-oriented conversations can also be organized upon the child's initiative.

If the child feels they are being treated unjustly or being bullied by other children, if they are unable to cope with the school's requirements or they are bored, they can ask for them.

Often, teachers consciously delay arranging these conversations or avoid them altogether. The same is true for parents. In both cases, this leads to these conversations being postponed, which makes finding possible solutions more difficult.

In the following we describe qualities that problem-oriented conversations need to have in order to reach satisfying results. *These conversations are about working together and nothing else.* They may reveal a need for parent or family counseling or family therapy or collegial reflection and supervision on the part of the teacher. However, these needs go beyond the scope of problem-oriented conversations. Even if teachers may also have the competence to offer parent counseling this should not be conducted in this setting. Offering this kind of advice and counseling would take the content and goal of the conversation to an entirely different level. Changing the setting should never be done without consent and knowledge of everyone involved. Similarly, all parties must agree on possible references to educational psychologists or family counseling centers[7]

These *necessary conversations* are often end up in mutual accusations. Who is to blame? Who is the problem? Is it the institution or the family? This not only destructive, but also not objective. There is no doubt that a child's personal and psychosocial development depends on the family with the parent-child relationship having the largest constructive and destructive potential. And there is equally little doubt that other relevant adult-child relationships have a high influence on the development of a child's inner and outer behavior.

A child's ability and willingness to cooperate may cause them to behave very differently in school than in their family. Some children openly share their pain with the family, while teachers perceive them as *well-functioning*. Other children behave difficult when they are in the institution because they actually feel comfortable there. This is also because of their trust in the adults who work there, that they try to be seen and seek support.

Again, others have real conflicts in the institution because they do have conflicts with the adults there.

In our opinion, parents and teachers alike should treat children as appropriately as possible. Should they fail, both of them have to change their interaction with the child. In the majority of cases, parents can provide their children with sufficient help and support. But often the teacher's commitment determines whether the parents' and child's attempts are rewarded. The adults are dependent on each other and, for the sake of the child's existential needs, need to acknowledge and cooperate with the child.

It is painful and stigmatizing for children, if there is a lack of contact or negative contact between the parents and the teachers in their environment. Thus, the solidarity among teachers can be just as destructive to the child's developmental potential as parents showing solidarity with their children by fighting the institution. This does not mean, however, that parents and teachers have to agree on everything. It just shows how important it is for adults to take care of the quality of their mutual relationships.

The process of a conversation in itself can lead to changes in difficult relationships by trading correctness, sobriety and objective distance with contact, closeness and authenticity.

Responsibility and Power

In conversations with parents, teachers have the *processual* responsibility – the responsibility for the general tone and atmosphere as well as the mood during the conversation. The reason for this is the relational asymmetry we spoke about above (because the teacher is in a more powerful position). To be sure, this does not always correspond with the personal perception of the teacher involved. And there may also be situations in which the parents appear extraordinarily powerful. Only very few teachers actually think about power as an intrinsic part of their daily work and position. Being employed by a public system and meeting individuals as an institutional representative bestows actual power on teachers regardless of whether they are aware of this power or not. Parents feel very vulnerable when confronted with this kind of power if the behavior of their child is criticized.

In everyday language, we see the teacher's role in *necessary conversations* as a host, even if the conversation is upon the initiative of the parents and/or at their home. In the latter case, parents are the hosts on the formal and social level. The responsibility for the content and the way of interacting (process) still lies with the teacher.

Since relational competence develops over the course of work life. Conversations like this are an ideal opportunity to learn complementary to collegial reflection, supervision and further training. This also means that it is impossible to have a perfect process in every conversation and that perfection is *not* a constructive relational quality anyway.

If a conversation does not run smoothly, either of the sides may feel uncomfortable, attacked, overlooked or ignored. The can feel forced to become defensive or feel criticized. If the teacher recognizes these negative qualities in a conversation, the reaction necessary is *openness*:
- I realize, I've been criticizing your daughter, and of course you want to protect her. So, please let me try to start over…
- I am prepared to accept your criticism if you think I've treated you badly, but I'm not willing to become the scapegoat for things, which have nothing to do with me!
- I realize that you feel uncomfortable with what I'm saying. I'd like to know why this is the case.
- Today I don't seem to be a good moderator. Do you think you could help me?
- I find it very hard to talk to you about this because I feel like it could hurt you.
- It often sounds like I want to criticize parents, when I try to address a difficult issue. I hope you'll be able to have a little patience, which helps me make myself clear.

What is special about problem-oriented conversations is that the content is always personal to at least one of the parties involved. When meeting for the first time this can prove utterly difficult. Consequently, people always try to create a respectful and polite tone when approaching each other. This, however, also brings up two problems. Firstly, it hardly ever helps to be polite on the surface because serious issues always break through eventually. Secondly important personal considerations and messages that would enable reasonable contact and change are suppressed or only given indirectly. Therefore, it is necessary for the teacher to seize any opportunity to be open about personal messages and, thus, create an atmosphere of acceptance and support.

Otherwise, the meeting becomes a *non-meeting*, the encounter of two administrative bodies (the parental body and the teacher body). This rarely leads to constructive outcomes.

Productive meetings require openly addressing essential issues in an atmosphere which is accepting of both irrational or spontaneous action as well as embarrassment. Teachers have the overarching responsibility and power to ensure this atmosphere with all its encouraging qualities.

Preparing Necessary Conversations

In preparing it can be helpful to consider the points listed below, either on one's own or together with a colleague. Sometimes it can also be effective to put important aspects down on paper.
1. Should I talk to the parents alone or ask somebody for assistance?
2. Should the child concerned participate?
3. What do I want to talk about with the parents? And how can I address the issues?
4. What kind of help do I need from the parents?
5. How do I feel before the conversation?

1. Talking to parents alone or together
There may be several reasons why assistance can be helpful in the conversation:

- The presence of a colleague may provide a feeling of security. But it is important to avoid a common front in the sense of 'we are several that think …' The clarification and solution of relational problems are not to be solved with help of democratic processes. They are creative processes which rely on empathy, experience, fantasy and sensitivity.
- A colleague may have a different perception of a child than the teacher concerned and, thus, add valuable nuances. Should all persons in an institution share the same perspective and attitude, there is no good reason to involve several people at once.
- A colleague might have a better contact with the parents concerned than the teacher directly concerned.
- The involvement of a colleague may also give the teacher leading the conversation an opportunity to use the experience in their own learning process. If this is the goal, the colleague should assume the role of an active observer and ensure the procedural quality. In their role as observer the colleague is responsible that both sides are granted the possibility to say what they want to say, and to explain if and how they have understood the statements of the other one. The colleague supports both sides in getting the most out of the meeting.

Caution: If a single parent is involved, he or she may easily feel inferior or overwhelmed by being confronted with two experts depending on their ability to approach authorities as equals.

2. Children participating
The decision to involve children in problem-oriented conversations has both a democratic and a psychological dimension.
Democratic values are about children's rights. This includes the right to hear what is being said about them, the right to express their own opinions and the right to influence their own lives.

From a purely psychological standpoint, the participation of children in problem-oriented conversations can be problematic. This is true, especially if teachers are insecure about leading the conversations without exposing the children to negative criticism or are concerned about affecting the contact to the parents in a destructive way.

Teachers can openly express their wish for a child to participate. But it is up to the parents to make the final decision. If the child participates and the teacher realizes a destructive tendency, he or she is responsible to end the conversation and draw attention to the problem: *I'm afraid I've lost control over this conversation and I really don't think it is any good for you to continue listening to us. What do you think? And what do you think as parents?* Although the parents, again, have to take the final decision, the teacher can give valid arguments for their position. Their argumentation may, in fact, be helpful for the child who witnesses an adult openly expressing their discord.

In our opinion, it is beneficial for children to be included as often as possible with respect to their right as well as existential and social development. It is not about official laws or regulations prescribing the children's right to be included. The moral right arises from empirical knowledge about the discomfort humans in general experience knowing that others are talking about us and taking decisions for us while we are not present.

Being allowed to witness and experience the processes adults go through when they are frustrated, sad or worried, enables emotional and existential development. Younger children may not be able to understand what is being said exactly, but they can understand the tone of the conversation and clearly react to what they observe. For older children, their involvement may be an opportunity for them to seize and develop their competence as active participants in a conversation.

EXAMPLE

Holger was in fourth grade. After the summer holidays, he got a new class teacher. As soon as, Holger heard the news, he was sad. At home, he told his parents that he felt like the new teacher did not like him, criticized his participation in class and even scolded him. Holger's pa-

rents took him seriously. They took time to talk about how much he liked his previous teacher and that he would need time to get used to the new situation. They wanted him to give the new teacher a chance, but nothing helped.

At the next parent-teacher meeting, the parents mentioned that Holger at the moment seemed to be rather vulnerable. Yet, this message was too subtle to take any effect. Soon, the parents asked for a meeting with the class teacher and Holger insisted on coming along. His parents were well-educated. They knew how to express themselves. The intended conversation, however, quickly turned into an intellectual discussion about pedagogical methods and principles. After having watched his parents' desperate attempts to protect him, the boy took over responsibility. Shakily, and with tears in his eyes, Holger said to the teacher: "I've just had enough of you criticizing me every single day. Can't you just stop, so that I can enjoy school again?"

This exact and personal message, in fact, made the teacher think. He fell silent and took a second to process what he just heard before he responded with the same openness: "I'm sorry to hear that this is the way you feel. I didn't realize that I was criticizing you. But now that I know, I'll pay more attention to what I'm saying."

Not only does this dialogue improve the relationship between Holger and his teacher, but the result also provides an invaluable base for Holger's way of building good relationships in the future. Conversely, destructive conversations can influence future relationships negatively:

"No, Holger, I think you must have misunderstood the situation..."

"Yes, Holger, that may be right, but don't you think it's partly your own fault?"

"I can't agree with you, Holger. Remember that I'm also responsible for all the other children in your class!"

In cases where adults invalidate the child's perception of reality and personal expressions, they will not be happy about having been allowed to participate in the conversation.

On the social level, these experiences become an intrinsic part of the child's way of interacting. Children inevitably imitate the structures they have experienced in future relationships, and this becomes their approach to solving problems, to cooperating and in other aspects of social competence.

3. What to say and how to say it

As the host and moderator, the teacher is required to think about how they want to address a topic or problem. Problems they have with a child personally, issues they see in the child's interaction with other children or difficulties concerning a specific subject or behavior.

At the same time, the teachers have to be aware that the reality of the parents may be a different one, and that they have had less time to prepare themselves. They might have additional issues. Therefore, the teachers have to be prepared to *also* include other topics in the conversation. It is easier to be open, if one's personal agenda is clear in advance.

In addition, the actual phrasing of the issue makes a big difference. Teachers feel and react just as spontaneously, prejudiced and irrationally as any other person. But since they are responsible, they must be committed to using constructive language. Constructive language is not to be mistaken for polite and diplomatic language. (see chapter 10 personal language p.241)

EXAMPLE

Trine, four years old, was very stubborn, aggressive and dominant towards other children in kindergarten. Her teacher could inform the child's parents about her problem in several different ways:

"I need to tell you that Trine's behavior in kindergarten is really inappropriate. She just won't listen to what we tell her. Of course, this also has negative effects on the other children. They often are sad when Trine wants to decide everything on her own. Sometimes, she is very aggressive and even violent towards others. They are afraid of her. Last week, for example, we watched Trine as she was..."

This tirade is full of negative descriptions and would overwhelm most parents and spark negative counterattacks. The negative tone of the language used is reinforced by the teacher's unwillingness to show any kind of co-responsibility for the situation.

> *"I've invited you to come here, because I don't know how to help myself or Trine in the current situation. I'd like to give you some examples of our daily interactions together. I'm afraid they may sound rather negatively, because I feel rather helpless. Do you think you'll be able to handle some of the stories I've got to share?"*

In this statement, the teacher assumes co-responsibility for the situation and carefully prepares the parents for bad news. Thus, she sets a tone that will also make it easier for the parents to take over their own responsibility and talk about their possible helplessness. All parents are aware that you often feel helpless as an adult and that what you do in difficult situations may not always be the right thing to do. Confronted with the above statement, the parents know that even highly qualified teachers know this feeling. Just like everyone else, they do not have the answer to everything and, sometimes, are unable to find a solution. This provides a realistic and positive base for further cooperation and prevents mutual accusations because of incompetence.

Should the parents come to the meeting with a different topic on their minds, it is advisable to talk about their concern first. Since the parents are not at home in the institution, they may need some time to adjust before they are ready to be confronted with serious issues. However, sometimes this is not possible:

> *"I'd like to talk to you about this too, but I'm afraid that I'm too concerned with a different matter to be a good listener right now. So, I want to talk about something else first if this is okay with you."*

The values needed for conversations like this contradict many values that are an essential part of everyday teaching. For teaching it's inevitable that the teacher has a plan of what a lesson should look like in its individual phases and what the desired goal should be. This professional approach enhances the quality of teaching as well as the outcome for students. In problem-oriented conversations, however, the situation is very different. We have experienced a lot of conversations in which the teachers already defined the problem along with its solution in advance. The parents' role was thus reduced to either giving consent or refusing the teachers' suggestions. Such an approach to problem-oriented conversations prevents the parties involved meeting as equals and relies on manipulation. Conversations are equally manipulative if the teachers' primary intention is to simply fulfill their professional duties. It is essential to distinguish between the responsibility to convey a message and the responsibility of guiding a dialogical process. If this differentiation is missing the progress and result of the conversation will not be satisfying for either side.

4. Parents' support

In a time dominated by experts, the public system has the idea that quite a number of parents need help from specialists either in their partnerships, in raising their children, or both. Experts and statisticians support this idea with facts. Yet, if you ask parents themselves, most of them, do not think they need help at all.

The special nature and function of the family needs to be better understood. The family is a systemic entity in which the behavior and wellbeing of the individual consistently influences every other member, as well as the nature of interactions. The majority of familial processes that influence the wellbeing and development of the children is unconscious. The parents' conscious attitudes, values, emotions and actions only make up a fraction of what shapes the personality and the self-concept of a child. Every single parent literally does the best he or she can to raise healthy, happy and well-adapted children. Should they fail to reach this goal, or have difficulties on their way, this is mainly due to relational phenomena that are beyond the parents' (and children's) daily awareness. Therefore, they are also beyond their immediate control. (Obviously, this does not include failure to provide care as well as active physical and psychological violation.)

In addition, the family plays a decisive role in creating and solving problems, as described earlier in this book. In most cases, the family's creative potential as *problem solver* is much larger than the experts'. This does not mean, however, that experts do not have valuable knowledge, experience and suggestions to contribute. It just means that the parents provide the soil from which children grow and thrive.

For reasons given above, parents sometimes need external help. But whoever tries to help individuals *always* need the assistance of parents or the rest of the family. As long as they are unwilling to talk to and share their personal life with experts, the expert's idea of a child's living circumstances is left to chance and remains fragmentary. This further reduces already limited possibilities to intervene constructively.

The willingness and ability to accept this fact and take one's own attitude towards parents into account, are crucial to achieving a constructive clarification and solution for specific problems and conflicts. This ability also decides if parents consider themselves as equals and worthy or not.

Over the course of time, parents have been labeled as *unmotivated* or as *unwilling to cooperate*, if their conversational behavior was determined by the fact that they did not feel like they were important to their children or the experts who cared for, treated or taught their children.

If Trine's teacher in kindergarten fails to productively interact with Trine, she needs the parents' assistance. If she wants to discover the causes for Trine's violent behavior she needs parents who are willing to openly describe their own approach to Trine, their perception of their daughter's character and their strategy of dealing with failures and successes.

There is little parents can do to change their child's behavior in institutions. They can talk to the child about their good or sometimes bad behavior, they can scold them, lure them, threat them, bribe or punish them. But (self-)destructive behavior patterns only rarely come from a lack of awareness of what the adults expect. Thus, parents and professionals (teachers or psychologists) need to cooperate and examine the child's living conditions in the family and in the institution in an unbiased way. If this reveals new insights, the parents can try to improve specific and general living conditions. This is only possible, however, if experts are humble and professional enough to create a dialogue between equals.

5. Personal feelings

We recommend reflecting on personal feelings, expectations and other people involved, prior to an important conversation. It helps to question whether the dominant feelings are a hindrance to contact. For example, fear, nervousness, pressure, anger, reluctance, irritation in previous conversations or empathy for the child are all feelings that can give rise to prejudice. *It is human to have feelings; and it is professional to know one's feelings.*

In addition, general prejudices can endanger developing positive contact. As we have mentioned above, some teachers have difficulties with parents who have the same education and profession. Some have problems with talkative marketing managers who drive big cars. Others have problems with insecure, shy single mothers. All of us have peculiarities (parents as well). These are not morally wrong or inappropriate professionally. But experts are responsible for avoiding that they dominate and interrupt important and *necessary conversations.*

Sometimes, it can be enough if the person responsible describes their situation with a few personal remarks at the beginning of the conversation:

"I've only started work as a teacher recently, which is why I'm a little insecure about whether I'll be able to bring this conversation to a conclusion which is satisfying for both of us. I hope you'll let me know if you feel like I'm on the wrong track."

"The thought of meeting you here today to talk made me a little nervous. I've met you at some of our parent-teacher meetings and realized that you are very good at talking and augmenting. So the idea of matching my rhetoric skills against yours frightens me. I hope I'll be able to interrupt if I feel overwhelmed. This is also why I asked a colleague of mine to join us as an observer. I'm just not sure about how well I'll be able to manage this part of my job."

One specific attitude or self-image which is always difficult, is if the teachers see themselves as *representing the side of the child* or as *attorney for the child.* In most countries, the law clearly stipulates that public employees are obliged to interfere in cases where a child's wellbeing and integrity is in danger. This obligation is sometimes part of a sentimental and complacent identity some experts like to take on. The problem is that this attitude is immediately obvious for the parents confronted and heard as: *I'm more concerned about the wellbeing of your child than you are yourself.* Thus, a competitive situation arises, which effectively prevents fruitful cooperation. Teachers are best able to help children by providing sufficient support for their parents. Otherwise, children have to cope with a painful conflict of loyalty, which in most cases causes them to turn against the experts.

Parents also have feelings and attitudes which can impede fruitful contact to varying degrees. Some parents burst out with their emotions and prejudices immediately. Most, however, try to remain nice, polite, correct and objective.

This is the reason it is important for the teacher to assume leadership, establishing a personal and honest tone, and be interested in the parents' irrational emotions and thoughts. *Being nice* has never contributed to solving serious problems. The alternative to being nice is not being unfriendly, but being as authentic as possible.[8]

Authentic Contact as Prerequisite

The more authentic (open for the thoughts, attitudes, values, and feelings of others) everyone involved is, the better the contact. It is important to distinguish between *good* contact in problem-oriented conversations and what we commonly refer to as good social contact. Good social contact does not necessarily include personal aspects. They are built on friendliness, good will, politeness and not least on the fact that both sides are free to choose the distance between them: a distance they both consider appropriate. Many people describe social contact as *superficial* and, in doing so, see it critical. We do not agree with this. Social contact has a peculiar function and a peculiar value. What is most important is to be aware of its limitations. These include the fact that *social contact is unable to clarify, process or solve personal and interactional conflicts and problems.*

If a child is so unhappy with their life that their performance in school and/or social behavior is influenced, this is of personal significance for the child concerned. If parents realize that their child's behavior causes frustration for other adults, they are affected personally too. If a teacher fails to establish a productive way of interacting with a child, this is a *personal professional* reality. All parties involved are emotionally touched. Consequently, the personal dimension is an active component of the conversations. Otherwise, personal aspects will accumulate and affect what is being discussed and decided on the rational and professional levels destructively.

If we receive the opportunity to express ourselves and our identity in an appreciative and open atmosphere, we can develop further and assume personal responsibility. Authentic and personal expression also makes us vulnerable to putting our self-image and the image others have of us at risk. In asymmetric relationships like the context of this book, parents and children are the most vulnerable.

If a teacher reduces their way of interacting to social and formal aspects, the contact is thrown off balance and becomes uncomfortable for the parents and children involved. In addition, the central problem will not be solved efficiently. We insist on taking the personal dimension seriously, because it does not undermine professional competence but lifts it to the respective level of the professional identity one has created.

Personal contact is not always harmonious. If we are confronted with situations that threaten our value as parents, children or teachers, it is only natural to react with anger, frustration and aggression.[9] These feelings oppose most people's desire to remain friendly and cooperative. Yet feelings are an unavoidable component of any kind of interpersonal problem. They are actually just a sign of being seriously committed and human. Over the years, teachers can learn to use the energy of frustration and aggression for the positive. For parents, however, the situation is always new. Presumably, there are few other situations capable of unsettling parent's self-esteem and self-image more than hearing that their children *do not function well* in kindergarten or in school. Immediately, this gives rise to self-reproach and feelings of guilt. Usually it takes some time to regain the confidence to participate in reasonable and rational discussions, thoughts and actions. Some parents withdraw and feel depressed during this initial phase, whereas others immediately become active and even aggressive. All of these thoughts and feelings are an intrinsic part of good contact.

An essential quality of personal statements is that they almost always take immediate effect on the other side. If somebody or something has an effect on us, it often is the beginning of change. Of course, criticism, moral judgement and humiliation have an effect because inappropriate behavior is reinforced and entrenched.

Many problem-oriented conversations between teachers and parents have taken place in an atmosphere in which personal aspects were hardly welcome, if not to say shunned. This has created the habit of concluding conversations with the demand for a promise or agreement on behalf of the parents or child. Yet, very often promises were not kept and agreements broken. In some cases, they did not lead to the desired outcome. There are three reasons for this:

- Conflict and desired changes always have a personal component, and these are the basis for personal and interpersonal changes, which in turn are prerequisite of behavioral changes of the child or their parents. Therefore, conversations in which personal aspects are ignored have little potential to achieve change.
- If the personal dimension is ignored, agreements made in the process will neither correspond with the problem nor with the measures necessary for a solution.
- Concluding a conversation on the basis of an agreement or promise conveys an indirect message; *we have gathered to induce a change, but we do not believe that our conversation has been sufficient. Therefore, as a precaution we will make an agreement.* Of course, specific agreements may be necessary and part of the solution, e.g. who is to report to other teachers, the educational psychologist, or the welfare authority or commitments of the teacher. However, the agreement itself is not a solution

We know from experience that it is wiser for teachers to rely on their gut feelings telling them if a conversation was successful or not and to wait and see what happens next. If nothing happens, there is a chance of improving the conversational quality next time, aiming to enable relevant change. Subsequent conversations can, for example, be introduced by the words: *"After our last talk, I actually had quite a good feeling. But seeing you now, I feel like nothing has really changed – maybe also not in my own reaction to the problem. Let's see if we can find a different approach to the issue today".*

As a teacher, you cannot avoid meeting parents with whom you are unable to establish good contact. Such parents may be people whose appearance and behavior touches our own *blind* spots and/or whose general attitude towards teachers is obviously arrogant and negative or even aggressive. They not only make you feel hurt but actually violate your professional integrity and dignity. In some cases, the problem can be solved by transferring the contact to a colleague with a different approach. In other cases, you have to open up: *"Unfortunately, I have to tell you that I feel treated badly in every one of our conversations. I don't know whether you generally dislike teachers or whether it's just me. But I know that I don't want to put up with you making fun of me or humiliating me as if I was an idiot. If you have a problem with me as a person, we can talk about it, but otherwise we have to put an end to our cooperation right now."*

Irrespective of how much you try to be responsible, and irrespective of your level of experience, you will time and again meet parents, children and colleagues with whom you find it difficult to develop constructive relationships. In these situations, it makes sense to withdraw to prevent any damage to either side. We have the experience that collegial reflection and supervision are helpful in resolving a large part of problematic relationships. In some cases, however, you may simply have to give up.

Who is Responsible for What?

Parents are responsible for their children's wellbeing and development until official authorities decide differently. The parents' responsibility includes deciding which educational institution their children should attend and seeking help in cases where their children feel bad.

Together with local authorities, politicians and public assistants, teachers are responsible for creating the best possible educational, professional and relational quality in working with children and parents. Also, they are responsible for seeking help in case of personal failure.

Children are obliged to attend school. Therefore, they are neither responsible for the quality nor for the quantity of their stay. This actually contradicts to children learning to take on responsible for their own learning and going to school. Therefore, by the fourth or fifth grade the latest teachers and parents need to provide a framework, so children can develop taking decisions concerning school and education and, thus learn to assume personal responsibility.

Seek help, if you fail, regardless of how responsible and committed you are, is an overarching guideline. As teachers or parents, we embarrass ourselves on a daily basis and, thus, create more difficulty in the lives of children and adolescents than would be ideal. Children have to come to terms with this fact, while we have to assume full responsibility for our behavior. What often happens instead is to praise our own commitment and to question the other side's contribution and thus make the individual child pay for it. As long as this is a common strategy of daily practice, we have an ethical problem. Whenever children are criticized for mobbing others and for their lack of social competence, this is shows how adults feather their own nests at the expense of others.

For good reason society trusts schools for primary prevention to ensure life quality for children and adolescents. In many countries, this means that a ministry (usually the ministry for social affairs) must rely on a second ministry (the ministry for education) to appropriately fulfill its duties. This division certainly does not make it easy for staff to face their responsibilities.

Necessary conversations in daycare centers and schools are important opportunities society provides for children and parents who are under great pressure. And these depend on the relational quality provided by teachers. Consequently, it is important to increasingly focus on communication and relational skills in the basic education and training of teachers, and to give conversational skills an important place in pedagogy.

CHAPTER 9:
Understanding Conversation

As mentioned before, we use the word *conversation* synonymous with *dialogue*, in the sense of two parties exchanging personal *truths* to create a new and expanded common *truth*.

Conversation according to Johannes Sløk's understanding builds on the concept of truth. A conversation is the sum of the possibilities as well as limitations of two people relating to this *truth*. K. E. Løgstrup[1], a Danish theologian, describes conversation as a *spontaneous manifestation of life*, directly arising from our human existence and the fact that openness and trust elicit openness and trust. The psychologist Jette Fog[2] summarizes this reasoning:

> Openness, trust and love spring from the fundamental human nature of being mutually dependent. Whereas mistrust, hate and caginess as spontaneous reactions to reality require justification and explanation due to their derived nature. We are able to act contrary to and evade sovereign manifestations of life, but the negative reactions only define us in a negative way to what has always been present: the origin of fundamental human nature. From a logical and psychological point of view, mistrust and lies are parasitical to trust and truth[3] Psychologically speaking, mistrust and lies originate from a lack. The sovereign manifestation of life is a condition which we choose to decide against, yet the *natural* response to trust is equal trust and openness.

In pedagogical relationships K. E. Løgstrup emphasizes that the *child's approach of openness in conversation* must be answered by *picking up the child's ton*e and by realizing that a child surrenders by giving trust. This is the real *ethical challenge* for teachers. Because of this we suggest replacing Johannes Sløk's idea of equality with the concept of *equal dignity*. The fact that adults have more power influences the mutuality in conversation and challenges adults to take responsibility for the nature and the quality of conversations. In the end, this responsibility decides whether a conversation is shaped by trust or mistrust, by truth or lie, or by development or violation.

A peculiar aspect of conversations between teachers and children is that the adults almost always have *intentions* or goals which go beyond the immediate conversation. Often, adults talk to children and adolescents to bring them closer to goals, they have defined on behalf of the children. This does not necessarily mean that the adults' goals are not also in the interest of the children, but *ethically the adults have to question and clarify the goals with the children, to ensure that they are common goals, that are described and defined from the child's point of view.*

Parents are often criticized for not taking sufficient time to talk with their children, and the teachers' ability to talk to children in a relevant way is questioned. Part of this critique has good reasons, but has led to the assumption that only parents *are capable of* leading conversations with their children, and professionals *should know how to*. Both are wrong. Parents' love for their children fuels the wish or desire for conversation. Since teacher training does not focus on conversational competence, both sides can only rely on their personal willingness to talk. This willingness is, in turn, based on the individual's own experiences during his or her childhood as well as related possibly opposing views. 25 years of practice as family counselors and supervisors, however, has clearly shown that willingness alone usually does not suffice.

Historically, there is little substantial evidence to prove that teachers and parents have a natural ability or willingness to talk *with* children, in a way that shows interest in who the child is and what the child's is experiencing. On the contrary, there are plenty examples of talking *to* children, of interrogating, questioning, interviewing, instructing, enlightening, reprimanding, criticizing and blaming them. In everyday life, adults talk about their own perception or reality. Exceptions can be found in psychological institutions or child psychiatry, where some experts have success by talking *with* children. As a basis for talking with children, professionals invite children to draw a picture or play a game. This can help children express *themselves* and gain trust in the contact. In private life, grandparents have proved to be excellent dialogue partners for their grandchildren. An explanation might be that grandparents have more time available than most parents, or consciously take time. Yet, it is more likely that many modern grandparents have simply let go of their parenting role. Thus, they are able to freely converse with children without any intention beyond establishing and fostering a relationship.

Our experience suggests that now a days more meaningful conversations take place between children and adults in families and institutions than ever before. Today's adults approach children with a seriousness and interest which seems unique in many ways. And they in return talk about thoughts, feelings and experiences whose open expression was still a taboo a generation or two ago. The modern problem is that the children's behavior determines the tone of the adults. The openness, interest and empathy seems to decrease in proportion to the way the behavior is perceived: disturbing, problematic, or wrong.

Consequently, exactly the adults and children whose relationship really rely on good conversations fail to lead such conversations. Many of these conversations also fail due to a fallback into experienced patterns. Usually, this is compensated for a while, but the necessity to talk about serious issues arises, both adults and children are confronted with the emptiness and deficiency of their conversational habits.

According to our experience the qualities necessary in both private and professional situations are largely the same. Paradoxically, one of the most important qualities is the adults' ability to *forget about* their own intentions. That means the ability to put the quality of the current interaction over the goals, as well as the process over the content of the conversation. *The quality of relationships increases with the quality of the conversations.*

In Torquato Tasso Johann Wolfgang von Goethe wrote: *They feel the intention, and are hence constrained.* There probably are only two exceptions to this fact in interpersonal relationships. One is erotic seduction and the other therapeutic conversations, in which the personal wish for change can determine the conversational motif.

Putting the intention aside when starting a conversation does not mean having hidden or secret objectives. It rather acknowledges the fact that the adults' plans and perceptions only make up half of the *truth*. Thus, they are the half which can be influenced to change the progress of the conversation.

The adults' intentions can be openly expressed at the beginning of a conversation or at any other point in the process:

EXAMPLE

"I'd like to have a talk with you, Thomas, because I don't like you being so mean to other children and because I want you to stop behaving like this. But I don't know how you feel about this and what you think about this. So, I hope we can talk about it."

"But I'm just mean because they always tease me..."

"I see – they're teasing you? I hadn't realized that. Can you tell me more? Maybe you can tell me about a specific situation?"

In this brief sequence, the teacher succeeds both in describing her own truth and intention but also in including the boy's truth and, thus, demonstrating her willingness to take him seriously.

The more common thing we see in schools regularly is that the conversation develops into a competition about who is right, and the adult devalues or even disqualifies the child's *truth*. Both our human values described previously as well as a pedagogical approach expecting Thomas to use language, discussion or negotiation rather than his body in the conflict with other children needs a conversation of this kind of quality. Otherwise it is an attempt to *motivate* the child in a similarly aggressive, albeit subtler manipulating form, thinking the goal justifies the means.

Nowadays, children and youth are more open and articulate than in earlier times. But they are not necessarily more apt of expressing themselves in a personal way. It can be helpful to know that most children and adolescents use their own *code* of language when trying to express serious conflicts or dilemmas in their lives. There is no official key to these codes. Our experience is that both young children and adolescents have a tendency of understating the pain and seriousness of their problems. Often, the need to be *seen* in their distress is neglected in favor of being *normal* and to not causing their parents to worry.

In the following we introduce basic conversational principles and concepts which are equally successful in individual conversations with children, adolescents or adults and in dialogues with groups or whole school classes. We have decided, however, to place the main focus on the one-to-one relationships. The professional contact to the individual child determines the contact and interaction to a group as a whole.

Personal Language

We have searched in vain for researchers and theoreticians whose work is devoted to what we call personal language. Below we therefore attempt to delimitate and summarize experiences of personal language in the context of our long-term work with private, educational, counseling, supervisory and therapeutic interactions. We are interested in personal language as a medium in interpersonal contact, conflict resolution and mutual development. But before starting in, we will take a look at other *languages* relevant in pedagogical context.

Social Language
Social language is the language code best suited for less personally committing areas: when we meet someone in front of the cinema, a stranger on the train, colleagues in the cafeteria, our hairdresser or when we get to know new people. The main characteristic of social language is that it allows regulating the degree of personal distance. It is a way of speaking which enables keeping a maximum distance or to slowly allowing close-

ness to develop without making oneself vulnerable. This type of language is what most parents expect when they tell their children to *speak nicely*. It includes generalizations, common phrases and stereotypes. It is entirely unsuitable in situations seeking the resolution of personal and interpersonal conflicts.

Academic Language

This type of language is appropriate for analyzing specific problems, formulating hypotheses and establishing theories. Its value lies in creating standards and facilitating communication and understanding within and between different theoretical disciplines. Academic language strives for objectivity. It helps analyze conflicts which we are not part of, but it is also entirely unsuitable for processing personal and interpersonal conflicts.

Subject-Specific Language

This type of language, like technical terminology or pedagogical terminology, is a necessary component of establishing an identity inside and on the outside of a specific subject. It establishes security by giving words and concepts the same significance for everyone involved. In addition, subject-specific jargon is a less precise and more stereotypical version of subject-specific language. It is valuable as a type of tribal language used by a small circle of insiders. Subject-specific language strives for the same level of objectivity as academic language and is equally unsuitable for the processing personal and interpersonal conflicts. Both subject-specific language and jargon are valuable for understanding relationships from the outside, e.g. within the framework of supervision. Subject-specific language is particularly important for mediation competence, but not for relational competence.

Pedagogical Language

In its current form, pedagogical language is primarily characterized by its evaluative, suggestive and advisory expressions, which range from objective to manipulative and instructive to complacent. When it is used objectively it supports the teaching competence but it can have destructive influence on relational competence. The objective form can also aid solving conflicts to a certain degree, provided that the teacher is not involved him-/herself. This language, however, is not helpful in individual professional relationships to children and parents.

Personal Language

When talking about *personal* language we use language in the broadest sense of the word.

Personal language conveys personal thoughts, values and emotions of the individual as authentically as possible. This means that internal feelings and external expression correspond. In addition, speaking in this way always enables a process of insight for the speaker him-/herself. Personal language is the most authentic way of expressing the individual's integrity in any kind of situation.

Personal language differs from other languages in two ways. For one it focuses on *subjectivity* and *individuality* opposed to objectivity and generalization, and for the other it seeks *expression* rather than analysis and description. It is similar to the personal expression of musicians making their own music rather than playing according to the notes, or actors enacting a role in a personal way rather than merely replicating text.

In the professional context, it is an important component of relational competence and most relevant for establishing contact, expressing appreciation and managing daily short-term conflicts, including real problem solving. To better understand inter-relational dynamics, we have differentiated the concepts: conflict and problem. A *conflict* is about having different opinions or needs. This can be between people within a relationship as well as an inner conflict within an individual. *Problems* are an accumulation of related conflicts which have not been solved, at least not sufficiently. In this understanding, conflicts are a natural and necessary component of life and relationships. Problems however show the quality of relational competence.

Why do we need personal language?
- It gives *presence* and *clarity* in contact.
- It increases the speaker's self-esteem.
- It inspires personal acknowledgement and response of the one listening, which in turn increases their own self-esteem.
- It does not hurt the feelings nor does it devalue the wishes and needs of another.

Personal language is the first language. It is how children express themselves. By teaching obedience, personal expression is repressed to benefit learning a social language: *speaking nicely*. Both languages exist side by side. Usually, however, the development of personal language is neglected from school age onwards. The ability to discuss is generally appreciated more than the ability to express one's inner life. Consequently, in a way our capacity to speak personally slips into oblivion. What adds to this, is that the terms *personal* and *private* often get confused. In the educational world, there is deep skepticism about connecting the concepts behind *personal* and *pedagogy*, as well as *personal* and *professional*.[4]

Personal and Private

What is personal, and what is private? The terms fundamentally differ in their original meanings. In practice, however, they are often used as synonyms. We may, for example, rightly say that each personal reaction is private, for it is always partly triggered by a *personal* (= individual) pattern of behavior which originates from *private* relationships. Historically this discourse in pedagogy has polarized the personal and the professional dimensions. This became most obvious when training courses for early childhood education and social work were introduced and had to prove their usefulness over untrained staff. This polarity is still shows, for example in the treatment of addicts or the view on private foster families versus socio-pedagogical institutions, or in the way *mentoring* concepts are used in social work.

These debates have led to attempts to delimitate the personal dimension and determine synonymous terms, such as personal *dedication, humanity, passion* and *life experience,* to name but a few. Such terms closely relate to self-representation and moral judgement. Often, they imply that the others are comparably *un*dedicated, *in*human, cold, and ignorant. This inevitably leads to an irrational and subjective polarization of passion and *science* or *vocation* and *occupation*. Our definition of professional development and way of understanding the professional as a *personal-professional* or *professional person* is an attempt to avoid this and to see how far the teacher's personality should and can be developed and consciously integrated into professional behavior as an asset.

It is not sufficient to *just be yourself* in educational practice. In addition to theoretical knowledge experts and autodidacts alike need insight into the way their individual characters impact their professional relationships and into their personal ability to develop the quality of relationships. The alternative is to ignore, suppress or hide one's character. This, however, entails losing control over personal reactions as well as diluting personal responsibility.

We suggest understanding the *personal dimension* as the current ways of interacting of a person. In this case the interactions a teacher has as a person relating to another person, e.g. children or a group of children. The *private dimension* however are all experiences, thoughts and feelings a person has.

We see the personal dimension as an essential component of professional behavior. The private dimension is usually not relevant and if it substitutes the personal it is often destructive to professional relationships. This happens when private aspects create an illusion of contact and closeness, while not really enabling *personal* contact. They then only give more or less detailed knowledge of the private sphere of the other. The social basis of personal contact can possibly be strengthened if the teacher chooses to invite students to their home or to tell them about their private background. This, however, is neither a sustainable compensation for personal contact nor does it establish it.

We have seen numerous examples of children knowing very well how to take spontaneous private expressions of their teachers. For example, a teacher whose child was critically ill burst into tears one day in front of his students and explained his private situation. The response of the children was: *It's good to see that he's human too*. His tears - his *personal* expression – was a gift to the children and improved their relationship more than the private story about his sick child stirred empathy. Children often react very positively to distinct emotional outbursts, which give them a glimpse into the character beneath the role. The children's desire to know the *person* of a teacher is the need to see the personal part behind their professional role, and not the need to interact with the *private* person.

Personal language has both verbal and nonverbal interacting aspects, that we describe in more detail below

Verbal Aspects

Personal language is marked particularly by use of the personal pronoun *I* (followed by an *active* verb) as introduction to or delimitation of a personal statement. This is the clearest distinction from other ways of talking. Compared to academic language, personal language can appear unprofessional because of its subjectivity. Compared to social language, personal language may even appear offensive due to its intimacy and self-reference.

The verbal core of personal language is:
- I like/I dislike…
- I want to have/I don't want to have…
- I want to participate in/I don't want to participate in…
- I believe/think/guess/find/hear/feel/see…

These core phrases can be reinforced or nuanced depending on the situation and the person's character and sound like this:
- I would like…

- By no means do I want to participate in...
- I can imagine that ...

Impersonal expressions, however, cannot simply be personalized by using I as an introduction: *"I really can't see that you have any interest in this at all, Simon."* This utterance can be both a masked, impersonal judgement meaning *"You are not interested"*, or an empty, personal expression like *"I feel like I'm wasting my time on you, Simon, and I would like to know whether you are interested in what I'm saying or not."*

Similarly, personal expressions do not depend on *I* to be personal:
"It's so nice to see you working together like that ..."
This sentence creates a very different tone than the expression *"You're working together well today."*

I must be motivated from within, otherwise it deteriorates to an educational cliché. Therefore, a certain degree of personal discipline is necessary when developing personal language.

Authenticity urges the speaker to be open and, thus, more vulnerable than colleagues who mainly draw on impersonal forms of language. Yet, we want to question if latter really gets hurt less than the first.

Nonverbal Aspects

Nonverbal expressions have to correspond with verbal expressions to ensure credibility and substance. If a person (adult or child) is angry, his or her counterpart has to be able to see, to hear and feel his or her anger. The same applies if we are even-tempered, nervous, pleased, happy, committed, tired, frustrated or touched. Body language plays an important role in our perception of the other, and we generally pay great (often unconscious) attention to nonverbal aspects. This also means that we tend to think there is a *correct* body language. We think that professionals should be open and inviting when they deal with children or parents. This thinking turns body language into social language. This way it no longer is the authentic expression of who you are but turns it into a strategy to have an effect on others. This is the way it is used to train politicians and business people for the media. It makes sense to be aware of one's own body language as the most reliable expression of the personal disposition in a conflict and adapt the verbal expression accordingly. Both easily visible body language such as posture, facial expression or manual gestures, as well as less visible body language, such as tension, energy or pain, are important signals we send to others.

Anyone can see a gap between verbal and nonverbal expressions if it is obvious, e.g. when anger is veiled by a smile, or nervousness is hidden beneath a distorted, sarcastic facial expression. The distinct effect of congruent or incongruent expressions on the dialogue partner is very personal and individual. Usually, a congruent expression activates feelings of relief, relaxation, harmony or joy, while incongruent expression stirs unease or tension. On the side of the speaker the own inner perception is the sole judge, and on the outside the response of the other person involved gives us insight to the way we appear. But we ourselves are the only ones who can take over responsibility for the congruence of our expressions.

Insight and Development

Personal language is by no means always friendly and pleasant. Sometimes, thoughts and experiences are clear and precise and we still cannot seem to find the right words. And sometimes speaking out words adequate to our feelings activates our body language. Adults and children alike are challenged to search for and experiment with words until they can sense a fitting connection. Finding personal words is an act of inner insight which expands and changes our self-concept and strengthens our self-esteem. A variety of different phenomena encourage this insight. E.g. the speaker's realization that their own words are inconsistent or sensing the other person's confusion, feeling misunderstood or ignored. When trying to convey a certain content, we have to be aware of the other's understanding of the issue and seek explanations or images which fit the intellectual and cultural understanding of the other. Sometimes didactical strategies can support this. In conversations, we have to search our inner experience to find ways of communicating *authentically*.

Thanks to the growing influence of psychological and psychotherapeutic knowledge, human emotions are gradually complementing cognitive reasoning as a relevant component of professional relationships. But both disciplines are also responsible a current linguistic impasse: we distinguish between thoughts and feelings, but speak about feelings instead of actually showing them. As a result, we tend to use a semi-personal language, which often turns into a monolog which reduces the interest of the other or stirs feelings of guilt.

To be able to experience comfort and a positive feeling in interpersonal relationships it is necessary that we are aware of where we stand in relation to each other and are able to question our positions in case of doubt or insecurity. Everyone is able to deal with short-lived professional relationships, such as with an attorney, a doctor or a tax accountant where the professional competence is most relevant and can be taken independently of personal dynamics. In long-term relationships, we cannot choose between the two. Both levels play an important role and our motivation and personal gain decreases if we cannot bring ourselves into the relationship in a personal way. Just the same within the pedagogical world both sides involved in adult relationships (colleagues and parents) are confronted with situations in which they have to decide whether to open up or to give up.

In professional adult-child relationships it is in the adults' responsibility to help children find and express their authentic feelings and thoughts. Although children in general are less inhibited in interacting with adults they usually do not have the courage and ability to express themselves in a personal way. They need to be *seen* and invited so they dare show themselves. Authentic adult interaction provides children with a rich source of

inspiration as well as important models. Adults sometimes need to *lend* children personal language:
- *"You look like you don't approve of what I just said. Is that right?"*
- *"I can see that you're angry with me. I'd like to know what about."*
- *"Although you just agreed to my proposal, it seems like you would have rather said no. I'd actually prefer an honest no to a vague yes, if this is your real opinion."*
- *"Your face tells me you're upset about this. I'd like to know more about how you feel."*

This way personal language can become an integral part of acknowledging communication and a concrete demonstration of what it means to take over responsibility for relational quality. Teachers often work with a less nuanced interpretation of this, they only feel responsible for creating a *positive* relationship, which is understood as the overall relational character. To illustrate this, we would will embed one of the above invitations in a dialog:

DIALOGUE 1

Teacher: *I can see that you're angry with me, Nikolai. I'd like to know what exactly you are angry about.*
Nikolai: *I just think it's unfair.*
Teacher: *What do you think is unfair?*
Nikolai: *Why am I given so much homework if I just can't manage it?*
Teacher: *I think you're capable of doing as much as your classmates. This is why I said that. But I see that you think differently, I can see that. Tell me what you think.*
Nikolai: *Yes, but I just think this is unfair.*
Teacher: *Alright. So, tell me about what you think would be fair.*
Nikolai: *I don't know.*
Teacher: *That's okay. Please think about it and tell me what you've found out later.*
Nikolai: *But why?*

> *Teacher: Because it's important to me to treat you right. It's no use if I'm happy but you're not.*

The teacher in this example will have to come back to the topic later during the day or week. It is her responsibility to keep the interaction open on this issue. It is not important in this situation that the teacher gets a clear and useful answer: the process is more relevant than the content of a possible answer, for the boy is learning to come to terms with the injustices in this world.

Before analyzing the relational qualities of this conversation, we would like to consider another possible version:

DIALOGUE 2

> *Teacher: What's wrong with you, Nikolai? Why are you so mad all of a sudden?*
>
> *Nikolai: I just think this is unfair.*
>
> *Teacher: This is nonsense! Why would you need a special treatment? You don't have to do more and you don't have to do less homework than anybody else.*
>
> *Nikolai: But what if I just can't do that much homework?*
>
> *Teacher: Well, I don't know what it is that keeps you from doing your assignments. Do you want me to talk to your parents?*
>
> *Nikolai: No, but...*
>
> *Teacher: You just have to make sure to get everything done in time. I can't treat you differently just because you think everything else is more important than school. That would not be fair towards the other children who do their homework in time. Just do what you're supposed to do so we don't have to waste any more time on this!*

(The teacher tries to remember to pay special attention to Nikolai's work in the future and to talk his parents at the next conference, if necessary.)

Analysis of Dialogue 1:

I can see that you're angry with me, Nikolai. I'd like to know what exactly you are angry about.

The teacher openly states that she thinks Nikolai is angry. She is aware that children have general difficulties expressing their anger towards adult authorities and that the boy's suppressed anger can have an adverse impact on their mutual relationship. She therefore helps him find words to talk about his anger and takes his feelings seriously.

I just think it's unfair.

Nikolai confirms that he is angry.

What do you think is unfair?

The teacher acknowledges Nikolai's subjective experience and assumes shared responsibility for the situation.

Why am I given so much homework if I just can't do it?

Nikolai is gradually moving from general to specific statements.

I think you're capable of doing as much as your classmates. This is why I said that. But I see that you think differently, I can see that. Tell me what you think.

The teacher clearly states her position and her motivation. At the same time, she accepts the boy's differing opinion of her well-meaning intentions. Consequently, she invites him to specify his position and clarify the problem between them.

Yes, but I just think this is unfair.

Nikolai lacks the words to express his thoughts, but he sticks to them.

Alright. So, tell me about what you think would be fair.

The teacher tries to invite a more nuanced and precise expression.

I don't know.

However, Nikolai feels stuck.

That's okay. Just think about it and tell me what you've found out later.

The teacher knows that children often feel uncomfortable if they are unable to make themselves understood: she recognizes this by stating that it is okay. Then, she refers to his inner responsibility and once again emphasizes her interest in the questions that remain unanswered.

But why?
Either Nikolai does not consider the situation so important, or he needs further proof of the teacher's honest interest.
Because it's important to me to treat you right. It's no use if I'm happy but you're not.
The teacher once again confirms her interest in their mutual relationship and, moreover, emphasizes the importance and validity of Nikolai's response.

In this example, Nikolai's teacher shows that she *sees* him, takes him serious and accepts his view on their relationship. She assumes full responsibility for the interaction, yet does not negotiate the content of Nikolai's anger, which is the amount of homework she assigns him with. She thus also makes clear that she does not question her professional responsibility. In doing so, she conveys a clear message to all other children, namely that they can expect to be taken seriously and can stick to their own inner responsibility and that she does the same for herself.

Analysis of Dialogue 2:

What's wrong with you, Nikolai? Why are you so mad all of a sudden?
The teacher here seems to urge Nikolai to justify his feelings, but at the same time using the word mad disqualifies his response in advance. Anger is one of the most fundamental human feelings; the word mad, however, is generally used to describe a person's reaction as childish and the expression, all of a sudden, signals that in addition the teacher considers his reaction out of place.
I just think this is unfair.
Nikolai still does not allow the teacher to disqualify his response and states his opinion.
This is nonsense! Why would you need special treatment? You don't have to do more and you don't have to do less homework than anybody else.
The teacher disqualifies Nikolai's thoughts even more openly than before. On top of this, she reveals that she has known what is bothering

him all along and that her interest is of pedagogical and strategic character rather than an honest interest in his problems.
But what if I just can't do that much homework?
Nikolai holds on to his integrity.
Well, I don't know what it is that keeps you from doing your assignments. Do you want me to talk to your parents?
The teacher's answer to his question is merely rhetorical, meaning: 'There is nothing more important than homework, and if you have a different opinion on this, I will team up with your parents.'
No, but...
Nikolai is slowly realizing that his contribution to the conversation merely is causing the teacher to get aggressive.
You just have to make sure to get everything done in time. I can't treat you differently just because you think everything else is more important than school. That would not be fair towards the other children who do their homework in time. Just do what you're supposed to do so we don't have to waste any more time on this!
The teacher immediately interrupts Nikolai and takes up the first word which fits into her approach, following the credo 'Anything you say will be used against you'. Afterwards, she declares him an outsider and signals that it is not important to her that he feels treated unjustly, because he is not one of the *good* children, while paradoxically claiming he is just like the others.

In this *conversation*, the teacher is only demonstrating her power and Nikolai can only lose. The teacher's moral approach is obvious: I give orders and you obey! Her message to the boy's classmates is equally obvious: whoever disobeys her is the scapegoat. She has thus conveniently created her own moral justification. From an ethical perspective, however, her behavior is highly questionable, conveying that anybody who does not behave in line with her moral expectations risks personal violation and social isolation.

The two teachers' moral concepts are not only different but also incompatible. Although both feel equally responsible for Nikolai's progress in school, the teacher in example one approaches the boy as an equal in a process of mutual development and the latter teacher only reacts to the boy's role as a pupil of hers. The first teacher refers to his inner responsibility and raises expectations; the other exerts power and demands obedience.

A main reason why these moral approaches are incompatible is that the demand for obedience can be increased, reduced, reinforced and democratized, while the demand for responsibility and integrity cannot. It is possible to be partly obedient to authorities and partly disobedient, but one cannot be partly or only temporarily responsible for oneself.

The majority of (Scandinavian) teachers would probably distance themselves from the abuse of power in conversation but tend to regress to this way of interacting for safety when feeling pressured or helpless. The same applies to many parents. As a consequence, children are confronted with two incompatible forms of adult behavior, which most children under the age of twelve or 13 are unable to read and react to cognitively, although they certainly feel the inconsistency. This experience is destructive to the children's self-perception as well as their perception of adults. What is even worse though is that this causes uncertainty and confusion about the idea of inner responsibility. This experience conveys that if it is easy for me to be with you, I have clear values, However, if it is difficult to be with you, your behavior defines the value according to which I react. In other words, the quality of my behavior is your responsibility.

Thus, the overarching responsibility for the adult behavior is transferred to the children, which is destructive to all parties involved. A similar situation can be found in couples, where one partner alternates between hot and cold, closeness and distance, affection and indifference without the other seeing the reason for these fluctuations. Children often lose their trust in the values of adults as well as faith in their own values. The lack of *consistency* in their own behavior tempts these adults into believing that it is necessary to let children feel the *consequences* of their behavior. Superficially, the situation may appear as if the children were in charge; but in effect, it is the adults' lack of integrity and authority, which has a destructive impact on both sides and is defining the situation.

The most effective means of preventing problems in the pedagogical context is teachers using personal language in connection with the expectation that the children need to develop their own personal language as well. This affects existential, individual and social issues and thus pedagogical issues.

To illustrate what we mean we will work our way *from the end to the beginning* and in a first step look at children and adults who are in need of socio-psychological or therapeutic treatment. Professional experience suggests that the long-term results of such treatments directly relate to the clients' ability to enhance their level of self-awareness and self-respect (self-esteem) and to personally express themselves in relationships. These abilities are just as essential to our existential and social quality of life as the ability to discuss opinions and as stepping in for personal issues is for the development of intellectual and democratic processes.

Many teachers are skeptical of this approach. They fear that this kind of *psychologizing* in school will foster egocentric attitudes. This skepticism is unfounded, for we can observe the following: the less a person is able to cope with or express personal conflicts and dilemmas, the higher the tendency for self-destructive or antisocial behavior and to shun dynamic interpersonal and social relationships. In this case, one's behavior is not determined by integrity and inner responsibility but by the chaos and the pain that destructive adult-child relationships leave. The phenomenon which is often referred to as self-centeredness is almost always a result of situations in which *significant others*[5] have failed to care for the *self* of the person concerned. Self-centeredness is necessary, yet is not dynamic, neither from an existential nor a social view.

According to our experience there is no reason to believe that showing respect for individuals gives rise to an unhealthy individualism. Rather, a substantial lack of respect and empathy towards others is one of the most reliable indicators for narcissism[6].

Differentiation and Respect

For a long time, adult-child relationships were built on the expectation that children have to learn how to respect adults. In reality, however, children merely learned how to fear adults, based on an emotional spectrum ranging from fear based on bad experiences and used as a strategy to deep seated angst. Over the past years, these phenomena have decreased, which is why room for honest and mutual respect is growing, respect for the personal integrity of the other. The use of personal language is a key factor in this development. Pedagogical consequences in turn become redundant, because they contradict *mutual* respect.

Children are no different than adults: they prefer to be with people who respect them and whom they have respect for. Two essential aspects enable mutual respect: on the one hand, the tone of the adult has to express respect for the child, and on the other hand this has to be authentic. This creates a foundation for developing respectful relationships, while at the same time teaching the child how to show respect other people and not the power they represent.

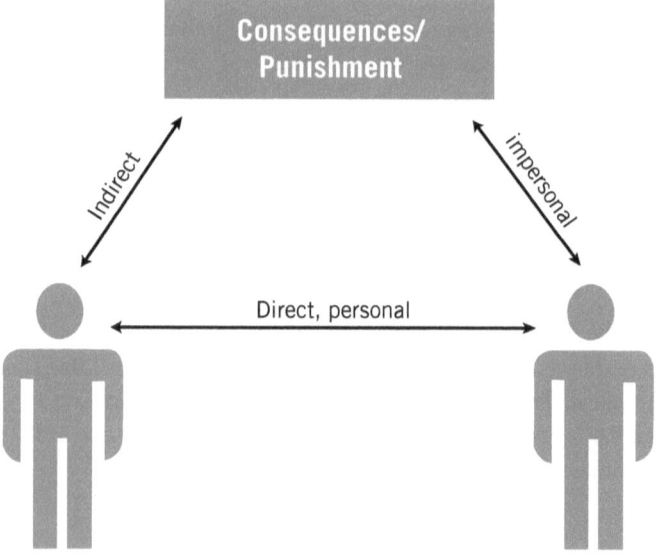

Direct, personal communication is replaced by indirect, impersonal communication that relies on consequences.

In this illustration, mutual respect is missing. Therefore, the adult relies on consequences and punishment, hoping to gain the child's respect. The message implied is: *I give up on asking you to respect me and, instead, create a situation between us which you have to respect.* This message is self-destructive, because it elicits discomfort, fear, strategically planned behavior or apathy rather than respect.

An integral part of traditional child rearing was the adult setting limits and in doing so also limiting their developmental possibilities. Today, adults are challenged to get to know their own boundaries if they want to remain intact while interacting with children and adolescents.[7]

Equal Dignity

Our intention using the terms equality and equal dignity is to draw attention to the fruitful and ethical value of ascribing equal human worth and of recognizing the equal amount of respect people deserve, even if they are not equal but differ in status and power.

Equal dignity means that the views, emotions, perceptions and self-concepts of the persons involved are given the same priority in establishing and developing the relationship. No one should be disqualified just because one of the parties involved considers the other's behavior childish, unrealistic, adult, mature, immature, typically female or male or the like.

Ensuring equal dignity as a relational quality is not necessarily easier in symmetric, than in asymmetric relationships. It may be just as difficult with a know-it-all or an extraordinarily modest colleague as with a five-year-old child.

The historical tradition of hierarchy, social pecking order and inequality is still much more visible than striving for equal dignity we are aiming for. One of the reasons why we do not see equality as an a priori moral demand but as an ethical quality we are free to choose, is that asymmetric relationships do not per se entail a tradition of equal dignity. Equal dignity is not a goal but a virtue that can be lived and nonetheless is out of reach sometimes.

Dignity is often defined from a *social* perspective. In this book, we talk about *personal dignity* and use the term as a synonym for personal integrity. People whose integrity is violated often feel like they are simultaneously deprived of their human value and dignity.

Relationships based on equal dignity arise from *mutuality*. This means that none of the sides involved can define rules that bear the risk of knowingly violating the integrity of the other. In everyday life, this is much more complicated than it may appear.

We can, for example, see a Muslim girls' reluctance (and of her parents) to use the communal showers with the other children after PE class as a cultural issue or as an expression of their personal integrity. The other children as well as their parents are likely to first and foremost base their argument on their religious and cultural integrity. And yet this cultural integrity is often also personal. This is true to the extent to which the individual *lives* religion instead of *having* a religion.

In practice, this means that the norms and rules of an institution have to be developed in a continuous dialogue with the children and parents concerned. Living and growing up in a traditional Muslim culture of obedience, parents and children *may* perceive this approach as undignified. In fact, relationships of equal dignity can be equally enervating and time-consuming as democratic processes. And it is up to the institutions themselves to elevate equal dignity to one of their central educational values.

Where both content and process are priorities of the agenda, equal dignity is reflected both on the large and on the small scale of relationships.

EXAMPLE

A group of children between three and six years was getting dressed to go outside. In passing, a father remarked:

"Aren't you too young to zip your coats yourself? You're way too young to do this on your own!"

"No, we're not – stupid", one of the boy's replied. This prompted the father to give a lecture about the importance of speaking nicely with other people. One of the teachers chimed in:

"You wouldn't like it either if we didn't speak nicely with you."

Another boy, who obviously disapproved of the situation, answered: *"Then my dad will come."*

The father involved said: *"Oh come on, as if he'd be able to take it up with us!"*

"Yes he would!", the boy objects with a confused and unhappy look on his face.

As the English saying *'never kid a kid'* says, self-adulation embedded in irony has never had a helpful effect on small children, and the dignity of all concerned is at stake.

EXAMPLE

An eighth grade was about to have a French class. France had just performed an atomic bomb test in the Pacific Ocean. Walking towards the classroom, the teacher already saw the children sitting in front of the door on the floor. They had decided to boycott French class to protest against France.

The teacher took this decision seriously: she talked to her students about the background and about how they could make their protest heard by responsible authorities. The adolescents decided to write a protest note in French addressed to the French government. They also created posters in Danish and French to express their opinion. Thus, they spent a perfect French class!

The teacher could have just as well taken the adolescents' protest personally and treated it as an attempt to duck out of French class. She could have made an effort to lure the pupils into the classroom, yet the class would have turned out very different due to a lack of a dialogue based on equal dignity.

EXAMPLE

Thea was a first grader in an international school. After two months in this school she came home obviously upset about something. Her parents got her to tell them about the reason for her anger, which turned out to be an educational invention of a teacher. This teacher had decided to hang up a board with the names of all the children in the classroom. Each day, she attached a small magnet, either with a happy face or an angry face, next to each name. Thea had watched this for a while and she just could not understand why she had gotten three angry faces in a row: "I've never been angry in class!"

Her parents explained: "The magnets don't mean that the teacher thinks you were angry on a specific day. They mean that she was angry with you."

Thea thought about this and concluded in a happy tone: "But why didn't she just tell me that?" Thea knows more about equal dignity than her teacher.

Acknowledgement

The word acknowledgement can have a double meaning. There may be doubt about whether it refers to *praise* or to the kind of acknowledgement which Berit Baa and the Norwegian psychologist and researcher Anne-Lise Løvlie Schibbye[8] described. This definition does not include praise, but exclusively describes acknowledgement which one might also call *affirmation*.

Acknowledgement is not a technique of communication, but a way of talking based on the ability and willingness to be open and sensitive to children's inner reality and self-concept and include it.

Openness is a teachers' way of understanding and accepting a child's perception of reality as equal to their own and seeing the fact that a child's perception can reveal essential information about the character and quality both of their relationship as well as the child's self-concept. As an adult, you have to give up control and the power to define *reality*. Openness also includes the adults' openness towards themselves, their own thoughts, emotions and views.

Sensitivity is the ability and willingness to react to a child's self-concept with curiosity, astonishment, interest, empathy and reflection. This sensitivity does not rely on knowing but on the possibility of paving the way to understanding.

If adults want to include the child's subjective perception of reality and self-concept, they also need to be willing to accept this perception and way of expression as equally valid to their relationship. In addition, they need to be capable of supporting a child's verbal expression.

Berit Baa writes:

> Acknowledgement is a *lifestyle* or an *attitude* and not a *communication strategy*. To show acknowledgement means to use one's full self, emotionally as well as intellectually. It is not about tricks or techniques but about that which comes from inside.[9]

In her famous novel 'To Kill a Mockingbird' the American author Harper Lee[10] provides a great example in the interaction between the father (Atticus) and his daughter, that shows the main difference between acknowledgement and traditional parenting very obviously:

> Aunt Alexandra was fanatical about my attire. I could not possibly hope to be a lady if I wore breeches; when I said I could do nothing in a dress, she said I wasn't supposed to be doing things that required pants. Aunt Alexandra's vision of my deportment involved playing with small stoves, tea sets, and wearing the Add-A-Pearl necklace she gave me when I was born; furthermore, I should be a ray of sunshine in my father's lonely life. I suggested that one could be a ray of sunshine in pants just as well, but Aunty said that one had to behave like a sunbeam, that I was born good but had grown progressively worse every year. She hurt my feelings and set my teeth permanently on edge, but when I asked

Atticus about it, he said there were already enough sunbeams in the family and to go on about my business, he didn't mind having me the way I was.

Acknowledgement is a foundation for developing self-esteem and personal responsibility as well as adult guidance. However, in many cases the pedagogical practice of *evaluative communication* impedes a positive development in all three areas.

Acknowledging Communication

Children are consistently confronted with experiences which make lasting impressions. While the children physically sense this, they lack words and concepts to describe their feelings. This is one reason they are often expressed in inarticulate ways. The first few months after birth, babies use gross motor activity and sounds. In time, they add to their body language by drawing on fine motor activity and their vocal cords as well as language. The expression of impressions is very individual and personal. Although most children cry when they fight with others, they have very different boundaries. Although all children experience frustration at one point or another, they all have their distinct way of showing it. Although all children have an ability to be happy and experience delight, the situations which spark these feelings vary from child to child.

The process begins with the children perceiving the impressions of their environment. Over time, these impressions are *cultivated*, that is, shaped by the culture and the family in which the child grows up. An example is *Boys don't cry*, while girls are allowed to cry. Culture plays a decisive role in how an impression is expressed by a child. Cultural norms categorize impressions in *right* or *wrong*. In the beginning, the parents as well as other caregivers are the most important cultural agents. They are responsible for the impressions children are allowed to express freely and the ones they suppress. They are also responsible for creating a balance between the child's self-concepts and the adults' perceptions. In the end, it is the adults' use of language which determines the right words.

The psychologist Agnete Diderichsen[11] uses yet another different terminology in her description of reciprocity as a necessary prerequisite for the development of the self, feeling of self and self-esteem in infants:

> In interdependency, the child expresses an internal stimulus, emotion or an inner tendency, which the caregiver reacts to. Thus, the child expresses a part of itself which Winnicott describes as 'original spontaneity' of the self. Through the caregiver's empathetic response, the child's self (and its emotions) is acknowledged and gets a frame of reference, which confirms the infant's existence. In interacting with the caregiver, the child gains two early experiences: 1. the experience of its own ability to influence the environment, e.g. by attracting attention or inducing contact, and 2. the experience of how others (the caregiver) react to the child (the self).
>
> These two experiences are important elements in the development of the self. From the very beginning, they are interconnected by a shared nucleus. They constitute the genetic root for the child's striving for, and perception of competence as a part of feeling of self and self-esteem. The child's feeling of self thus corresponds to its perception of personal emotions as real and an integral part of the self, where self-esteem corresponds to the feeling of being of worth.

There is probably not a more accurate way of explaining the relation between self-esteem, motivation and learning.

Parents and teachers are responsible for both the quantitative and qualitative development of a child's self-esteem. In our culture, we have a rather flexible approach to psychic values (e.g. crying is ok if you lose) in favor of moral concepts or other stereotypes related to gender and age. It is up to the individual family and institutions to determine norms and to decide what is healthy mentally and culturally acceptable.

Consequently, there can be huge qualitative differences in the adults' use of language when confronted with a crying child.

- *"Why are you crying?"*
- *"You sure are tired."*
- *"Now don't make such a fuss again!"*
- *"I can see that you're sad, but I don't know what about..."*

The last of the above statements pins down the child's emotional state with just one word and, what is more, does not contain an evaluation. The first three statements, however, confront the child with words that have negative connotations and indirectly judge their emotions. By giving wrong descriptions, which neither improve nor specify the personal experience and quality, words distort the quantitative dimension of the child's self-esteem. The child thus learns to distance itself from the feelings it experiences when confronted with sadness, unhappiness or frustration.

The last statement acknowledges the child's inner perception. In the long run, this enables the child to also correct adults in cases where they don't get the words right: *"No, I'm not sad. I'm mad at Karoline, because she..."*

EXAMPLE

Together with three other children three-year-old Mia was helping her teachers set the table in the red classroom. They learned how to arrange knives and forks and where to place the plates so that they were right in front of the chairs. Mia was getting tired and losing interest in the task. Realizing this, the teacher had two possibilities: Either providing an educational training or taking care of Mia's personal development. She turned to Mia and said: "I can see that you're tired, Mia, I'll help you set the table."

The teacher also could have said: *"I can see that you're tired, Mia, but you should finish setting the table before you leave."*
Also note that these are often said in different tones of voice.
Usual alternatives to the latter include:
"Mia, are you really done? Do you think we should use our fingers to butter our bread?"

"You can't possibly be tired yet. Come on, Mia, there's still one knife missing on the table."

In these cases, the tone of voice can be very hurtful, and convey that it is wrong to feel the way she does.

EXAMPLE

Emil's (3) language abilities were not well-developed. He was in a group of children whose verbal communication skills were considerably better than his. So far Emil had predominantly experienced that his signals were ignored, misunderstood or misinterpreted by the environment. He had tried to connect with other children by poking them, pulling their hair, hitting or biting them. The adults' reactions to his behavior were usually the same: "Emil, stop! You know that it's not okay to hit others. Don't you see that they won't want to play with you if you hit them? Why don't you just ask them if they want to play with you?"

Of course, the intentions are good: the teacher wants the child to change his way of connecting with other children and teach him manners so he will receive positive reactions from others.

But Emil is neither able to understand this message nor to learn from it. The teacher's tone of voice is reproachful, so the way she connects to the boy is very similar to the way he tries to get in contact. Moreover, her negative tone of voice conveys that the boy does not fit here the way he is. On top of this, her statement is simply too complex for the child to appropriately react to it.

If the teacher really wants to reach the Emil, she could start by saying: *"Hi Emil, you look like you want to play with someone. Is that right?"*

If Emil confirms this, she could continue: *"Is that hard for you?"*

If Emil's answers yes again, the teacher could say: *"I'd like to help you, if that is what you want."*

Thus, Emil might feel seen and acknowledged for the first time. This would automatically cause him to invest in his relationship with the teacher. Later, his relationship with the other children can also develop in a positive direction. Just like all of us, Emil needs at least one person who appreciates our very being, before he can change his behavior for the better.

EXAMPLE

Mads was in first grade. When his class teacher was around he was always boasting. He talked a lot and sought attention. The teacher thought of him as a boy who only felt comfortable in the center of the others' attention. She believed Mads was a typical only child, spoiled, ill-bred and without a sense for the boundaries and needs of other people – one of these 'little egoists' from postmodern families, as children like Mads are commonly called.

His family background fit this picture and was typical for children with this behavior. His parents were in their late thirties. They had a good education, made career, and now were leading the life they had always wanted to. They were thriving on the thought of being good parents. Just like any parent, they wanted the best for their child. They emphasized intellectual talent and communicative competence. Mads was naturally talented and quickly learned how to talk, produce arguments, complete puzzles, write his name and use the computer. He was used to being admired by adults.

Mads' parents are very much like the parents we described in Chapter 2: they do not want to limit Mads' possibilities and therefore rarely say no and, instead, halfheartedly agree to entertaining him, playing with him, reading or listening to him. They spend a lot of time working and don't want their time with Mads to be burdened by conflicts. In cases where they finally say a clear no, they are usually so exhausted and frustrated that their tone of voice tells Mads that he is out of place and the cause of their frustration. Since they simultaneously try to be perfect parents, they rarely are authentic in contact with their son. The boy's experience of this situation is that contact to him as a person is not worthwhile. As a consequence, he settles for the second-best option available: he is rarely seen for who he is, but often praised for his abilities and achievements, which his parents openly appreciate. His self-esteem has had little opportunity to develop. He is socially insecure and relies on what he is praised for, which is to talk and present his intellectual and his linguistic competence. He wants others to listen to and to watch him, hoping that he will be *seen* eventually.

His teachers react by pointing out what the boy is *not* able to do, like sitting quietly, keeping still, being just one of the group, speaking when he is asked, etc. These are the things they are trying to teach him, which would be reasonable pedagogical goals if the situation was actually about understanding math or sports. Yet, since it is about his personal behavior, this method is counterproductive and reinforces the problems instead of reducing them.

If the teachers start to give the boy what he is missing then positive development will occur. What he needs is authentic, warmhearted, differentiated, honest and acknowledging contact. This means that his teachers need to take time to relate to Mads as person (does not take more time and energy than they waste on telling him what to do). They have to establish eye contact with Mads when he comes to class, and acknowledge his presence with a friendly nod, followed by a *"Hello, Mads"*. In this way, they can show that they see him, that he has their attention and that they are willing to help him integrate into the class as good as they can. Since Mads has obvious difficulties expressing himself, it is important that his teachers react with sensitivity and help him find words to express himself. Of course, Mads is very articulate, but he lacks personal language. It is essential that the teachers' approach is reflective and not moralizing and instructive. In cases where the boy finds it difficult to sit still while another child is getting attention, they could say: *"I can see that it's difficult for you to wait. Just let me know if this is too much for you."*

In other cases, however, the teachers may also be challenged to confront the boy with their definite authority: *"Mads, I want you to be quiet now! No, Mads, I don't want to talk to you right now. I'm just talking to Sune!"*

(As in so many similar cases, all parties involved get the most benefit out of the situation if the child's parents recognize that they have to change their behavior as well and also show the willingness to do so.)

EXAMPLE

Amalie, two years old, went to see the head of the kindergarten, who was sitting in front of her desk.
"What are you doing?", Amalie asks.
"I'm writing. What about you?"
"I'm Amalie... What are you doing?"
"I just told you, I'm working."

In the above example, Amalie expresses a child's typical need to be acknowledged in their existence through adult presence, contact and appreciation. Amalie is likely to keep asking her question until the adult finally recognizes her need. If she does not recognize it, Amalie might give up or find a way of forcing her to focus her attention on the girl.

Obviously, the teacher has a lot of work to do and does not appreciate being interrupted. She feels like she cannot simply *reject* Amalie and therefore offers vague contact. Amalie might be sad if she were sent away directly, but it would not hurt her personally nor the mutual relationship. A clear, appreciative and personal answer is all that Amalie needs: *"I know you'd like to talk Amalie, but I don't, because I have to work. Why don't you go to Bente and see if she's got time?"*

This answer would provide contact as well as a clear message, which would not force her to react to an ambiguous statement. It may not be what she wants, but she will not feel out of place. At the same time, the director would show how to make one's limitations clear to others, without conveying the feeling that they are wrong.

Children who do not receive acknowledgement often have to cope with an inner critic for the rest of their lives, which is detrimental to their self-esteem and creates social insecurity. But the need for acknowledgment is not only a matter of childhood. Time and time again, most of us need it to develop new and empathetic perspectives on our existence.

To a certain degree, acknowledging communication is essential for children to develop so-called *personal/emotional competence*[12], which in turn is necessary to develop social competence. This is because the children's perception of how they are treated by their social environment is decisive for their ability to integrate into and deal with different communities.

Evaluative Communication

The above-mentioned quote about the *power to define* by Berit Baa describes the way a child's character and intentions are categorized based solely on the background of the child's visible behavior and its interpretation by the adults. Parents have done this for a long time. This way of communicating is characterized by evaluating what the child is like and what it should be like seen from the adults' perspective. The child's personal views are either ignored from the very beginning or disqualified during the process:
- *No, you're not being nice!*
- *You've been so nice and quiet today!*
- *Now go outside and play with the other kids. That's more fun than sitting in here and doing nothing!*
- *But you're really lazy today!*
- *Now don't you get cheeky!*
- *Alright, kiddo, but I'm the boss here!*

For obvious reasons, evaluative communication has prevailed in school more than in daycare centers. Schools have always prioritized the *content* dimension consisting of curricula and subjects and evaluated the students' performance as sufficient/ insufficient or right/wrong by providing precise subject-specific critique or positive feedback as well as formal grades.

Together with the absence of procedural thinking, this phenomenon has given rise to a simplistic and reductive conception of the human being, in which children (and by and large also adults) are reduced to their professional and social behavior. This conception still dominates schools and creates a culture according to which humans are either right or wrong. For many generations, the decision whether someone is right or wrong was based almost exclusively on moral guidelines. This moral basis, however, has gradually been complemented or replaced by psychological and psychiatric diagnoses.

But the actual problem is not whether a child's behavior defies current moral and behavioral rules, or whether a child is correctly diagnosed with Asperger's syndrome, ADD or Tourette's syndrome; the problem is that these facets of human behavior, which only make up a fraction of a person's character, suddenly define the entire identity. This violates integrity and prevents the human encounter which would provide the essential basis for a helpful relationship. Consequently, evaluative communication does not only reduce children to their most distinct problem, but also degrades the adult-child relationship to pedagogical strategy.

As it turns out, changing this part of educational culture is utterly difficult. The reason for this destructive behavior is not the adults' ill will, but rather to be found in the professional identity and self-image of teachers. They feel more committed to institutional goals than to the current relationships. This is partly due to personal insecurity and/or intellectual reluctance possibly related to the idea of having to give up the dichotomy of *right* and *wrong*. This is aggravated by the fact that most teachers believe that they represent the *right* side.

Educational goals should provide support, guidance and accompany a child to a stage they have *not yet* reached. In light of the interests and needs of society, and the need of children for inspiration, challenge and support in their social, motoric and intellectual development, these goals are absolutely justified. They only become problematic if they are given a higher priority than personal contact. This can impede a child's development of self-esteem and destroy the little self-esteem that weak and threatened children have been able to develop in their families. This shows how educational processes undermine educational goals.

We see two main reasons for this. The first reason is that children cannot distinguish the feedback they get for their actions and achievements from the feedback they get for personal qualities. If the reactions children get for their actions and achievements are judgmental or moralizing, they develop doubts about their value as a person; as a result, their self-concept is something that develops from the outside and not from the inside. This influences the way their self-esteem develops, it either stagnates or decreases. The second reason is a basic human reality that *personal development, (integrating new insights, findings and knowledge into our inner and outer behavior) needs self-acceptance as a starting point.* We are not able to develop or change anything personal on the basis of a negative self-concept. This is a fact, no matter if this negative self-concept is solely our own idea or something others confirm about us. Humans are neither *right* nor *wrong* – humans just are. We have to work with these humans exactly the way they are, to reach educational goals. The relationship is the way and not an obstacle on the way.

Pedagogical processes that focus on the future and specific goals are not only evaluative. And evaluations are not always negative. But these processes convey the message that adults are more interested in what you do or who you will become than who you are at this specific moment. Children with a healthy and strong self-esteem can be able to put up with this, however, most children have major problems doing so. Some cooperate *correctly* and use all of their energy to try and meet the adults' expectations. At the end of their time in school they have developed *good* character traits and low self-esteem. Others cooperate *in reverse* and stick to their right to be the way they are. They usually end up developing a *bad* character and an equally low self-esteem.

The intellectual reluctance to let the *culture of right and wrong* go, can also be the fear of going from one extreme to the other. The fear of having no guidelines and everything being indifferent. However, nihilism is not the answer. We are not talking about giving up attitudes or knowledge as part of professional identity. We are talking about the ethics of not abusing these attitudes or this knowledge to define others. Defining children and adolescents also gives them a problematic social role. Taking a child's self-perception seriously and integrating the relational perspective does not mean that adults have to ignore or step back from their own perceptions, goals and moral ideas and take on the child's views. It means creating a shared space, for who the child and the adult are *at this moment*, with opportunities allowing both sides to develop constructive interactions.

Part of teaching is conveying personal values and society's ideas about what is right or wrong. We do not question that this is a central educational task and are not interested in putting all moral values up for discussion. A successful transfer of moral values can only take place if these values are lived in professional relationships and this means enabling respectful, personal contact with each child.

The new development we see on a moral level is that children who are at the mercy of adults' power to define, have started to openly characterize adults in return. They call adults idiots, geezers, witches or similar things. The words used by children are not encoded academically, which makes them morally offensive. On a personal level, however, both the teacher's and the child's language are equally hurtful.

The daily praxis and contemporary professional demands (building on psychological healthy patterns) rely on acknowledging language. The listing below shows different areas, where change is occurring.

Then:	Now:
exertion of power	participation/inclusion
discipline	dialog/conversation
focus on the child's behavior	focus on the relationship
correction/instruction	empathy/care
Evaluative	acknowledging/reflected
role-based authority	personal authority

The Norwegian International Child Development Program (ICDP)[13], emphasizes the necessity for teachers' personal involvement similarly as we do. Here two teachers describe their experience:

"Due to this resource and relation-oriented educational approach and in particular to the eight issues of reciprocity, we have made progress in reaching an awareness that improves our personal communicative behavior and makes the humaneness of our educational approach visible. As special education teachers, we see that we can facilitate learning if we show interest and commitment on the professional, personal and social level."

"Being a teacher has become much easier and also more interesting once we recognized that things can be different. We now see problems as challenges instead challenges as problems."

These and many similar statements show that the program could be an International Child and Teacher Development Program.

The Quality of Contact

Children cooperate! If they do not feel in contact with a teacher, they start to behave as if the contact was bad or there was none at all. Many experts over the years have asked us: *How do we put this into daily practice if we are teaching a class of 28 students?*

The answer is that this is not possible all at once. If you want to have a thriving and dynamic contact with a class of 28 different children, you first have to get in contact with each one of them individually. Some children easily hear the tone of voice and *professional-personal* quality of a teacher and reach the calming conclusion that they are in good company. Others, however, need more than one piece of evidence of the teacher's competence to be sure they will be treated correctly. For some, this is the case because they are skeptical, while for others it is because of negative experiences.

When it comes to relational quality, children cannot be deceived over a longer period of time. They might be very interested in the appearance of a teacher, but it only lasts for a moment. There are numerous examples of older teachers who are *hopelessly old-fashioned* concerning their language and appearance, but whom children love after ten minutes and pay respect to throughout the whole time they work together. Little does it help to dress young and use teenage slang, if this disguises a person who does not dare act according to his or her age and personality.

Methods of establishing initial individual contact are countless and depend on the child's age. There are well developed, tried and tested methods: e.g. the tradition of the Italian village Pisoia, where children are given a small suitcase when they start going to kindergarten. Together with the parents and teachers the children are allowed to fill this suitcase with items that give their lives content and meaning: a doll, a photograph of the grandmother, holiday pictures or maybe a porcelain figure. Over the years, the same teacher regularly takes time looking through the content of the suitcase for about half an hour and listening to the child's stories and exchanging one thing for another to represent new stages or interests. When changing from kindergarten to school, a procession takes place in which the mayor leads the parents and children through the village to the school building. The new teachers at school take time right in the beginning to take a look at each child's suitcase. This effect reaches far beyond the first days at school. It is a practical interpretation of what the verb to relate means. Etymologically speaking, the root of the noun *relationship* means to *report about oneself*.

Another teacher built contact to his new pupils over the years by being interested in them. His usual approach was: *Listen, the idea is that I teach you sports. In order for me to be able to do this, I need to know two things. First of all, I need to know if you are interested in learning sports and, second of all, how you think you might be able to learn sports best.* Then he encouraged the children to draw their answers and explain the meaning of their drawings. The children's explanations always had an extraordinarily high quality and showed self-awareness and willingness to cooperate with the teacher.

The two approaches described only take about 15 – 30 minutes per child to be realized. This seems very efficient in contrast to the time which one spends later on conflicts and other difficulties arising from an insufficiently established contact. These methods or hundreds of similar approaches practiced by teachers are only effective if the method itself is not held for the *teacher* and if the adult's interest goes beyond *building contact for the sake of contact*.

The daily conflicts encountered in the first month are decisive for the common future. Should establishing contact not succeed, there is always the possibility to make a *break* and take a few hours (or less) to talk the matter through and start over. Should this fail, it is time to seek help from a colleague or a supervisor. The possible negative impact on a teacher's self-confidence is too high to let them go through this on their own.

Time and again the media reports on young teachers who have given up their job and looked for a new profession after only one or two years. They often refer to the bad manners of today's children which makes it impossible to establish an acceptable relationship with them. If we look at these reports in detail, we soon realize that many of the stories are examples of failed or misinterpreted collegiality and leadership. The same stories occur in adult education; but the child (and their parents) are missing as a scapegoat and makes it uninteresting for the media.

As advisors and supervisors, we experience that there is always a good reason why establishing contact with a specific child (or adult) developed in one way and not another. In most cases, failed contact has to do with the adult's lack of attention or insufficient training in relational issues. This does not mean that it is not difficult to establish fruitful contact with, for example, twelve-year-olds in an all-day school who have very different family backgrounds. Nor that it doesn't take a lot of effort to approach a class of seventh graders from eleven different nations and help them form a coherent group. But this is all part of being a teacher.

An interesting side note: teachers working with, for example, autistic, psychotic or physically disabled children hardly ever have complaints about difficult contact. In these areas, we usually see professionals with enthusiasm, commitment and heartfelt joy about situations in which there is good contact. This reveals how our *expectations* influence our perceptions of other people and the contact we establish with them.

We are convinced that children's and adolescents' trust, openness and readiness to be guided is the greatest compliment an adult can receive. Neither parents, nor teachers, have a natural entitlement to this.

Individual Student-Teacher Dialogues

Danish law, for elementary schools, does not specify the individual conversations between teachers and their pupils:

> §13 sect. 2: Evaluating the students' learning outcomes (output) is part of teaching. This evaluation provides the foundation for counseling the individual students and for planning future teaching.
> And §18 sect. 4: In each course and each subject, teachers and students are to work together to define the objectives that are to be achieved. The students' assignments are planned accordingly. Working methods and teaching materials are selected, as far as possible, in cooperation with the students concerned.

That means teachers need to decide for themselves whether they want to have individual conversations with students or not. Our experience, however, shows that implementing an annual evaluative talk with each pupil alone or as an individual in a group makes sense. We further recommend that children assume the role of the host and are allowed to plan conversations from sixth or seventh grade onwards. These evaluation talks have several advantages:

- From a child's perspective, ten years feel like an endless period of time, and although the end of a schoolyear and vacation divide this time into relatively clear sections, it is appropriate to set goals within specific timeframes.

- Evaluation, as used in this context, does not refer to grading but goes much farther. Evaluation is a *mutual* process: how are we doing in relationship to one another, to our job, socially and personally? What would we like to change the following year, and what are the wishes and needs we have concerning our relationship? Evaluative conversations encourage the personal responsibility of both the student and the teacher and helps keep the contact intact.
- Regardless of how the individual or group conversations proceed, the children involved get a chance to take their relationship with school serious and personal.

Our recommendation is to keep the conversations rather brief and focused, possibly under half an hour, and that the teacher openly expresses their opinions and observations right at the beginning. This usually makes children and adolescents feel more secure than if they are, expected to go first. Even if this might appear like a more democratic approach or conventional courtesy. Having them start, as explained previously, can take place later, once the children are familiar with the content, process and goal of the conversations. The fact that these have to be well-prepared is more obvious to teachers than it is to children in the beginning. Therefore, it is important to tell children that they have to prepare and what they have to prepare for. If a child still starts the conversation unprepared, it is not helpful to make a compromise. It makes more sense to stop and say something like: *Alright, Ole, you forgot it. This annoys me, because I basically wasted half an hour of my time. But let me know when you'll be able to come to this discussion prepared.*

It is usually more effective when adults take themselves seriously rather than telling the child about the seriousness of the situation. The first approach offers requirements and structure, while the latter conveys feelings of guilt. If aspects of both approaches are combined, the latter will always outweigh the first. During the first two to three years, it is also advisable to inform the parents about the conversations and ask them to help their children prepare, especially concerning the content. The teacher's approach in the conversation can focus on the aspects of their relationship which are presently most important to him or her.

EXAMPLE

Mette was attending fourth grade. She disliked math class and did not believe that she could handle it. From an objective point of view, her achievements were class average. The teacher therefore did not agree with her perspective. There are a few other children in her class who, unlike Mette, in fact had great difficulties with math and required the teacher's support. Mette was an insecure and careful girl who did not want to do anything which she had not clearly been encouraged to do. Therefore, she often asked for assistance.

The teacher was annoyed by this, because he knew that Mette was doing just fine and that there were other children who needed more help. Thus, his response to Mette's requests was not always appropriate:

"What is the problem now, Mette? Sit down and try it on your own, I know you can do it!"

"But I can't do this."

"Nonsense! Look, you just gotta do this... see, you got this."

The teacher was aware of his inappropriate behavior and, therefore, started the evaluative talk this way: "Listen, Mette, I'm sure you must have realized that I'm often annoyed with you, right?"

"Yes."

"This isn't because I think you're actually annoying; it's just because I can't understand why you think that you're bad at math, when I know for a fact that you are quite good at it. Do you know why you think this?"

"No, but I just feel like I'm not good enough."

"Well, I see. It's no use then if I think you're actually doing well. I can see that."

This was followed by a break in which both had time to think – and please note that breaks like this are essential!

"Mette, do you always get insecure about what you can do whenever you can't get it done in a first try?"

"Yes... maybe... not sure..."

"No, of course not, I don't know either. But we both have a problem that we need to try and solve together. You think you need help, I think

you need less help... Do you think it might be better if I, instead of getting angry with you, just told you: 'This is good enough, Mette, I will help you when I have more time.' Do you think you could continue on your own until I have time?"

"I guess..., maybe 'cause I really don't like it when you're angry with me."

"Okay. I'll try to change that. If I'm not mistaken, you're more insecure about math than you are bad at it. So, it won't be of help at all if I were angry with you all the time. Thank you for your help, Mette! Let's see if this will help us in future. Otherwise, we'll just have to talk again."

On the surface, this conversation may not have produced relevant results. Still, it bears the potential of reaching two important goals. First of all, it may help the teacher use his frustration in a more productive way by telling Mette about his expectations instead of just expressing his anger and reluctantly assisting her. Second of all, and as a direct consequence of this, Mette will find it easier to focus her energy on what she can do instead of on what she thinks she cannot do. In this case, it will be too long to wait until next year's evaluation conversation for a next evaluation of the situation. The teacher can talk to Mette for a few minutes along the way and see how things are coming along for both of them.

Evaluation conversations need to relate to problems dynamically and focus on the future rather than the past. It often happens that one party is unable to find a solution in the conversation, but can provide a relevant idea later on, if the conversation was of high quality. If it is difficult to relate to a student, it may be advisable to contact the parents and try and find common ground this way.

In kindergarten, there is no reason for this type of conversation. But occasional evaluations make sense.

EXAMPLE

Julie was almost four years old and had started going to kindergarten three months ago. She was rather quiet and the teachers were not sure about whether her interaction with other children was actually the way Julie wanted it to be.

"So, Julie, you've been in kindergarten for three months now. This is why I'd like to talk to you about how you like it here. I've talked to some of the other adults and we're all happy to have you here. What do you think? Do you like it?"

"Yes, it's much nicer here than in daycare... here we can do more."

"I'm glad to hear that... and I'm also a little surprised. I've been wondering about whether you think you can do all the things you want to do... like play with the other children or something like that?"

Julie looks out of the window and thinks for a while ...

"I play a lot... more than before... and it's my birthday soon. Do you know that?"

"Yes, that's right. I just wasn't thinking about it right now. Do you know how we celebrate birthdays here at kindergarten?"

"Sure! Do you really think I don't know that? Rikke just had his birthday."

"You're right. How do you celebrate your birthday at home?"

Julie received an opportunity to evaluate her first three months in kindergarten and the teacher got answers: Julie was ready to celebrate her fourth birthday in kindergarten.

Evaluation conversations assess relational processes and are part of the process at the same time. Moreover, they show children and adolescents that they are seen and are important. Children begin to differentiate early on between the two realities they live in: the inner, existential reality and the outer, social reality. Evaluation conversations are one of the few opportunities adults receive insight into this inner and existential reality of children and at the same time, they are a rare opportunity for children to be evaluated beyond their social reality. The professional content of these conversations can be structured; the parties involved can reach agreements and make plans. But the adults involved have to also leave space for personal and social and sometimes private matters.

Existential Conversations

Example

Niels, a twelve years old student, was sitting together alone with his special education teacher to learn Danish. All of a sudden, he said: "My dad died two months ago!"

His teacher was shocked. She knew that his father had been very ill, but she was taken by surprise by Niels sudden opening up about it, because he usually didn't say much. Many different thoughts crossed her mind at once: What should I say? This is awful? He might have a breakdown? How does he know that? Is it just his fantasy or really the truth? She was afraid to stir something in him she might not have been able to control afterwards. She started wondering about whether his class teacher was informed and what was to do. She decided he should talk to the school's psychologist, because she believed that Niels needed to talk to her about the situation.

Eventually she said: "Really? Is that what you think?" Niels responded by saying: "Yes, I know that, because he's not been eating, and if you don't eat, you cannot live longer than two months!" The teacher told Niels that today there are many ways to help, and that this wasn't always the fact.

After their conversation and over the course of the following days, the teacher thought a lot about Niels and his family. She talked to his class teacher, who decided to contact his parents and suggested talking to a psychologist. The parents, however, were not able to react at this point. they asked the class teacher to wait until they had regained some more energy.

As a short-term intervention, it can make sense if Niels talks to the psychologist. But first of all, he obviously chose his special education teacher as the one person he wanted to talk to most, and this with good reason. The teacher's thoughts about his situation were both precise and nuanced: she realized that he was afraid and had probably overheard some scraps of conversation, which made him draw his own conclusions. She realized that he was thinking about the situation a lot and had difficulty concentrating in school. She realized that he maybe was not able to sleep at night and that he must be angry and confused about what was happening to his family.

The main point is that Niels himself does not have a *problem*. He is confronted with the fact that his father is dying. This fact is overshadowing his entire life and will continue to do so for a long time. This is also the way it is supposed to be, when children lose their parents. Since the rest of his family does not have the strength to talk right now, Niels decides to cooperate with loyalty and willingness by contacting another adult whom he trusts. He acts in a very competent way and chooses a competent teacher whose only problem is that she isn't able to share all of her good and relevant thoughts and emotions with the boy. She obviously needs supervision more than Niels needs therapy. Supervision could help her find the courage to get back to Niels and tell him: *"I've had some time to think about what you told me about your father. I somehow couldn't tell you that I was really sad when I heard that your father was sick. I can imagine that you're thinking about this a lot and I'd like to talk to you about it if you're okay with that."*

When children and adolescents are confronted with sad events which deeply move them and bring about great changes in their lives, they need a person to talk with about their lives and their future. This person can be a parent, another family member or a teacher belonging to the child's closest social environment. But it can also be a more distant expert, such as an educational psychologist or social worker.

These existential conversations with children and teenagers draw on the same principles as all other conversations described in this book. However, concerning their emotional effects, they are different. They may stir up our own personal losses and crises and remind us of death, fear and loneliness.

EXAMPLE

As a young psychologist, Helle Jensen, co-author of this book, had the following experience:

I was asked to talk to a six-year-old girl who had just lost her four-year-old sister in a car accident. Just like many children in similar si-

tuations, the girl straightforwardly told me about how her sister was hit by a car after she had just gotten off the bus with her mother. I could easily imagine what it must have been like for her, but suddenly I was so overwhelmed by my own fear of loss that I was unable to continue talking to her. Since it was such an intense situation, I decided to get help from the child psychiatry department.

Today, I know that I would have simply needed a thorough supervision. I should have looked at my own way of relating to loss in more detail. I was able to put myself into the girl's situation, but I was not at peace with myself enough to be able to be with the girl and her pain.

Often, existential conversations with children about death, divorce or abuse not only confront us with our own existential questions and insecurities, but also with the content of the conversation per se. We have to acknowledge that we can be with the children, listen to them and be at their disposal as personally and authentically as possible. That we can acknowledge their feelings and thoughts, but that we cannot change anything about their lives. We can take care that they are not alone for a few moments, but we cannot take away their loneliness. We can hope that our presence will inspire them to go on and find their way. In many cases, children and teenagers are more aware of these fundamental facts than many adults. This also explains in part why they tend to withdraw in cases where adults seem too helpful or offer excessive comfort, or are unable to withhold their own pain and their personal loneliness.

EXAMPLE

Peter was in eighth grade and had always had difficulties with theoretical subjects throughout his time in school. Now he was supposed to discuss the possibilities for his future education together with the in-house youth counselor. Peter appeared disheartened and weary not having an idea and to not believing he there were any prospects he would like. When the counselor asked him about his ideas, the boy responded with 'don't know' and a resigned shrug.

This reaction can have different meanings. It may well be that the boy has lost the feeling for what he wants himself. It may be that he has lost his belief in the helpfulness of conversations with adults, when it is about himself. Maybe both apply, or neither. No matter what the reason, the boy's isolation and loneliness are so distinct that the youth counselor is urged to offer his help. The best way of doing this would be to express his personal thoughts: *Peter, I see that you find it difficult to talk about what you are interested in. I can imagine that you might have talked to a lot of grownups who wanted to help you but couldn't. I really don't know if I can be of any help, but I don't like that you're alone with all of this. This is why I'd like to try anyway.*

A more usual approach to handle this urge would be talking to the boy and emphasizing the importance of being a part of society and finding a way to enter into the labor market. But this is not helpful as long as the boy's personal situation is too serious for him to handle on his own.

In kindergarten, extended conversations are rarely needed. But, it is necessary to show a high degree of attentiveness and openness to the children.

EXAMPLE

Marianne was four years old. Her best friend had just died. She was allowed to stay home for two weeks and just came back to kindergarten. She spent the first two hours playing as usual, but then she sat down next to one of her teachers and, while watching the playground, asked: "Has one of your best friends ever died?"

"Yes, she died many years ago... but I still miss her. I could talk to her about everything."

"I miss my best friend too", Marianne said with tears in her eyes. The teacher invited the girl to sit on her lap and stroked her hair. Marianne burst out in tears and both of them fell silent.

After a couple of minutes, another girl came over and took Marianne's hand, laughing: "Come on, let's play!" Marianne readily jumped up from the teacher's lap and was fully immersed in playing again just seconds later.

We frequently observe similar behavior patterns in small children. One minute they plunge into sadness and then the next minute they act as if everything is fine. Marianne's kindergarten teachers have the opportunity to be there for her because she seeks contact. Other children, however, may not be this open and need to be invited actively to share their feelings.

Often, it is necessary to introduce existential topics to the entire group or in the classroom. This is very important, for example, when a child or a teacher falls seriously ill, dies in a car accident or is murdered. Such losses affect each and everyone in the class and, therefore, have to be talked about.

The following reasons show why we are convinced that institutions have the responsibility to offer space and conversations in these extreme cases and why the teacher's role is vital:

- Death is a relevant part of life, which is why it is absolutely necessary to talk about it and react to it if something happens.
- If a death concerns an entire community, it is important for this community to help one another cope with the manifold emotions and thoughts stirred by death. This may be feelings and thoughts related to the deceased, to one's own death and our closest relatives.
- An open way of talking about death builds a culture that makes a community and in specific the institutions to a place where the human being as a whole is welcome.
- Furthermore, it offers a great opportunity to talk to children about life and what is important to them in their own lives.
- It can be helpful for children whose parents feel at a loss, are overwhelmed or simply feel unable to talk with their children.

Death is a severe cut in our otherwise goal and action-oriented way of living, which gives adults unique insights into the children's reflective capabilities and their answers to the great mysteries of life. These insights facilitate keeping a sense for what is really relevant at a deeper level.

Conversation and Conflict Resolution

Today, there is plenty of helpful literature and guidebooks on classroom management available. Classroom management offers helpful ideas for common rules and structures required for larger groups of children so they function well in their learning environment. The success in implementing these rules, however, largely depends on the individual teacher's relational competence and professional presence. When visiting schools and day care centers, it is easy to see that there are no specific common rules that work better than others, that can be applied to all. Clear and simple structures along with a healthy working culture is all that is necessary. What is important is that the teachers and the principal are committed to both the basic structures and the way of working

A decisive issue though is the way the rules and structures are implemented. Rules that are implemented to solve existing problems are usually least effective. This is because they tend to be restrictive and not supportive and are negotiated or implemented by adults with a defensive approach. Existing rules that are controlled in an authoritarian way by teachers acting like police or on the contrary are hidden beneath a sweet and coaxing mask are similarly ineffective. In short, these ways of interacting undermine or entirely destroy any child's basic willingness to seek guidance in rules.

As we described above, interpersonal conflicts are best processed and resolved in dialogues. Rules prevent relationships from developing with help of conflicts. The following section is therefore devoted to how to intervene in group conflicts. The quality of conflict resolution determines both the way a child sees the teacher's competence as well as their own approach to dealing with conflicts. Role models do not always influence children as quickly as adults would hope for. And often other people than the parents or teachers themselves function as role models (for good and bad).

EXAMPLE A

The children of second grade liked to use nicknames. This caused conflicts, tears and even fights. The teachers had to repeatedly take time to talk with the children in the break.

Teacher: What's the matter, Anders?
Anders: They call me Shaggy, just because I got my hair cut.
Teacher: Who's calling you that?
Anders: Martin!
Martin: Well, and you called me Speedy. That's a nickname too.
Teacher: So, you're both responsible. Why don't we try and stick to the rule of not using nicknames in class? We all agreed on this rule together.

EXAMPLE B

The children of second grade were rehearsing a play in their Danish class. They were in the middle of it. Some of them were sitting in the auditorium, while others were on the stage and again others were backstage. The teacher was in front of the stage giving instructions. At the same time, she was trying to keep an eye on the rest of the group. Simon and Mikkel were standing on a stool watching.

Mikkel: Simon's teasing me – stop it!
Teacher: Simon, stop it – come down!
Simon: But why? Damn it!
Teacher: For God's sake, what's wrong with you? Just come down here and stop cursing!
Simon didn't move. And then here was a brief interruption of the discussion.
Mikkel: He just won't leave me alone!
Teacher: (got up and walked towards the boys): Who was on the stool first?
Mikkel: Me.

> *Teacher: Don't you think you'll find a solution that's okay for the both of you?*

Both incidents represent teachers who in a similar way clearly show that they consider conflicts superfluous. And they both react halfheartedly. In the first conflict between Anders and Martin, the teacher has several options, which depend on her own temper and professional principles, the general relationship of the two boys, her role in the classroom, as well as her own adherence to the rules she addresses.

The present conflict is not serious in the sense that one of the boys is physically or psychologically hurt. Children have always teased each other by using nicknames and will continue to do so in the future, regardless of how often teachers ask them to agree not to do so. The last sentence of the teacher signals that she actually thinks that the boys involved have broken an agreement. The teacher is referring half to rules, partly to psychological aspects, while at the same time referring to what she had planned to teach today. This does not provide a safe basis to solve the conflict. Her intervention is a waste of time at best. At the worst, it destroys the children's trust in the teacher as an independent support in their conflicts.

One extreme on the intervention scale would be the teacher deciding to give her teaching priority and state: *'I can see that you don't like this Anders, but I want you to clarify this yourself after school. I don't have time to help you now.'*

On the other end of the scale, she could interrupt her teaching for ten minutes to support the *students' overall development.* She could sit down with the boys and help them sort things out:

> *Teacher: Anders, I'd like you to tell Martin about how you felt when he called you Shaggy.*
> *Anders: It annoyed me...*
> *Teacher: Yes... and...?*
> *Anders: And it also makes me sad when he...*
> *Teacher: You should look at Martin and directly tell him.*

Anders: You're annoying me and it makes me sad... That's what you wanted, right?
Teacher: Okay, let's stop here, Anders. Now we need to hear what Martin's got to say. Martin...?
Martin: It was just for fun!
Teacher: That's good to know, but what do you think about Anders being sad about it?
Martin: I didn't mean it, it was just cause ...
Teacher: That's fine, Martin, you just got to tell Anders and not me...
Martin: It was just for fun, Anders. I didn't want to make you sad...
Teacher: Anders, what do you think about this? Do you want to let Martin know what you think about what he just said to you?
Anders: But I don't know...
Teacher: Are you feeling better now or are you still sad, or maybe even sadder?
Anders: I'm feeling better.
Teacher: Good enough to be friends again or is there anything else you'd like to say?
Anders: No...
Teacher: Look at him and tell him.
Anders: Don't call me Shaggy again...
Martin: If you don't call be Speedy again!
Teacher: Okay, I think we should talk about this as well, but right now I'd like you to give Martin an answer.
Martin: Yes, I said that I'll stop.
Teacher: Is it ok, for both of you?
Both: It's fine.

If there is time, the teacher can involve the other children in the class to comment on what is on their minds to the issue. Otherwise there is nothing left to say. Every attempt to moralize the issue or bring it to a general level will only undermine the process she just went through. Neither of the boys had the feeling of being out of place. And they received a first basic training in how to solve interpersonal conflicts.

Rules like prohibiting nicknames are an attempt to save children from unpleasant situations that are part of being a child. Such attempts never work out according to plan. Where children call others by their nicknames to tease them, flirt with them or consciously hurt them, they can only draw conclusions about their own boundaries after having experienced these situations themselves. Over the course of life, prevention does not protect us. We learn from experience how to deal with certain situations, e.g. with the help of relevant guidance provided by adults. Only in rare cases is it helpful to address phenomena in general. *But it is always effective to react to specific situations personally.*

In the second example, the conflict between Martin and Simon, the teacher involved has to make two decisions. The first one is whether to direct her attention to the trivial territorial conflict, or to the actors on the stage. The second and superior decision concerns the teacher's belief in the value of predefined compromises for solving children's conflicts. From our experience, compromises like this are a waste of time and energy. If the teacher really wants to invest time in the conflict, she could say: *You both want to stand on the same stool, but you don't want to share it. Find a solution and let me know about it when you are done.* In the most cases, children will find a solution, but forget about reporting it to the teacher because the conflict was not important anyway.

Both of the above conflicts require taking the nature of the boys' daily relationship into account. If the general potential for conflict increases and causes harm to the boys and the atmosphere of the class and the teaching, there is little use in a quick intervention. Instead, the teacher needs to take time to help the children look into their mutual interaction and clarify issues between them. A similar approach is also helpful in conflicts between adult colleagues, that inhibit a positive atmosphere in the institution and their relationship.

Experience shows that one of the most effective methods to reduce conflict potential is to welcome conflicts instead of rejecting them. Conflicts are an absolutely necessary component of interpersonal relationships. They teach us very valuable aspects of ourselves and others. Schools and Kindergartens simply need to get used to the idea that children may need their entire childhood to develop the strategies necessary for handling conflicts constructively.

If we succeed in establishing a culture which takes this seriously, we are able to influence *when* and *how* conflicts are processed. If adults introduce certain structures, children can handle many situations on their own:

- Sofie and Lene, listen. I realize that your conflict is serious. I'll help you find a solution, but I need you to wait until later.
- I can't really find out what is making this so important to you. But why don't you leave it alone for a second and I'll get back to you later.
- Knowing the both of you, I trust that you can sort this out on your own. Would you like to go outside for ten minutes or can you wait until after school?
- I don't have time to help you right now, but when the others go to the playground later today, Sören and Rikke can stay here to talk about it. Now, I'd like to continue showing you how to ….

Another advantage of welcoming conflicts is that it creates a positive atmosphere in classrooms and groups of children. It also prevents senseless conflicts between adults and children. The adults' respect for life and its manifold irrational manifestations encourages children to respect adults. This respect develops through practice and experience.

CHAPTER 10:
Challenging Children

The hyperactive child is a term used for both a distinct group of children who have serious existential issues, children with attentiveness disorder (e.g. ADHD, attention deficit hyperactivity disorder) as well as children who merely are full of energy, eager to learn, and are used to being included in the family as active, equal and valuable members.

The flexible structures and less educational approach can give day care institutions an easier time working with challenging children.

In schools where *quiet children* are *good children*, it is difficult to establish meaningful social and professional relationships to hyperactive children. In addition, many teachers' lack experience in differentiating the causes of hyperactivity. This gives rise to many myths about modern children and their parents. Some teachers tend to evaluate the child's behavior by the influence it has on the working situation. They cannot see the conflicts and challenges an individual child might be going through.

A nationwide survey conducted by the Danish ministry of education in 1996[1] showed that approximately ten percent of the pupils regularly distract themselves and others during class. A little below two percent interrupt class constantly and not quite one percent of the children are such a problem that their teachers wish they were not in their class at all. Comparable surveys in Norway provide very similar results.[2]

This chapter could have also been titled *strenuous children, misbehaving children, ill-mannered children, children with psycho-social issues, different children, children with learning difficulties* and *children with behavioral problems* and the like. Yet we chose *challenging*, because this term describes the relational aspect and does not characterize the individual child. These relationships challenge the framework and rules of institutions, the relational competence of teachers, expectations as well as prejudices with the same intensity as they challenge the child themself.

History provides us with ample attempts to define and categorize children whose inside and outside behavior deviates from the norm and thus both challenges and is challenged by limitations, expectations and prejudices of teachers and the norms and rules of institutions. A growing part of these children are sorted out and offered additional support or special education. In this context children and adolescents are constantly and largely seen as *the* problem and often treated like scapegoats.

Within the framework of this book, we do not question well-established diagnoses nor analyze categories such as ADHD. Some of these diagnoses are, without doubt, fitting, relevant and helpful. Many children and adolescents have testified that having a diagnosis rather than just feeling different and out of place, has brought great relief to their lives. Moreover, it is can feel very constructive and helpful for teachers and children alike, if pedagogical methods are adapted to the potentials and limitations that the diagnoses implicate.

Keeping these advantages of diagnoses in mind, we have the experience that it is essential to be aware of four circumstances:

1. certain diagnoses are rather vague and leave a lot of room for interpretation. A wrong diagnosis can be as much of a burden as a correct diagnosis can be helpful.
2. Seen from a social perspective, diagnoses appear in waves, based on new findings and shifts of attention of experts. But in some cases, they can also be considered passing fashions, which violate a child's integrity.
3. Reducing children to their diagnoses and thus making them an object in educational relationships, inhibits mutual development.
4. Last but not least, often the experts who make a diagnosis are not sufficiently qualified to assess the quality of a child's closest daily relationships.

We are able to cope with being treated as the *appendix* during a brief stay in hospital, although even this requires humor and leniency. But both children and adults suffer greatly if important relationships are reduced to specific aspects of their behavior over an extended period of time. Even well-meant reductions are not bearable.

If all attention is directed at a child's *functionality*, the child's experience is similar to the experience of being bullied by peers. The essential difference is that this type of *mobbing* by responsible and committed adults is accompanied by a positive undercurrent tone and a general moral acceptance. This causes chaos in the child's self-perception, way of understanding the world and, in addition, weakens their self-esteem. This happens independently of whether the intellectual, physical or social function is in focus.

Children with identical diagnoses differ from one another as much as they differ from children without diagnoses. Therefore, the larger the *functional* difficulties, the more attention and affection their individual *existence* and *being* needs. Not only as part of educational perspectives and goals, but also as the foundation for their development. Although parents and other people in the child's private network play an important role, it is not advisable to split up educational and existential issues between parents and experts. *Both the integrity and the self-esteem depend on every relevant adults' ability and willingness to establish contact with the whole child.*

Often experts divide their tasks so that one person is responsible for general education, another for remedial teaching, a third one for the emotional support, a fourth for working with the family and so on. This specialization, which gained momentum after World War II, has brought about advantages for professionals in the form of increased knowledge, understanding and expertise. This specialization though tends to inhibit professional relationships and children (and adults) affected are often left alone with their emotions. They are made into objects or mere background actors in a multi-act drama.

Again and again, we have experienced that challenging children can receive treatment, and that their teachers can help make a permanent difference if they take in both interdisciplinary findings and a systemic view. This chapter is devoted to the approach and the competence children benefit most from and which offer the opportunity to improve destructive educational relationships. Our main focus is on the psycho-social dimension and on children with psycho-social issues, behavioral problems, adaptive disorders or similar. Regardless of whether they are children attending kindergarten, school or special facilities. Our aim is not to develop new methods, but to describe a new approach to provide a foundation for developing alternative methods.

A New Approach

At the beginning of this book, we offered three concepts:

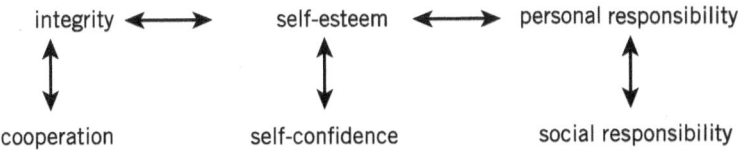

Above we described the correlation between a person's personal integrity, self-esteem and personal responsibility. The other side of these concepts is not interconnected as strongly.

There is a clear correlation between integrity and cooperation, a limited correlation between self-esteem and self-confidence and a varying correlation between personal and social responsibility. Moreover, we went into detail on how a person's personal integrity consists of the elements: integrity, self-esteem and personal responsibility.

Pedagogy for challenging children often is a reaction to qualities and characteristics these children (apparently) lack. These included the ability to
- cooperate
- trust in themselves
- develop social competence
- assume responsibility

In other words, these children and adolescents are labelled as not willing to cooperate, as insecure and antisocial. And the educational goals defined that build on these observations are:
- *make* them willing to cooperate
- *give* them self-confidence
- *turn* them into social beings

Numerous socio-pedagogical institutions and projects in the last decades have tried new methods for treating and supporting children and adolescents. Some of them have proved to be helpful and brought about adolescents who have been able to cope with the world outside of the educational institution in a better way. Others depended strongly on individual educational pioneers and were hard to be taken over by the next generation. General educational thinking has often been open to the ideas and methods of alternative enthusiasts. This, however, only seldom induced a revision of fundamental values to really support child development.

For this reason, we suggest no longer relying on the idea of modifying a child's behavior to influence their willingness to cooperate, their self-confidence and their social responsibility. Instead, we focus on creating an approach that strengthens integrity, self-worth and personal responsibility. Our goal is to enable individual and social development so even challenging children can feel comfortable and accepted by society.

If we look at the life course of a mal adapted and unhappy child, we see that the reasons for their uncooperative behavior are either that they have had to cooperate with their parents' behavior in a self-destructive way, or that they have been hurt by their parents or other adults in such a serious and/or ongoing way that its personal integrity was at risk. These violations can be severe – physical or psychological violence, sexual abuse – or in a subtle but daily way. Especially if, what Daniel Stern calls *present moments* violate a child's integrity[3]. These interactional moments of active violating or passive failing can show up both as an accepted part of authoritarian child rearing as well as in pedagogical institutions, that see themselves *advanced*.

We know that many of the children and adolescents in need of serious treatment come from families which try to set boundaries in an authoritarian way. In addition, there is a large group of children and teenagers who are not in need of intense treatment at first, but fall victim to what we know as *public failure of care*. The expression comprises both vulnerable children whom the social system meets with passivity as well as those who are confronted with actual attacks by the educational or welfare system.

No matter the primary cause we see for a child's problematic behavior, their message to the environment is not *'Teach me how to cooperate and conform!'*, but rather *'Take care of my integrity and teach me how to get to know myself and how to make other people stay with me.'*

A child's self-esteem develops in a continual, dialectical process between the child's desire for integrity and intellectual interests. To develop this a child needs to experience educational relationships in which the adult is interested in, open and sensitive for its personal integrity, as well as able to abstract from the child's immediate behavior, To the extent to which a *challenging* child is enabled to recover, express, recognize and stimulate its integrity, it will also be able to develop a healthy self-esteem and foundation for intellectual and social developments (not however for intellectual and social obedience).

It is both a developmental process (growing in age) and process of understanding (intellectual development), which enables the child to assume growing personal responsibility and thus also enhances its social responsibility. This, however, also needs relational competent adults which are sensitive to and appreciative of the human aspects of a child's existence. This specifically means all emotions related to sadness, pain, blind fury and deeply rooted distrust. This way of interacting also inspires adults to learn to act both as a sparring partner[*****] and as a source of inspiration according to the child's needs.

Social competence and responsibility is an outcome of this way of interaction. Boundaries and rules are not educational in and of themselves. They are nothing more than boundaries and rules. Adults decide which boundaries and rules are appropriate and reasonable in the context of the institu-

---

[*****] This term stems from combat sports where it describes a training partner who provides maximum resistance and minimal damage.

tional culture. Conforming with these boundaries and rules is neither the goal nor the success of education. The pedagogical success lies in the way teachers treat those children who disregard established rules and boundaries. The challenging task is supporting the disobedient on the path to him- or herself. It is not about teachers acting more reasonable than parents, providing more stable and trustworthy commitment and being stricter about their rules.

Sustainable values and principles for working with challenging children are not much different from those for all other children. But challenging children need a little *more of everything*, regardless of their behavior or possible diagnosis.

What experienced teachers find most confusing about working with challenging children is that they feel the urge to start backward, namely with personal responsibility. But as we described above, one needs to feel real needs and limitations and be able to think about them before one can take responsibility for them. This is the main reason social responsibility starts with personal responsibility. Regardless of how paradoxical it may seem, we are forced to start exactly at this point. Especially with older children who either continuously make self-destructive decisions or appear passive and apathetic. We have to see that their decisions make sense (from their point of view) and offer an empathetic contrary perspective. That is an opposing view which does *not* describe the adults' wishes, but reflects the child's present being. If the teacher concerned has real *adult* alternatives that are personal, he or she may offer them to the child, but only at the end of a dialogue upon being asked by the child itself. What is very difficult is watching the trial-and-error process in the child's own pace without getting involved. But new options and approaches have to be based on new experiences, otherwise they cannot be integrated.

To be sure, there are children and adolescents who suffer being in ordinary kindergartens or schools as much as these institutions suffer having to deal with these children. Our clinical experience with challenging children shows that, being treated with high relational quality, quickly relinquishes or at least reduces symptomatic behavior. It therefore makes sense to adapt this relational competent way of interacting for institutions in general. In addition, this kind of treatment confronts children with essential qualities that can play a decisive role in their lives in the long run. The is also true for hyperactive children whose behavior is determined organically. Coherent long-term studies and research to focus and evaluate this general experience are still needed.

Although challenging children only make up a fraction of the whole, they occupy a large portion of teachers' awareness. The examples provided below offer a small selection of teacher-child relationships, which we have ourselves closely accompanied as supervisors and counselors. The following teachers' emotional involvement, which ranged from empathy over anger to helplessness, was always very high. It is interesting to note that all adults involved were originally looking for *solutions*, but soon felt inspired and pressured to change their ways of interacting.

Examples and Analyses

EXAMPLE 1:

Allan was fifteen years old and in ninth grade. Ever since he started school, he had been a quiet and inconspicuous boy whom the teachers never paid much attention to. Allan was silent, friendly and able to keep up with the rest of the group. He always did what was expected of him. But when he entered fourth grade, the class teacher realized that he appeared sad and unhappy. After a conversation with him, the teacher contacted the welfare authority.

As it turned out, Allan had grown up in a family with an alcoholic mother and three younger siblings as well as a father whose current location was unknown. With his mother's approval, Allan moved in with a foster family, where he had been living ever since. His foster parents loved the boy dearly, and he loved them. They were very surprised how quickly he managed to integrate into the family and the new school as well as with his helpfulness and thoughtfulness. The only problem they had with Allan seemed to be the long period of up to four or five days the boy needed to recover emotionally after the monthly weekend visits of his mother and siblings.

In ninth grade, Allan, just like many of his friends, was confronted for the first time with his future after school*******: should he enroll for high school, begin an apprenticeship, or opt for a technical school? Responsible and committed adults, like his foster parents, talked with him a lot about his future. They took him to different youth counseling sessions. His foster parents were open and impartial. Their idea was that Allan should decide for himself which option would suit him best.*

After several months, Allan's behavior started to change. He started skipping school, coming home late and one day he stayed away all night. He also became more withdrawn and reserved. He suddenly preferred to be alone. Although his foster parents were worried, they did not panic and comforted themselves with the thought that he was neither doing criminal things nor taking drugs. But on the school's request, the welfare authority put increasing pressure on Allan's foster parents demanding that Allan should be sent to school regularly and should make a decision concerning his future. With the rising pressure Allan's problematic behavior escalated.

Analysis:

Allan grew up in isolation. Addicts like his mother quickly lose the ability to recognize, assess as well as fulfill their children's needs. Furthermore, he grew up with an enormous burden of social responsibility. Where parents are either physically or psychologically absent, and in Allan's case both applied. The oldest of the children (or the only child) usually steps in and tries to compensate for the adult(s) absence. In his family Allan assumed the role of the prime caregiver and was already a model of social competence when he started kindergarten. He knew just about everything about cooperating and conforming.

Therefore, his behavior also perfectly matched the requirements and expectations of his school and foster family. Early in his life, he gave up his personal integrity without resistance, and the adults' praise for his character

---

****** In the Danish school system, school is compulsory for 9 years (starting at the age of 7).

were daily proof that this was the right decision. During the monthly visits, his pain surfaced, even if he mostly felt concern for his smaller siblings.

After 15 years of struggling to live up to the standards and expectations of society, the boy was suddenly confronted with the first and largest personal decision which he had ever had to take: *What do you yourself want to do with the rest of your life?*

Nobody even considered that Allan might be confronted with a vast emptiness when trying to find an inner answer, and that he had given up his identity long ago to cope with the demands of his life. He readily listened to the ideas and suggestions of his foster parents, the youth counselors and specialists. But since none of these ideas resonated with his *self*, he was unable to make a reasonable decision.

Instead, Allan chose isolation and loneliness. This happened partly because this was familiar and partly because, lacking a relevant inspirational environment, he expected to finally find his *self* there. Thus, he did what thousands of adults do in similar life and identity crises every day. However, he got pressured and punished for retreating. The adults surrounding him could have simply smiled at him and said: *We can see that you are withdrawing to take an important decision and we know that this is the most difficult task you ever had to solve. We understand that you need time for yourself to find out what to do, and that's fine. We'll make no more suggestions about possible schools, apprenticeships and the like, but we'd like to talk to you about who you are. You don't need to worry about all the pressure you experience in school and through the authorities. They are all just trying to adhere to the law. But the law is made for common children, and you are not a common child. So, just take all the time you need.*

The boy would have probably also been satisfied with less psychological expertise and a minimum of relational responsibility on the part of the school director or the responsible counselor: *Allan, we don't know how to help you. We already tried our best. All we can offer is more of what we have already given, but none of us would be really happy with that. I hope that you'll be able to find a way out of this situation yourself. I'll just try not to embarrass you anymore.*

EXAMPLE 2:

Marie was attending third grade. She had always gotten along with her friends well and been able to cope with the demands and challenges in school. Yet, around Christmas time, her behavior in school suddenly changed. When she came to school one morning, she refused to take off her coat and just sat there, trying to hide beneath a popped collar. She soon developed difficulties in school. Her performance dropped and she often cried, balling up the paper and railing against 'stupid math class'. Every time classmates passed by her desk, just touching it lightly, she claimed they pushed her and burst out in tears.

A conversation between the class teacher and the girl's parents could neither clarify the problem nor solve it. The parents only knew Marie as a good, polite and cooperative child and thought that her changed behavior in school may be more the teacher's problem than Marie's. The teacher tried to speak with Marie: "What's wrong with you, Marie? You've never had any problems before. Has anybody teased you?" No matter how many helpful suggestions the teacher made, Marie's answer was always the same: she sniveled, shrugged her shoulders or denied the suggestions. The teacher was stuck and decided to focus on teaching instead. Marie was stuck too and ran the risk of getting stuck in the role of a difficult child.

Analysis:

At home, Marie's situation was the following: her mother had recently fallen in love with one of her colleagues and developed doubts about her marriage. She was deeply in love, but at the same time sad about the consequences this might have for her entire family. Her husband was angry, unhappy and just as confused as his wife. None of them spoke to their children about the situation. They agreed on talking about the issue when their children were not home. They also agreed on first telling them once they know more about what the future might look like. The parents attempted to act as if nothing had happened and to treat their children as usual. Still, Marie felt that the atmosphere at home had changed. Both parents were mentally and emotionally absent, and Marie experienced this absence as if she was not existent for them.

On an existential, yet unconscious level, Marie thus experienced herself as less valuable for her parents than before. She reacted just like any child would react, trying to restore their feeling of worth, and cooperated.

For many months, Marie felt her family change. Her father was angry and developed a temper. Even when the parents tried to converse over dinner, she could sense the difference. Marie took the blame and tried everything in her power to change the tense and bad mood. She tried to tell funny stories to lighten up her family's mood. She tried to remember what her parents appreciated most. She put her plate in the dishwasher, hung her schoolbag and coat where they belong, and so on. But that was only of minor significance. Marie really tried everything she could, and she went way beyond her own limits without ever changing her parents' reactions. The less valuable she perceived herself in her relationship to her parents, the more her frustration grew. Just like many other children, she remained loyal towards her parents and was forced to express her frustration in school.

Of course, her parents could not see Marie's behavior. In their reality, Marie was just as good, nice and cooperative as usual. Since they lived in the illusory belief of being able to keep their crisis a secret until deciding on their own what to do. It did not even occur to them to inform the teacher about the situation or to see a connection between the family situation and Marie's unexpected difficulties with school and other children.

Very often, teachers do not know any details about the background for a child's behavior. Marie's teacher was hamstrung and thought he needed to know more to help Marie. It is rarely helpful to ask children in Marie's situation about what is going on. Marie merely needed her teacher's empathy and acknowledgement, which could be expressed like this: "*I see that you're going through a difficult time, Marie. I don't know why you're sad or what you're worried about, but I do know that it is not nice to feel like this and to be alone.*" The teacher could have sat down with Marie, just to be with her and to show her that he recognized what she was going through and that he liked being there for her.

Many teachers find this very difficult. They would rather solve problems and see them pass. Yet, children in Marie's situation do not need a solution to their problems from outside. And this is the first of many crises to follow over her course of life. The teacher's empathetic closeness could have offered Marie an ideal opportunity to direct her attention inwardly and find words for her present feelings. This would be a basis for her to start to distinguish between her needs and the needs of her environment. Even if Marie's parents will sooner or later be able to resolve their dilemma or open up to their children and their teachers about the issues, (regardless of leading to a divorce or not), the situation will still affect Marie's inside and outside behavior over the course of the next two years. The school can decide to, either be another burden or a rest area in her life, where she can regain her life's balance herself.

In addition, her class teacher has two options: he can, either just been frustrated and consider himself a failing teacher, or he can act like a relevant part of Marie's social environment.

EXAMPLE 3:

Thomas was four years old and had always been a problem for his teachers ever since he first started kindergarten. He insisted on the adults' attention. He interrupted other children playing and ran away again, and acted just like he wanted to. Obviously, he was not able to integrate the general rules of the institution into his awareness. If he did not get what he wanted, he was either truly unhappy or angry. He threw himself on the floor, held on to adults or punched other children. He was unable to stay focused on a specific task for more than a couple of minutes and quickly got restless and demanded new input. The other children in his group started keeping their distance to him. Only on rare occasions, Thomas got invited home to one of the other children's homes and hardly ever did he bring one of them to his home.

His teachers put great effort into trying to explain to Thomas that it was inappropriate to hit other children and that he was not the only one who requires the adults' attention. They led two long conversations with his parents to address the issues. Thomas's parents recognized their son in the teachers' accounts, but they merely tended to trace his reactions to his character and the fact that he had been alone at home with his mother the first three years of his life. They thought that this might be the reason why he was simply not used to being around other children. The parents were committed, caring and friendly. Still, the teachers found it difficult to establish a productive way of cooperating with them. Therefore, the kindergarten suggested a psychological observation, yet the parents did not agree to that. They thought that his problems were nothing more than minor 'initial difficulties', which would disappear once the teachers had gotten to know Thomas better. The teachers, on the other hand, advised them to set clearer boundaries for Thomas.

After one year in kindergarten, Thomas was isolated. Neither children nor adults truly sought contact with him. They all treated him with rejection and critique.

Analysis:

Thomas is one of these modern *planned children* which stir prejudice about the well-educated parents' tendency to spoil their child with the wrong form of attention. Thomas's parents are parents who allow their child's wishes to guide them and act according to the misconception that by giving their child what it wants they will also give him what he needs. Thomas's parents did not take this approach out of indolence or a lack of interest in their son's wellbeing. On the contrary, they are parents who take their responsibility for Thomas very seriously and see themselves as opposing to parents who do not spend enough time with their children and sacrifice family life for their careers. They could understand the teachers' complaints, but they still felt provoked by their angry tone of voice. Consequently, they reacted by trying to protect their son. The more negative reactions Thomas met from the outside world, the more positively they tried to react to him at home.

Thomas had always been at the center of his parents' attention. Yet, being in the constant focus of others' attention only encourages loneliness. The boy's parents misunderstood their role in his life and reduced themselves to service providers. As a result, Thomas did not receive an opportunity to learn that living in a community also entails being thoughtful to others and finding a balance between the needs and limitations of several parties involved. All parents offer their children love to the best of their abilities and knowledge, and all children adapt to the specific forms of love they receive. For Thomas, love meant to have all of his wishes fulfilled immediately. But since this form of love never really met his actual needs for love and cohesion, he did not know any better than to ask for more and more. As a consequence, his parents' genuine love for him diminished, and Thomas was soon all on his own and isolated, unable to reach out to others.

Thomas's teachers face two major challenges. First of all, it is a challenge to get in contact with his parents and suggest competent family counseling. Secondly, it is a challenge to find a relevant way to interact with Thomas in everyday life. Thomas does not need pedagogical lectures, reproaches or critique, no matter the tone of voice. He needs adults with sufficient personal authority to set boundaries and energy and willingness to personally confront him. These are the same qualities missing in the relationship to his parents.

Both of these challenges are linked closely. The teachers will be able to establish relevant contact with the parents after treating Thomas in a competent way. Otherwise, they will not be trustworthy enough to convince the parents to change their way of showing Thomas that they truly love him.

If the teachers fail to meet these challenges, Thomas's future will look rather dark. Schools are generally much less flexible and, in addition, his inner anger will rise tremendously. Moreover, occasional expressions of anger would be judged negatively by most people in his life.

Thomas' anger is, of course, understandable. He is the victim of two-fold deception in his primary relationships. His parents express their love and care for him in a form which he cannot experience as loving and caring, and his teachers react to his *symptoms* instead of his *existence*. The fact that both parties have good reasons to act the way they do, does not help Thomas at all.

Even if the teachers' attempt to create meaningful contact with the boy's parents fails, they are still challenged to adapt their own behavior. This can have great effect on the boy and offer him essential social experiences. And taking on this challenge will spare the teachers the feeling of failure, which always leaves a bad taste. Moreover, it will improve the social culture of the institution and teach the children an important lesson about commitment, respect and conflict resolution. In the end, everything comes down to whether the kindergarten defines Thomas as a pedagogical problem or as a relational challenge.

EXAMPLE 4:

Charlotte was in fourth grade. She was charming, talented and eager to learn, but undisciplined. Ever since first grade, her teachers had tried to teach her how to sit still, to raise her hand if she had something to say, to ask before leaving the classroom to go to the toilet and similar rules, but without success. Because she was good at school, and showed a sense of humor, her teachers just let Charlotte have her way. They patiently corrected and reminded her of what to do to no avail. Charlotte was very popular with the other children, especially the girls, but recently she has become more aggressive than charming. She started answering her teachers' corrections with, "I'm doing it the way I want!", or "Don't tell me what to do". One day, she reacted to a teacher by saying "Why don't you just mind your own business?", her teacher had had enough and decided to invite her parents for a talk.

Charlotte's parents, in particular her father, could relate to the teacher's frustration. Charlotte had an older brother who had always been cooperative and never caused any trouble. Their debates with their daughter had also taken a toll on them. They supported the school's expectations, yet they had no idea how to get the girl to stick to the rules. They agreed on having a serious talk with Charlotte and once more trying to convince her to adjust to the situation at school and behave just like the other children. Charlotte carefully listened to what her parents had to say and then answered in a serious tone of voice: "But what if I'm just not like the others?"

Over the next few weeks, the situation at school didn't change. And Charlotte's teacher asked for a supervision. The teacher soon realized that he never really considered that Charlotte may be just the way she behaves. He saw that he had divided her into positive and negative sides and used all of his energy to change the aspects that he considered negative. After four years, Charlotte's negative qualities had been reinforced and now threatened to undermine her positive characteristics. Charlotte had been given clear signals from both her teachers and parents that if she wanted to get on in life, she would have to give up part of her character. Both parents and her teacher made a classic 'mistake' in their relationships with Charlotte. They saw a pattern of behavior which they did not approve of and decided to change it. Since their approach did not bring the desired result, they reinforced their measures instead of questioning what was going on.

The class teacher decided to talk with Charlotte and openly stated: "I figured out that I have difficulty getting along with you because I've never really accepted you the way you are. From the very beginning, I've worked against you, and now you've started to work against me as well. This is why I've decided to work with you. I still think that you should respect our rules, but I know that I'm the one who has to make the first step, if we want to get along better."

After the teacher's first few words, Charlotte started to cry and said: "I'm just the way I am. I can't change, even if I sometimes wish I could."

Soon after the conversation, Charlotte started to use her energy surplus in a more productive way. She still did whatever she wanted, but with less temper and less aggression. In addition, the teacher's fear that the other children could follow her example turned out to be unfounded.

Analysis:

Charlotte belongs to a group of children of whom we see more and more frequently. She has an inborn aura of sovereign independence, which appears rather provoking to most adults. Her personal qualities are ones we would expect from an 18-year-old, but seem very unusual and alienating in a four or nine-year-old. Many of these children grow up in families and institutions with adults jumping back and forth between delight and annoyance, pushing children into emotional chaos. Nonetheless, most of these children decide to fight for their integrity and, eventually, pay for this with loneliness.

Although these children appear independent and self-confident, they have the same needs of being seen, acknowledged, included and taken seriously as any other child. Charlotte's teacher therefore did the right thing in assuming responsibility for both their frustration with their mutual relationship and acknowledging her right to be who she was, without making her have to give up her personal integrity.

In the above example, the teacher sought help in supervision. Yet he could have come to the same conclusion on his own, if he had considered the fact how pronounced Charlotte's desire to be herself was. The need is so strong, that she would rather accept consistent criticism and irrational comparisons with her brother than change her behavior. This is the way children (and adults) behave who do not experience their right to be who they are in their close relationships as self-evident. To cooperate with these persons in a productive way, demands acknowledging this right first.

EXAMPLE 5:

Line was five years old and the kindergarten's police officer. She kept an eye on her teachers and the other children and was fully occupied making sure that each and every one of them was doing what they were supposed to do. Her teachers were annoyed with her attitude and started explaining that telling tales is wrong. They often reminded her to mind her own business rather than caring about what others are doing. Sometimes, Line tried to justify her actions. Other times, Line turned sad and confused, but her behavior did not change.

Analysis:

Line is the oldest of three siblings. Her parents' relationship was tense. They were too preoccupied with their own problems to have any energy left for their daughter's needs. Line thus reached the same conclusion as any child in her situation would. She believed that she was doing something wrong and cooperated by being as *right* as she could, hoping to finally be seen and acknowledged. Her message was: *Look at me! Don't you see, I'm trying everything I can to have my most fundamental needs fulfilled. My needs to be seen and accepted as the person I am. I do see that it's not working out, but I don't know what else to do. So, I need your help to get on. I can't get out of this myself.*

Approximately half of the children in similar situations cooperate with their environment exactly the same way. The other half cooperates *in reverse*, starting to behave in a way which is just as *inappropriate* as the way they feel in their essential relationships.

Since Line's teachers were only able to moralize and reinforce her feeling of being out of place, the girl of course is not encouraged to adapt her behavior. Knowing about the circumstances in Line's family could have been helpful but is not essential. Objective reasoning would have helped the teachers realize that a child who strives for correctness and praise, usually feels out of place and lacks acknowledgement.

What is detrimental in these situations is the tendency to feel limited by educational possibilities and turn to psychological expertise. Instead of drawing on their personal experience and talent this can cause teachers to send challenging children to experts, who do not have personal and daily contact with the child. In doing so, they often create two obstacles for a constructive development.

The first obstacle comes from underestimating personal contact when feeling helpless and turning to other professionals for help. Existing scientific[4] research about the influence of psychotherapy for example, shows that helpful interventions are closely tied to the perception of having had a meaningful, personal contact to the therapist, psychologist, doctor, psychiatrist or the like – the respective person's profession or approach were not significant in this context. We have every reason to expect that the same is true for the children's and adolescents' feelings towards teachers. If we send a child to an unknown adult for help, we run the risk that the child may not experience the new contact in a meaningful way and cannot profit from the otherwise impeccable qualifications of the expert.

The second obstacle arises from the fact that most experts belonging to the system *around* schools treat children on the basis of diagnosis. However, a major part of children and youth referred to these experts do not actually need to be treated and therefore clash with a person trying to provide treatment. What these children actually need is an improvement in their familial and educational relationships, not the treatment by external experts.

We are aware that many people disagree with us on this aspect, as our society relies more and more on experts and is dependent on their knowledge. As we have observed, the need for experts seems to increase with the number of experts available not vice-versa. Please note that we do not object to expert knowledge, but we would like to see pedagogues getting equipped with helpful strategies with the help of experts, rather than relying on another persons' knowledge.

EXAMPLE 6:

René was in ninth grade. One day, he wanted to see the school nurse to get his hearing tested. The test did not reveal any hearing problems, which is why the nurse wondered why he wanted to get tested.

"Sometimes, I see people talking, but I can't really hear what they're saying."

The experienced nurse was interested in getting more details: "Well, René, do you know that, sometimes our ability to see or to hear is affected if we have problems or have to think about something a lot?"

René started to think. He took a quick look at the nurse's friendly and clear eyes, as if trying to reassure himself that he could trust her. Then, he told her that he had a smaller sister only two years old – and that their father went mentally ill after going bankrupt several years ago. His father was hospitalized from time to time and had to take medication. His mother was trying hard to prevent her family from needing help from public authorities and wanted their problems to stay in the family. The boy also remarked that he likes to go to school and could easily handle the workload.

Since the school nurse is also a part of the social system, she felt obliged to send the boy to a psychologist instead of relying on her personal feelings and experience as well as René's trust in her. This was also despite the fact that she was aware that the boy would have to wait for at least three months for an appointment. She asked: "René, is there something you would like to talk about to someone?"

René was puzzled: he was talking right now. Yet, he answered: "Well, yes…"

"Alright. I'll try to get you an appointment with the school psychologist, but in the meantime you should ask your mother to confirm that she approves of you seeing a psychologist."

René agreed and left. The nurse looked into René's records and discovered that, in the past three years, there were three incidents where the boy acted violently and once even attacked his teacher.

The following day, René's mother called, obviously upset, and demanded an explanation why her son should see a psychologist. She wanted to know whether her son was having mental issues. The school nurse eventually managed to calm her down and even get her consent. When she came back from a meeting the following day, she found René waiting in front of her office. He told her that, the other day, his mother had been so mad about being asked to send him to a psychologist that she forbade him to go to his best friend's birthday party. So, he ran away to celebrate with his friend anyway. The nurse could clearly sense his helplessness and his need to talk with somebody, but she was unable to give the boy more than the weak advice to respect his mother's requests and at least let her know where he was going. He promised to do so and tried to calm the nurse down by telling her that his mother would be 'nice again' when he got home because it was his own birthday.

When the school nurse told the school's psychologist about this incident, he promised to take René in for a conversation soon. Moreover, he urged the nurse to write a report about the family and submit it to the welfare authorities, particularly because of the younger child.

Analysis:

René is a healthy and sufficiently talented boy whose father's mental illness is a great burden. Sometimes more and sometimes less, he has had to assume his father's role in the family. He cooperated with his mother's wish to not seek help from outside and therefore did not tell anyone how difficult the situation was and how much he was worried about his father's health and his mother's wellbeing, or about his fear of becoming mentally ill as well.

Over the next three years, René's emotional pressure grew and grew because he sacrificed his own integrity (his need to express his thoughts and feelings) for the sake of cooperating with his mother. He also reflected her sense of being strong enough to cope without help. His high pressure showed in three individual incidents where classmates and teachers provoked him for no reason. At that time, nobody was interested in why an otherwise reasonable and balanced young boy simply exploded just like that.

In the end, the boy just could not take any more of this and sought help. Luckily, he got a chance to speak with the smart and sensitive school nurse, in whom he trusted enough to be *disobedient* and open up about his problems. Yet, he did not need professional help or treatment. He needed a person that could listen to him, recognize his difficult situation and be there for him in this rare moment in which he could not bear his loneliness anymore. This person could have been his mother, another family member, a teacher, a friend or, as in the present case, the school nurse.

The nurse's decision to ignore her own intuition and experience and instead do what the system expected her to do had fatal consequences.

- Her referral to a psychologist turned René into a client and thus increased his fear becoming mentally ill himself.
- Ideally, the boy can develop the same level of trust in the psychologist as he had in the nurse, but since his mother considered the new status of her son as a client as another failure, his chances are not good.
- René's healthy disobedience caused the welfare authority to become aware of the family's situation. This affected the mother's pride of having been able to deal with the situation on her own. This pride had previously fueled her energy to be able to care for her husband and her

children. Of course, René concluded that it would have been better to have kept his mouth shut. Because of this his mental stability is, in fact, endangered.
- With the values in mind with which he had grown up, he felt betrayed and *out of place* rather than *seen*.
- René opted for the healthiest way to relieve his personal pain, but with the result of causing even more pain and chaos in his life. This opens up to other ways of getting relief from emotional pain: cynicism, aggression, violence, alcoholism, drugs and similar.

René's relational status as a 15-year-old, was that he had been at the mercy of adults' failure very often, especially concerning the protection of his personal integrity. The first one to fall short was his mother who simply did not know any better. Then psychiatry fell short by reacting solely to the ill individual and not considering the fact that mentally ill also have families[5]. His teacher also fell short because he judged his signals rather than taking them seriously. And finally, the school nurse failed him by refusing to help when she could have helped most. René was able to handle life in his family. He performed well in school and in social contacts with a minimum of support. He could have developed into a healthy, empathetic, responsible, well-functioning and clever adult. But from what he experienced in the above example, we can assume that his future might turn into an extended series of conflicts with professional adults who try to teach him exactly those qualities, which he already had a surplus of. Their ability to see his person as a whole, decreases with the social seriousness of his symptoms.

Psychology and Education

We are convinced that psychology should play a more relevant role in pedagogical training and that the psychological aspects available do not connect enough to practice. They need to interact in a new way. Educational relational competence could be a suitable title for this fusion, which could facilitate drawing on psychological knowledge and inspiration as needed and relevant. In this book, we have primarily referred to contributions and inspiration from developmental and relational psychology. But recent findings of cognitive psychology[6] also provide an essential input for the content-focused part of teaching. Both research areas are based on a new paradigm. Instead of treating the child as an incomplete version of the mature, adult human being and comparing the two, they look at the child based on his/her own conditions and the essential interpersonal relationships seen from the perspective of a child. Although every attempt to put oneself into a toddler's world of thought and emotion will never be more than speculation, modern technology like video recordings have produced more and more reliable data[7]. These developments could be very rewarding to improve professional adult-child relationships.

The key for this improvement is not in the adults' increasing self-recognition nor in a larger psychological understanding for children, but rather in the increased awareness for relational qualities, which enable healthy and productive relationships, which are the basis for academic learning as well. For teachers, it can be an advantage to know things about family psychology, developmental psychology or a child's personal development. But the best place for professional development and relational competence are playgrounds, classrooms or rooms for talks with parents – all shared spaces with children, parents and colleagues.

We appreciate seeing more and more psychologists in schools and daycare centers that share the children's, adults' and other professionals' space as analysts, advisors, and as a security net for active and living relationships. They have begun withdrawing from providing intellectual reactions to the incomplete and biased picture drawn by one party or another, or – even worse – abusing their power by judging children or adolescents and their parents without even having met them, solely on the basis of written reports.

Final Words

Educational experts are faced with the complicated and complex challenge which, despite politically relevant statements of intent, are not given due priority by the political agents in charge. The fact that Nordic countries invest a comparatively large amount of money in educational institutions does not oppose this. It merely confirms that we have become used to receiving too little for what we pay for and that we tend to mistake quantity for quality.

With the growing relevance of professional adult-child relationships for the quality of life of children and youth, we have long crossed the point where we can no longer treat schools as mere suppliers of qualified students for institutions of higher education and of a workforce for the labor market. Today, the quality of these relationships has a decisive influence on society and social ethics. Children and adolescents grow into responsible human beings if confronted with responsible adults who do not violate the children's and adolescent's inner responsibility and also refuse to be violated themselves.

Notes

Chapter 1: The Educational Landscape
1 D. *Riesman*: The Lonely Crowd, Yale UP, New Haven 1961.
2 http://www.un.org
3 D. N. *Stern*: The Motherhood Constellation, Karnac Books, 1995.
  L. *Cozzolino*: The Neuroscience of Human Relationships: Attachment and the Developing Social Brain, W.W.Norton, 2014.
  P. *Fonagy, G. Gergely et al*: Affect Regulation, Mentalization, and the Development of the Self, Oxford University Press, 2016.
4 S. *Hart*: Brain, Attachment, Personality: An Introduction to Neuroaffective Development, Karnac Books, 2008.

Chapter 2: Family
1 J. *Juul*: »Familien– nye roller, nye funktioner" in: Den sociale dimension i pædagogikken, P. Schultz Jørgensen (ed.), Kroghs Forlag, Vejle 2002.
  J. *Juul*: »Fra opdragelse til inddragelse«, in: Aschehoughs store babybog, Aschehoughs, Copenhagen 2001.
2 E. *Christensen, M. H. Ottosen*: Børn og familieliv. Resultater og perspektiver fra Socialforskningsinstituttets forskning om børn og familier, Socialforskningsinstituttet, Copenhagen 2002.
3 K. *Killén*: Barndommen varer i generationer, Hans Reitzels, Copenhagen 2001.
  L. Dencik & P. Schultz Jørgensen (eds.): Børn og familien i det postmoderne samfund, Hans Reitzels, Copenhagen 1999.

Chapter 3: Integrity

1. *R. E. Helfer, C. H. Kempe (eds.)*: The battered child, Chicago UP, Chicago 1968.
2. *C. Collodi*: Pinocchio, G. Brock (trans.), New York Review of Books, New York 2009.
3. *Grimm Brothers*: The stubborn child, in: The complete fairy tales of the brothers Grimm, All-new third edition, J. Zipes (trans.), Random, New York, 2003.
4. *D. N. Stern*: The motherhood constellation, Basic Books, New York 1995.
5. *B. Bae*: Voksnes definitionsmagt og børns selvoplevelse(1988).. Tidsskriftet Social Kritik, 1996, 47, s. 6 – 21.
6. Hvis jeg fik bestemme …, Video recording, Pedagogisk Forum, Oslo.
7. *D. N. Stern*, The Present Moment in Psychotherapy and Everyday Life, 2004, W.W.Norton & Company
8. *J. Juul*: Selvtillid og selvfølelse, den indre familie, in: Tidsskriftet FAMILIEN, No. 14 and 15
9. *J. Juul*: Your competent child. Toward new basic values for the family, Farrar, New York 2000.

Chapter 4: Personal Responsibility

1. *A. Phillips*: Saying no. Why it's important for you and your child, Faber & Faber, London 2008.
2. *J. Juul*: Here I am! Who are you? Resolving conflicts between adults and children, AuthorHouse UK, Bloomington 2012.
3. *P. Schultz Jørgensen*: Hvad er kompetence?, in: Uddannelse 1999/9 Årgang 32 København: Undervisningsministeriets Tidsskrift
4. *M. E. Kerr & M. Bowen*: Family evaluation. An approach based on Bowen Theory, W. W. Norton & Company, New York 1988.

Chapter 5: Interpersonal Relationships

1. Projection (or transference) is the process by which we attribute our own internal qualities to external objects or persons. These are qualities which cause such great tension on the inside that we perceive them as stemming from outside. It is then a type of defense mechanism employed by the ego.
(Sigmund Freud: Metapsychology I and II)
2. *W. Kempler:* Experiential psychotherapy within families, Brunner/Mazel, New York 1981.
J. B. Burnham: Family Therapy: First Steps Towards a Systemic Approach, 1986, Routledge
T. Marner: Familieterapi – Milanometoden, Hans Reitzels Forlag, Copenhagen 1992.
T. Andersen: The reflecting Team. Dialogues and Dialogues about Dialogues. 1991, W.W: Norton & Company
3. *I. D. Yalom with M. Leszcz*: The Theory and Practice of Group Psychotherapy, 5th ed., Basic Books, New York 2005.
4. *J. Juul*: Et æble til læraren – om skolens overste dimension, Schönberg 1993.
5. *K. Tomm*, Interpersonal Patterns – Inviting relational Understandings for therapeutic change, 2014, Routledge, New York
6. *B. Lenneer-Axelson & I. Thylefors*: Arbejdsgruppers psykologi, Hans Reitzels Forlag, Copenhagen 1993.
M. Thorning: Lær at løse konflikter, Forlaget Frydenlund, Copenhagen 2001.
7. Prof. Dr Phil. Johs. Sløk was the renowned founder of The Institute for European ideas at the University in Århus DK and this text was one among many, which he shared with his students during lectures and tutoring.
8. *D. Bohm*: On Dialogue, Lee Nichol (ed.), Routledge, London 2004.

Chapter 6: Relational Competence

1. *D. N. Stern*: The interpersonal world of the infant, Basic Books, New York 1985.
D. N. Stern: The motherhood constellation, Basic Books, New York 1995.

D. N. Stern: Diary of a baby. What your child sees, feels, and experiences, Basic Books, New York 1990.

K. G. Hansen: Kometencebarnet og den professionelle pædagog – et nyt syn på børns udvikling, Forlaget Børn & Unge, Copenhagen 2000.

2 M. Berg Brodén: Psykoterapeutiska interventioner under spädbarnsperioden: det empiriska underlaget för boken »Mor och barn i ingenmans land«, Swedala, Trelleborg 1992.

3 D. Sommer, A childhood psychology: Young Children in Changing Times, 2012, Palgrave

4 J. Juul: Your competent child. Toward new basic values for the family, Farrar, New York 2000.

5 O. R. Jørgensen: Tænk fremtiden, Borgens Forlag, Valby 2000.

6 S. Bayer: »Relationer – en pædagogisk kompetence«, in: Pædagogens kompetencer, D. Cecchin & E. Sander (eds.), BUPL 1996. København

Chapter 7: Professional Development

1 E. Spinelli: Terapi, magt og mystifikation, en afdækkende analyse, Hans Reitzels Forlag, Copenhagen 1998.

2 K. Kildedal: En mennskelig opvækst? Om voksnes oplevelser af at være anbragt i familiepleje og/eller på institution i barndommen: en kvalitativ undersøgelse, Ålborg Universitetscenter, Aalborg 1995.

3 B. Jacobsen: Eksistens psykologi. En introduktion, Hans Reitzels Forlag, Copenhagen 1998.
   I. Yalom, Existential Psychotherapie, 1980, Basic Books

4 Bang Susanne "Rørt, ramt og rystet. Supervision og den sårede hjælper." Gyldendalske Boghandel, Nordisk Forlag A/S, København 2002

5 M. E. Kerr & M. Bowen: Family evaluation. An approach based on Bowen Theory, W. W. Norton & Company, New York 1988.

6 H. Dreyfus, St. E. Dreyfus with T. Athanasiou: Mind over machine. The power of human intuition and expertise in the era of the computer, Free Press, New York 1986.

7 S. Bang & K. Heap: Skjulte ressourcer. Supervisionsgruppen og dens arbejdsmåder, Munksgaard 1999.

8 see e.g.: *P. Westermark*: »Realtionsarbejde i institution og skole – metodeovervejelser«, in: Skolen i morgen, 1999/4. Dafolo A/S, Frederikshavn
9 *M. A. Lund*: Konsulentarbjede og supervision i skole- social- og s undhedssektoren, Schönberg, København, 2000

Chapter 8: Teaming up with Parents

1 *H. Anderson*: Conversation, language, possibilities. A postmodern approach to therapy, Basic Books, New York 1997.
2 *J. Fog*: Saglig medmenneskelighed, Hanz Reitzels Forlag, Copenhagen 2000. E. Spinelli: Terapi, magt og mystifikation, en afdækkende analyse, Hans Reitzels Forlag, Copenhagen 1998.
3 *Andersen, F.* (director of the University of Education in Denmark), Vera nr. 2 in 1998:
4 *D. A. Schön*: The reflective Practitioner: How Professionals think in Action, 1983, Basic Books.
5 *E. Erikson*: The nature of clinical evidence, in: D. Lerner (ed.): Evidence and inference, Free Press, New York 1958.
6 *E. H. Schein*: The corporate culture survival guide, rev. ed. John Wiley & Sons, San Francisco 2009.
7 *J. Juul*: Familierådgivning. Perspektiv og metode 3rd ed, Schönberg 1996.
8 Ibidem, p. 106.
9 Ibidem, p. 35.

Chapter 9: Understanding Conversation

1 *K. E. Løgstrup*: Solidaritet og kærlighed och andre essays, Gyldendal, Copenhagen 1993.
2 *J. Fog*: Saglig medmennskelighed, Hans Reitzels Forlag, Copenhagen 2000.
 K. E. Løgstrup: Ophav og omgivelse, Metafysik III, 1984, p. 175.
 See e.g.: Social Kritik, p. 78–107, 57/58 Oct. 1998.

5 Woelfel, J. & Haller, A. (1971) Significant others: The self-reflexive act and the attitude formation process American Sociological Review American Sociological Association: 36(1), 74-87
6 *Svinth Lone* „Nærvær i pædagogisk praksis." Akademisk Forlag, København 2010
7 *J. Juul*, Here I am! Who are you? Resolving conflicts between adults and children, 2012, AuthorHouseUK
   J. Juul: »Nytt perspektiv på grensesetting«, in: A. Dyregrov (ed.): Et liv for barn, Fagbokforlaget, Bergen 2001.
8 *A. L. L. Schibbye*: »Fra begrennsning til avgrennsning: Synpunkter på grensesetting og barns utvikling av selvreflekjon«, in: J. C. Jacobsen (ed.): Refleksive læreprocesser, Politisk Revy, Copenhagen 1997.
   B. Baa & J. E. Waastad: Erkjennelse og annerkennelse, Universitetsforlaget, Oslo 1997.
9 *Bae, Berit* (1988). Voksnes definitionsmagt og børns selvoplevelse. Tidsskriftet Social Kritik, 1996, 47, s. 6 – 21.
10 *H. Lee*: To kill a mockingbird, Popular Library, New York 1962, p. 85–86.
11 *A. Diderichsen*: Den professionelle omsorg og børns udvikling, in: Social Forskning, special issue, March 1997. Socialforskningsinstituttet, København
12 *B. Ravn & T. Holst Mortensen*: Empirisk forskning i bløde kompetencer: www.f2000.dk.
13 Uddannelse, 7, 1999, København. Undervisningsministeriets Tidsskrift

Chapter 10: Challenging Children

1 *N. Englund & K. Foss Hansen*: Urolige elever i folkeskolens almindelige klasser, Undervisningsministeriet, Copenhagen 1997.
2 *T. Nordahl & M. Sørlie*: Skole og samspillsvansker. En studie av 4. Og 7. Klassingers adferd, kompetense og læringsbetingelser i skolen, in: NOVA, Oslo 1997.
3 "Critical [present] moments, …, are moments in which the parties are fully in the present or the "now," caught in a pivotal space where any action, or even inaction, will change the destiny of the situation and the actors themselves."
   D. Stern, The present moment as a critical moment, Negotiation Journal, 2004, Volume 20, Issue 2, Pages 365–372

4 *D. Stern*, The Present Moment in Psychotherapy and Everyday Life, 2004, W.W.Norton & Company
5 *K. Glistrup*, Talk bout it … with every child: a book about anxiety, depression, stress and trauma 2014, PSYKINFO Frlaget
6 *A. Gopnik et al.*: The scientist in the crib. What early learning tells us about the mind, 1999, Harper Perennial, New York.
7 *D. N. Stern*: The motherhood constellation, Basic Books, New York 1995.
   D. N. Stern: Diary of a baby. What your child sees, feels, and experiences, Basic Books, New York 1990.

www.ingramcontent.com/pod-product-compliance
Lightning Source LLC
Chambersburg PA
CBHW051208300426
44116CB00006B/479